PREJUDICE

ACROSS

AMERICA

PREJUDICE

ACROSS

AMERICA

www.upress.state.ms.us

08 07 06 05 04 03 02 01   4 3 2

⊗

Library of Congress Cataloging-in-Publication Data

Waller, James, 1961–

    Prejudice across America / James Waller.

      p. cm.

    Includes bibliographical references and index.

    ISBN 1-57806-269-1 (cloth : alk. paper)—ISBN 1-57806-313-2 (pbk. : alk. paper)

      1. Prejudices—United States.   2. Racism—United States.   3. United States—Race relations.   I. Title.

E184.A1   W216   2000

305.8′00973—dc21   00-035195

British Library Cataloging-in-Publication Data available

To my mother, Billie Jean Waller.
It's not a Silver Star, but every page reflects your loving guidance and influence on my life. Thank you.

Contents

Foreword   ix

Preface   xiii

Acknowledgments   xxv

Introduction: The Making of "Prejudice Across America"

1. The Preparations   17

2. Los Angeles: Taiko Drums, Blues, and the Banana Bungalow   41

3. San Francisco: The Goodness of Uncle Guy   75

4. Chicago: Arvis Tells It Like It Is   101

5. Memphis: A Grief Observed   137

6. New Orleans: An Interlude   161

7. Birmingham: "Bombingham" Revisited   175

8. Atlanta: "Don't Tell Me It's on Peachtree, Again. . . . "   201

9. Washington, D.C.: The Beginning of a Country
   and the End of Our Line   237

   Afterword   279

   Appendix A: Itinerary of the 1998 Tour   289

   Appendix B: Bibliographic Essay   295

   Index   305

Foreword

"O Public Road . . . you express me better than I can express myself." I first read Walt Whitman's *Leaves of Grass* as an Ohio schoolboy. The great Democratic chant struck me hard, a lightning bolt of simple, authoritative words proclaiming that only in motion do people really have a chance to turn dreams into reality. Even as a fourteen-year-old, I had already suspected such. After all, my favorite reading, be it Jack London's Alaska stories, Mark Twain's Mississippi River tales, or Jack Kerouac's highway antics, had adventurous escape as a subplot. What sense did it make to be trapped in Perrysburg Junior High School reading *Huckleberry Finn* when the white bass were running in the Maumee River? If Huck had the good sense to discover the river by "lighting out for the territories," then why shouldn't I be exploring along the banks of mine? As London wrote in *John Barleycorn* about his own youth, "I wanted to be where the winds of adventure blew." Although this was obviously an immature perspective on what constituted an education, it is also true that I learned more about American history by taking field trips to Thomas Edison's birthplace and Johnny Appleseed's grave than I did in a traditional classroom setting.

Memories of childhood longings were swirling around my mind when I created a new kind of course at Hofstra University in New York in 1992. With universities being run like failing businesses and the art of teaching often considered antiquated, it seemed important to inject the joy of learning back into the college curriculum. A solution that appealed to my sense of adventure was to abandon the classroom altogether and take to the open road in a forty-foot-long sleeper coach with my students. Instead of fidgeting in a Long Island classroom reading about the Civil Rights movement, we would visit the Ebenezer Baptist Church in Atlanta and the Dexter Avenue Baptist Church in Montgomery, hold political seminars on Martin Luther King Jr. at the Lorraine Motel in Memphis and his crypt in Atlanta, and discuss the African American struggle with

Amiri Baraka in Newark and Toni Morrison in New York. The challenge was to turn a bus into a classroom and learn about our nation at the close of the twentieth century. Instead of merely studying prejudice in America we would grab it by the scruff of the neck. I called the course "American Odyssey" and wrote a best-selling book about our highway adventures titled *The Majic Bus* (1993), spelled with a *j* to avoid confusion with The Who, a British rock group, who had a title hit song by that same name. Today, the course is taught from the Eisenhower Center for American Studies at the University of New Orleans.

Now, in addition to taking college students on Majic Bus road courses, I've expanded the program to take high school students on two-and-a-half-week Civil Rights tours. The Civil Rights movement is still less than a generation from us, but too many young people today are growing up largely ignorant of that heroic struggle. So each year twenty Louisiana high school students, along with their history teachers, join me on a historical discovery trek to Central High School in Little Rock, Medgar Evers's home in Jackson, the Edmund Pettus Bridge in Selma, and Ingram Park in Birmingham.

Given my own road course history, it's a true honor to introduce readers to James Waller's wonderful *Prejudice Across America*, inspired, in part, by my book *The Majic Bus*. Waller, a professor of psychology at Whitworth College in Washington state, took twenty-one students on a journey across America in 1998, visiting Los Angeles, San Francisco, Chicago, Memphis, New Orleans, Birmingham, Atlanta, and Washington, D.C. to study the corrosive legacy of racism in the United States at the end of the second millennium. "The students, who were rapt with attention, finally were able to augment their 'classroom' understanding with the authentic face-to-face legacy of prejudice and discrimination," Waller writes in his preface. "They saw that although the face of hatred may change from generation to generation, the inheritance remains the same—forbidden opportunities, unfilled dreams, inner guilt, tension, fear, societal strife, and diminished productivity."

These lucky students profiled in the fascinating pages, with Waller serving as their intrepid guide, studied the ugly face of racial prejudice, and learned first-hand the power of redemption, while simultaneously forging a lifelong bond with their compatriots. With a different purpose than my own Majic Bus trips, Waller is on a multicultural mission to understand America today, to introduce his students to Hispanic activists in Compton, learn about the Native American experience at Alcatraz, contemplate manufacturing in Chicago, grapple with the Jewish Holocaust in Washington, D.C., and listen to blues musicians on Beale Street in Memphis. Waller is a champion of diversity, an avatar of the "salad bowl" metaphor who truly believes a better America is just around the bend if only we would learn to "care." While historical reflection makes up a good part of *Prejudice Across America*, the most moving passages, for me, occur when Waller explains the students' reactions to this intense educational odyssey. The entire class—and book—should be read as a mission for justice. Or as Waller so eloquently puts it, "We must recognize the beauty of our melange. We must see promise where we have typically seen peril."

There is great wisdom in this book because Waller is a great teacher. Honesty is his modus operandi. After riding in a Texas elevator, for example, with a couple of white racists, Waller chastises himself for not speaking up, for seeming to agree with their anti-black statements. "In my silence, the two bigots assumed companionship," Waller writes. "My silence sent the message that I was in agreement with them. They thought I was one of them. However, I was not one of them, and I should have summoned up the courage to let them know that."

By retelling this elevator episode, Waller gains the readers' full confidence. He is not a preachy, pious, self-righteous liberal, but a concerned and compassionate teacher who is unafraid to reveal his own embarrassing shortcomings. We all have them. And yet, by exposing his personal vulnerabilities, Waller allows all of us to confront our unfortunate complicity to racism in its many insidious guises. I say . . . forget William Bennett. In my opinion, James Waller should be made education czar for both living and writing this uplifting book.

Douglas Brinkley
Bay St. Louis, Mississippi
Easter 2000

Preface

Education is not the filling of a pail, but the lighting of a fire.

W. B. Yeats, Irish poet and dramatist (1865–1939)

I am always hesitant to tell people what I do. As soon as I mention the word "psychologist," they immediately conjure up images of Frasier Crane and try to hide their inner child from my ever-probing Freudian mind. I *am* a psychologist, but not the kind who can explain why your mother insisted on giving first and last names to the radishes in your garden. Nor can I prescribe drugs for your gray moods or maniacal shopping sprees (that largely remains the province of psychiatrists). Nor am I paid by the hour to head off your next divorce. In short, I am not a counselor or clinician. Even my best friends shudder at the thought that I ever might be "that kind" of a psychologist.

At times, I wish I *were* "that kind" of a psychologist. Recently, I was a career-day guest in my son's second-grade classroom. I thought how simple it would be if I could steal the line used by one of my colleagues, who *is* a counseling psychologist, when she explains her occupation to children: "I bandage people's emotions like a doctor bandages their scraped knees." Of course, it would have been even simpler had I not followed a fireman who proudly rode in on his bright red fire truck.

So, I fit none of the common conceptions of a "psychologist." What *am* I and what *do* I do? I am a social psychologist. I work in a fascinating field that explores how our thoughts, feelings, and behaviors are influenced by our interactions with other people. Take a course in social psychology and you will study how "social loafing" seduces a committee of twelve to produce work equivalent to a committee of six; how your choice of the shirt or slacks you wore today was influenced by implicit and explicit pressures to conform; how the faulty group decision-making that led to the *Challenger* disaster could have been avoided; why you married the person you married and why you may, or may not, regret that choice; why thirty-eight residents stood by and did nothing while a young woman was assaulted and eventually murdered outside an apartment building in New York City.

In this incredibly rich field, I have been most drawn to understanding how we "misrelate" to each other. For example, one part of my teaching and research life is spent studying perpetrators of the Holocaust and other cases of genocide. How can ordinary people become capable of such extraordinary cruelty? It has been a fascinating area of research and has provided humbling self-insight about fundamental human nature and the inhumane actions of which each of us is capable.

The other significant part of my professional life is spent studying the psychological dynamics of why we hate and exclude others simply because of what they look like, where they come from, or what they believe. This puts me in the arena of "isms"—racism, sexism, ageism, antisemitism, ableism (prejudice against disabled people), and the ever-expanding field of fatism (prejudice against overweight people). Over the past several years, I have become increasingly intrigued by the "ism" of race in America. Race is and always has been our most divisive issue. It is the conversational equivalent of water on a grease fire. Bring it up and you are guaranteed, at best, to become the center of attention and debate or, at worst, a charred island of social desolation. Race is the fault line running beneath our nation's landscape. It is the only problem that ever sent us to war against ourselves, the only one that periodically requires troops to be stationed on the streets of our cities. It is the most frightening tear in our social fabric, the most important domestic dilemma we face. Finding our way toward racial reconciliation is the crucial social challenge of the new millennium. Our success in meeting this challenge depends, in large part, on our appreciation and understanding of people who are different from us—our ability to see with the other's eyes.

As a college professor in a field that directly engages this challenge, I have the obligation to assist my students, most of whom come from white, middle-class backgrounds, to see with the other's eyes. However, accepting an obligation to do something does not always include detailed instructions on how to meet that obligation. This is a "rubber meets the road" issue. Generally, college students are notoriously egocentric. The world *is* as it appears to them. Teaching them to perceive *their* egocentric world more accurately is daunting enough. Teaching them to understand and appreciate how *others* perceive the world is even more formidable. Ultimately, however, understanding others' perceptions of their world is pivotal to clarifying our own.

Now, when I am even more convinced of the obligation, the question looms even larger. How do I move students to see with the other's eyes? How do I translate the experiences of racial, ethnic, and religious minorities in America to students who, like me, are not regularly victimized by prejudice or discrimination? In my teaching, I followed the standard operating procedure in higher education. I worked zealously to expose students to primary source testimonies, novels, documentaries, and guest speakers who could detail the legacy of pain and suffering caused by hatred in this country.

Although a clear improvement, this approach still allowed students the luxury of retreating to their dormitories, same-race friends, kindred minds, and comfortable relationships. Despite what they were exposed to in my class, my students could easily remain at a safe distance from the reality of what they were studying. Consistent with the nature of higher education, the students and I live our lives in an intellectual environment that is wonderfully nurturing, but also perilously enclosed. My constant admonition that "prejudice is a problem in America coast to coast" just did not leave the intellectual, moral, and emotional impact I expected. My students were hearing others' voices, but they were not going beyond that to see with the other's eyes.

I simply had not yet risen to the challenge. Sure, I could embrace the lie that I had done my best and no one would be the wiser. I could retreat to the tenured comfort of the life of the mind. Tempting as that was, a part of me knew that I could not leave this particular challenge unmet. I was drawn to accept the dare to be more innovative, creative, and resourceful than I had yet been in my teaching career. I felt called to dream big and to find ways to turn that dream into reality. I am tempted to label that call as "intellectual courage" and disguise it as purely virtuous. In truth, however, I was drawn to the challenge for some deeper, more personal, and even selfish reasons, reasons that I would not begin to discover until months down the road—literally.

How could I, even for a short time, immerse students in a learning experience that would compel them to see with the other's eyes? In the fall of 1995, I began to plan a month-long, cross-country study tour, "Prejudice Across America," that would focus on the history of prejudice and discrimination in America. Obviously, study tours are nothing new in higher education. However, a tour on this specific topic that ran literally from coast to coast was unique. It would be an extraordinary opportunity to move students from the sheltered environment of higher education and to engage them, however temporarily, in the experiences of racial, ethnic, and religious minorities in America. I hoped that they would be drawn closer to the daily realities faced by victims of hatred and would more fully realize the persistence of prejudice across America.

In January 1996, sixteen students and I met in San Francisco and traveled by rail to Los Angeles, Denver, Chicago, Memphis, New Orleans, Atlanta, and Washington, D.C. At each stop along the way, we heard firsthand from members of various minority groups regarding their history, culture, celebrations, and personal experiences as victims of prejudice and discrimination. I lectured very little on the tour. The direct testimonies of the people with whom we interacted—unfiltered by my experiences, thoughts, and biases—were the keynotes of the course. The students, who were rapt with attention, finally were able to augment their "classroom" understanding with the authentic face-to-face legacy of prejudice and discrimination. They saw that although the face of hatred may change from generation to generation, the inheritance remains the same—forbidden opportunities, unfulfilled dreams, inner guilt, tension, fear, societal strife, and diminished productivity. Yes, these encounters only gave us a gauzy approximation. However, they did move us closer to seeing with the other's eyes than anything else I had ever done or seen done in higher education.

Quite unexpectedly, the 1996 tour captured an incredible amount of interest. We drew national media attention from CNN, news wire services, and the *Chronicle of Higher Education*. In each city we visited, we were featured on local television and radio news reports. Later, the White

House would select the tour as one of the national "Promising Practices to Promote Racial Reconciliation." I have enjoyed recurrent opportunities, both in writing and speaking engagements, to discuss our experiences. The tour has now spawned similar trips in colleges and universities across the country. Something about the tour, and our experiences on it, has resonated with a diverse range of people, both as news and as pedagogy.

Bolstered by the success of the 1996 tour and wanting to correct some of the omissions and mistakes of the initial trip, I planned a second tour for January 1998. In this book, I want to take you along on that tour. You will join us on a month-long trip that took us from the beaches of Santa Monica to the foot of the "closed for renovation" Washington Monument. You will share in the vitality of eight great American cities—their history, identity, food, unique challenges, and accomplishments. You will eat beignets with us in New Orleans, walk the cheerless halls of a South Side housing project in Chicago, experience the agitated resettlement of post–Olympic Games Atlanta, sit in with us at a briefing with President Clinton's Initiative on Race. You will also drop in on our wide-ranging group discussions and join us in the unpredictable adventure of traveling cross-country by train, plane, and public transit.

However, this book is not simply a travelogue. In joining us on the trip, you also join us on a *journey*. A journey to confront issues of race in America. A journey to face your stereotypical thoughts, prejudicial attitudes, and discriminatory behaviors. A journey that raises more tough questions than easy answers. A journey of introspection and self-discovery in the urban reality of an America where diversity is not simply a buzzword, it is a way of life.

Any journey of self-discovery is laced with tension-filled dualities: pleasure and pain, insight and denial, honesty and deceit, hope and discouragement. This journey is no different. It is a journey with peaks of promise countered by deep depressions of despair. Why go on such a journey? The alternative—to stay home in the comfort of whom we appear to be—is certainly easier. But does that alternative promise anything of substance? As Annie MacGuire, a lead character in Oscar Hijuelos's powerful novel *Mr. Ives' Christmas*, states: "The troubles in life were started by people who never looked into their own souls." We choose to embark on a journey of self-discovery because we recognize the promise of growth. To be sure, it is a journey that takes courage to commence and commitment to continue. However, we can also be sure that only by looking into our own souls will we begin to see with the other's eyes.

For whom is this book written? It is easy to write it simply as a chronicle of the journeys of some white college students, led by a white college professor, to study prejudice across America. It is also easy to let our white voices and reactions dominate the text of the book. However, I refuse to let this book be that shortsighted.

As best as I am able, I bring the voices of blacks, Hispanics, Asian Americans, and American Indians whom we met on the tour into these pages. Also included are other voices of ethnic, religious, gender, and socioeconomic diversity. As a result, I believe there are two specific ways *each* of us—regardless of race, ethnicity, religion, gender, or economic class—can expand our understanding of the world from this book. First, like any book, reading this one will pull you into a "quasi-conversation" with the voices on the pages. Most of these voices are ones with which you do not typically converse in your day-to-day life. Research tells us that the vast majority of Americans set very specific boundaries about the people with whom they interact. Most of us set these boundaries around obvious characteristics—skin color, age, political affiliation, religion, social standing—and tenaciously avoid crossing over them. If you are like most Americans, you are hard-pressed to think of the last time you engaged in a significant and meaningful conversation with someone from outside of your boundaries. However, it is such cross-boundary conversation that sets the stage for empathizing with, listening to, and understanding others. Although "only" a quasi-conversation, this book can be a safe place for *all* of us to begin to understand the framework—both cognitive and experiential—in which the sensitive issues of racial, ethnic, and religious diversity are embedded.

Whites reading this book, for instance, may resonate with many of the questions, fears, and challenges expressed by the students and me. In addition, they may realize that the legal successes of the Civil Rights movement were not the death knells of racial stereotypes, inequities, and persecution in America. Whites may come to recognize their unearned privilege and, perhaps, even begin to understand the extent to which race *does* still color the vast majority of life experiences for racial minorities in America.

Similarly, racial minorities reading this book may resonate with much of the frustration, bitterness, and, perhaps, hope expressed by other minorities across America. They also may have an opportunity to connect themselves to a larger narrative by recognizing the similarities and differences in the historical and contemporary experiences of other minority groups. This book intentionally does not speak *for* racial minorities—too many books by white authors have that tendency. However, I do hope that many of the voices we met on the tour can speak *to* racial minorities about others who are waging similar battles on different fronts.

This conversation for racial minorities is particularly relevant when one realizes that, as the 1992 Los Angeles riots demonstrated, animosities *between* racial minorities in America are at an all-time high. Some surveys reveal a "horizontal hostility" in which minorities harbor even harsher views of each other than they do of whites. A recent poll by the National Conference, a nonprofit organization that promotes racial dialogue, reported that nearly fifty percent of Hispanics and forty percent of blacks agree that Asian Americans are "unscrupulous, crafty, and devious" in business. Only twenty-five percent of whites agreed with that statement. More than sixty-five percent of the Asian Americans and fifty percent of the blacks and whites surveyed believed Hispanics tended to "have bigger families than they are able to support." Meanwhile, Hispanics are almost three times as likely as whites to believe that blacks "are not capable of getting ahead" even if given the opportunity.

The individual voices in this book do not presume to speak for any particular racial, ethnic, or religious group. Taken as a whole, however, they say a great deal about the contemporary state of racial, ethnic, and religious relations in America. I expect that your reactions to this book will run the gamut. You will agree with some voices and disagree with others. At times, you will think I have given a balanced perspective; at others, you will think it is biased. You even may be so struck or infuriated by something in these pages that it drives you to conversation with someone of a different skin color, age, political perspective, religious belief, sexual orientation, or social standing. If so, then the book has accomplished its purpose of initiating cross-boundary conversation. Only by taking the impetus and having the courage to initiate such dialogue will we begin to break down the barriers that divide us.

Second, I hope this book can speak to all of us on a basic informational level. The voices that form the heart of the book are complemented by an in-depth analysis, drawn from interviews and research, of each of the cities we visited. These analyses explore the role of minorities in the past and present of the city; their contributions made and sufferings endured; their stories as told by local museums, exhibitions, and activists; and the social and political challenges still facing each of the cities as they enter the twenty-first century. You will see where these cities have healed racial divisions and what remains to be done in the struggle for racial reconciliation. You will read about some incredible programs that you may decide to borrow for your own community. Just as instructive, you will learn from some flawed programs what types of strategies to avoid.

If you know a particular city well or even live in one of these cities, I suspect you will still discover some new information. For the cities you do not know as well, I hope the taste you get in these pages drives you to visit for a full meal. However, more than being simply travelogue introductions, I want these analyses to make clear the general state of racial, ethnic, and religious prejudice across America as well as provide some specific strategies for building coalitions and learning to live, and thrive, in diversity.

To fix our fluid experiences on the page is a daunting task. The tour was a time so busy that I could not step back to see it until several weeks, even months, later. Fortunately, my recollections have been refreshed by the student journals and the voices of our docents, lecturers, interviewees, fellow travelers, and new friends made on the tour. The students have graciously given me permission to excerpt portions of their journals in this book. They recognize the importance of sharing their life-changing experiences and reflections with others. In so doing, my students complement the intellectual courage that led them on this journey with an even deeper courage that allows them to share their journeys of self-discovery with others. They did not always ask the right questions in the right way, hear what they needed to hear, feel what they needed to feel, respond as they should have responded. There were moments of selfishness, immaturity, and impatience. Through it all, however, my students chose to put their minds and hearts on the line in a discussion that is among the most divisive in contemporary America. It would have been much easier for them to remain on campus and take a "safe" course that required less preparation and less effort and offered less risk of painful self-insight. Instead, these students chose to step out and let their lives be changed. For that, and for sharing their journeys with you, I applaud them for the integrity of their unselfishness and thank them for their permission to use their journals.

It would be wonderful to say that *every* one of the students had dramatic journeys of self-discovery. Certainly, most of them grew. Some grew in ways that were penetratingly life-changing. However, some did not respond to the challenges posed by the tour in ways that readily reveal themselves as growth. Perhaps growth occurred in areas not noticeable to me. Perhaps seeds for growth were sown that will blossom months or years from now. I prefer to believe either of these two alternatives because they absolve me of any nagging questions about the tour's effectiveness and my own efficacy as a teacher. In truth, however, I must remain open to the reality that some students were not challenged by this tour in the ways I had hoped. Their stories are also part of this book's collective journey.

However, I can speak about my journey with certainty. Both study tours have been an explosion of personal self-discovery. Removed from the hierarchy of privilege inherent in academia, I am reminded that I do not always ask the right questions in the right way, hear what I need to hear, feel what I need to feel, respond as I should respond. I am reminded that my age and advanced degrees do not make me immune to incredible bouts of selfishness, immaturity, and impatience. While I grow, I am reminded that growth does not come easily. Nor do I always choose the grueling journey of growth over the comfortable decline of stagnation. So I try to follow the model of my students and be honest about my own journey of self-discovery through these tours.

The thread of transparency that runs throughout all of our accounts leaves an unusual book—one that raises more questions than it answers. These questions, however, compel us to continue our conversation and ultimately may lead us to answers that will help make a fragmented society whole.

In most cases, the other voices we encountered on the tour have not given explicit permission that their comments and experiences be identifiable. In consideration of this, I have chosen, where appropriate, to use pseudonyms and to modify some details (for example, gender, age, location) to protect their privacy and confidentiality. This does not compromise the accuracy or integrity of the book. It is simply an ethical courtesy to the people who so kindly opened their hearts to us.

I have refrained from cluttering the book with footnotes or chapter notes. As an academic, I have a natural inclination to document. I am driven to avoid the worst of all academic sins: UFFS (unidentified flying facts). As a reader, however, I also recognize the joy of clean, uninterrupted prose. I want this to be a good read that encourages you to see with the other's eyes and, at the same time, romances you into the promise of our incredible country.

In hopes of finding a middle ground, I conclude the book with a bibliographic essay of selected resources. These resources, which are extensive but not exhaustive, represent the significant books and articles I consulted while writing this book and are recommended for additional reading. In selecting these resources, I wanted balance in accessibility and perspective. Some of the resources are easily accessible to the lay reader, others are meant primarily for professional scholars. I also wanted to include as broad a range of perspective in the resources as possible. The issues raised in this book are contentious, to say the least, and I intentionally selected resources that convey that tension rather than simply support my own arguments. Although I have not included footnotes or chapter notes, I clearly indicate portions of the text that are heavily dependent upon the work of a specific writer.

Finally, a word about the format and pace of the book. The format of the book directly reflects the structure of our tour. After a brief introduction about the origins of the tour, the first chapter describes our fall 1997, on-campus preparation course. This is followed, in the order of the itinerary, by the eight cities we visited during January 1998—Los Angeles, San Francisco, Chicago, Memphis, New Orleans, Birmingham, Atlanta, and Washington, D.C. Thus, there is not a continuous historical narrative to take you through the book. You will read, for instance, about Martin Luther King Jr.'s death in Memphis several chapters before you read about his birth in Atlanta. However, I choose to sacrifice a continuous historical narrative in hopes of a format that more easily brings *you* on the trip with us.

Similarly, the pace of the book directly reflects the pace of our tour. We did not spend the same amount of time in each of the cities. Nor did we have the same types of learning experiences in each city or at each listed itinerary stop. Some of this unevenness was mediated by variations in our moods, expectations, and levels of fatigue. Some of it was impacted by the quality of program or speaker. In short, the pace of the tour—both in quantity of time spent and quality of experience received— was mixed. Thus, some chapters are longer and more detailed than others. Some experiences are more nuanced and "chewed on" than others. Again, I choose to have the pace of the book reflect the uneven pace of the tour in hopes of more easily bringing *you* on the trip with us.

Acknowledgments

When I was an undergraduate, I remember a professor telling me that writing a book is a marathon, not a sprint. After finishing my second book, I think he was wrong. It is a little of both. All I know is that for the past year, the book has felt a little too much like Inspector Javert and I have felt a little too much like Prisoner #24601.

I am indebted to many people who have been influential in the development of this book. My great colleagues in the Psychology Department at Whitworth College—Karol Maybury, Adrian Teo, and Noel Wescombe—have again picked up more than their fair share of extra responsibilities so that my time could be freed to write this book. I especially appreciate Karol Maybury for her wonderful service, once again, of being a primary reader for the manuscript. Any flaws in the book are only because I chose to ignore a piece of her wise advice.

I also give thanks to Bill Morkill and Doug Sugano, both of whom, within hours of each other, first suggested that a book about the 1998 tour would be a perfect follow-up to my first book. Fortunately, Craig Gill, the senior editor at the University Press of Mississippi, agreed and offered to publish the book. I am grateful to him for his patience in the early stages as I struggled to find my voice for this particular book. I am grateful as well to the two reviewers who read a first draft of the manuscript. Their comments gave a focus and direction to the book that was sorely needed. Finally, much thanks to Lisa DiDonato for her exceptional editing in the final stages of the manuscript preparation.

I also thank Whitworth College for its continuing support of the study tour and a minisabbatical granted by the Academic Affairs Office in January 1999, during which the crucial first chapters of the book were completed. In addition, thanks go to Nicole Polen and Andrea LeGore, both of whom were indispensable as research assistants for the book. Marie Beard of Kahala Travel in Phoenix, Arizona, is the world's best travel agent, and these tours will only go on as long as she does.

I especially acknowledge all of those who met with us on the study tours. The gifts of their time and experiences were the foundation of whatever we learned. Equally important, I send thanks to the thirty-six students of the 1996 and 1998 tours. Without their interest, passion, and enthusiasm, the tours would never have been possible. Thanks to Sarah Armstrong, Mindy Beard, Stephen Brashear, Jody Carlson, Sarah Chickering, Joy Crawford, Nicole Earin, Heather Eiffert, Hanna Ganser, Christian Gunter, Sarah Hostetter, Tiffanie Hart, Nathan Henry, Jennifer Langlois, Jennifer Lee, Krista Leeland, Megan McEwen, Kendra Nickerson, Erika Oestreich, Amber Palmer, Monica Parmley, Penny Pearson, Nicole Polen (again), Chrisanne Roseliep, Aaron Russell, Melissa Schnase, Joe Schneller, Jeremy Schossow, Sheri Schueler, Carolyn Stamy, Justin Visser, Ann Walker, Mandolyn Waln, Jeremy Watson, Melinda Wenny, and Jeremy Wynne. A very special thanks goes to Joy Crawford ("She-Ra"), who was incredibly helpful as a teaching assistant for the 1998 tour. All of these students are living reminders that I have the best job in the world.

My deepest appreciation, of course, goes to my wife and children. Once again, they have been willing to share me with the computer keyboard. To Patti, Brennan, Hannah, and Noah—thank you and I will always hold you in my heart.

PREJUDICE

ACROSS
AMERICA

INTRODUCTION

The Making of "Prejudice Across America"

The importance of seeing with the other's eyes was brought home to me on the last Sunday of our 1996 study tour. On that morning, we attended a worship service at Mount Zion United Methodist Church, a predominantly black church in Georgetown on the western fringe of Washington, D.C. Mount Zion has a rich heritage reaching back to its pre–Civil War days as a stop on Harriet Tubman's Underground Railroad. Following the service, an elderly black woman pulled me aside. She asked if I had enjoyed the service. I responded positively and expressed my deep appreciation for the congregation's warmth and hospitality. Still clutching my arm, she looked searchingly into my face and said, "I hope you felt the pain. I really hope you felt the pain." She was communicating a central truth about issues of race in America. This truth is that until we can understand the pain we inflict on each other because of hatred and exclusion, we will never fully understand why racial reconciliation is so essential to the future of America. The pain is not meant to be a destination in and of itself. Recognizing that pain, however, is a crucial step in the healing of America.

When we face the depth of this pain, we understand that we are closer to the threshold of racial hostility than we are to the threshold of racial reconciliation. Sociologists Joe Feagin and Hernan Vera offer the bleak recognition that at "sometime in the not-too-distant future a racial war between the haves and the have-nots in the United States is not inconceivable. The hour is already late to take action to prevent such a racial war." Similarly, journalist Carl Rowan recently has argued that the "so-called American melting pot has become a tinderbox that seems ready to explode. Before the end of the century, this country seems destined to look more like the South Africa of a decade ago than any dream of racial and ethnic tranquility." Those of us secluded by position and privilege—earned or unearned—must heed such voices of forewarning.

I will borrow an analogy to illustrate my point that there is much to

be learned from these voices. Like any analogy, it is a broad-stroke caricature with obvious limitations. However, I do think it illustrates another
reason for you and me to be moved to see with the other's eyes. Picture
American society as a large ship with two main decks, one upper and
one lower. On the upper deck are the privileged of our society. You can
fill in the blanks of who is on this deck. In my mind, I see whites, males,
heterosexuals, Christians, and those who are economically advantaged.
On the lower deck I see the traditionally excluded—the nonwhites, females, homosexuals, non-Christians, and economically deprived. Further imagine that this ship rams the edge of a submerged iceberg (a
stretch, but it is just an analogy). A devastating hole is torn in the hull
and, as a result, the ship is doomed to sinking. Although the *entire* ship
is in danger, the first to know are the ones on the lower deck. The last to
know will be the ones on the upper deck. By the time the persons of
privilege on the upper deck realize the extent of the damage, it will be
too late to save the ship or themselves.

I like this analogy because it reminds us that knowledge does not
always come from the top down. We cannot always assume that if something is really important, someone at the top knows about it and it will
eventually filter down to us. Rather, sometimes knowledge comes from
the bottom up. In this analogy, the people closest to the damage—those
on the lower deck—are the ones with the most accurate information. If
you and I want to do something about the damage before it is too late,
these are the very people to whom we must listen. Do I think that racism
is the iceberg that has torn an irreparable hole in the hull of American
society? Not necessarily. However, I do think that the hole may be much
bigger than many of us realize.

The rapidly changing face of Americans intensifies issues of race in this
country. Between 1920 and 1965, legal immigration to the United States
averaged about 206,000 per year, with the major flows coming from
northern and western Europe. Since the passage of the 1965 Hart-Cellar
Act, the volume and origin of immigration have changed dramatically.
Between 1965 and 1995, legal immigration averaged more than 500,000
per year, with the most dominant flows coming from the Asian Pacific

Triangle region. As a result, the nonwhite population grew more than seven times as fast as the white majority population during the 1980s. Today, at least one-third of Americans do not trace their origins to Europe.

Because of heightened immigration—legal and illegal—and high rates of birth among the newly arrived immigrants, nonwhite minority groups are projected to surpass whites to become, collectively, the numerical majority of the U.S. population by the middle of the twenty-first century. Between now and the year 2050, the black population is projected to increase by 94 percent, the American Indian population by 109 percent, the Hispanic population by 238 percent, and the Asian population by a whopping 412 percent. In contrast, the white population is projected to increase by only 29.4 percent during that same time period. Even were we to curtail foreign immigration immediately, we would continue to become far more racially diverse over the next decades through natural population increases alone. Most of mid-twenty-first century Americans will trace their descent to Africa, Asia, the Hispanic world, the Pacific Islands, and Arabia—almost anywhere but white Europe.

In addition, the recent immigrants coming to the shores of America tend to be less inclined than previous immigrants to melt quietly into American society. They are not as quick to change their name, hide their religion, and lose their accent—all in the pursuit of becoming that amorphous thing called an "American" (usually meaning some close approximation of the white, Anglo-Saxon, Protestant ideal). More and more, immigrants are choosing to preserve and maintain their unique cultural heritages and identities. In so doing, they challenge and expand the conventional definition of what it means to be an "American." This "browning of America" is the most dramatic change in the racial complexion and cultural orientation of our population that we have experienced in history. The changing face of America is a reality. The issue is not *if* or *when* the face of America will change. That change is a given and it is happening now. Rather, the issue is how we will respond to the changing face of America. Will we perceive a threat in this reality and retreat into self-segregation? Or will we boldly step into the borderland of diversity and be challenged by its potential?

The results of many public opinion polls do not bode well. For instance, when asked about the effect of the increasing diversity in America, a July 1993 Gallup poll found that fifty-five percent of Americans said that diversity "mostly threatens" American culture. Only thirty-five percent opted for "mostly improves" it. A more recent *Newsweek* poll found that nearly half of those surveyed indicated that "immigrants are a burden on our country because they take jobs, housing, and [consume] health care." These strong negative perceptions of the impact of immigrants on American society can no longer be classified as "whites-only" reactions. Rather, they represent a rift between the foreign born and the native born. Native blacks and Hispanics, for instance, are just as likely as native whites to express negative sentiments about the impact of immigration on their lives and our society.

Our growing antagonism toward diversity is further evidenced by an alarming rise in state legislation aimed at curtailing social services for illegal immigrants and repealing affirmative action programs. Among other things, this nativist backlash is fueled by the perception that "American" culture and traditions are being imperiled, our level of education is being lowered, our jobs and housing are being taken, our political influence is being lessened, English is declining as the primary language, and our social and health services are being overburdened. There is clearly an apprehensive fear of the "browning of America."

In the face of apathy, ignorance, exclusion, and fear, the following questions remain. How do I give my students a chance to hear from people on the "lower deck"? How do I give them a chance to make their own determination about the size of the hole torn in the hull of American society? In late 1994, I found a strategy that sounded promising. While browsing the shelves of a Denver bookstore, I picked up a copy of Douglas Brinkley's *The Majic Bus: An American Odyssey*. Brinkley, a historian, provides an engaging account of a six-week, cross-country bus tour in which seventeen Hofstra University students explored American history. They visited thirty states and a dozen national parks. He was convinced that if he could take the students to see where history was made, to touch it, to live it, they would be hooked. He did and they were.

Brinkley's tour garnered widespread attention because of its alternative, action-based approach to traditional education. Today, Brinkley—director of the Eisenhower Center for American Studies at the University of New Orleans and hailed as the leader of a new generation of American historians—continues to expand the notion and scope of his tours. One year he took two buses cross-country for three months, traveling as far north as Alaska. During another trek, he went "clean across America" on a natural-gas bus with college students from Yale, the University of Virginia, Haskell Indian College, Kenyon College, Tulane University, American University, and the University of New Orleans. For each of the past several years, he has also taken inner-city high school students from various districts in Louisiana and their teachers on a three-week, seven-state Civil Rights tour of the Deep South.

Brinkley's tours represent the best of what higher education has to offer—innovation, stimulation, and life-changing instruction. I was inspired by his unique commitment to enlivening the educational experience. I also am fortunate to teach in a place with an academic mission and calendar that encourages pedagogical flexibility and innovation. It was Brinkley's example, however, that directly sowed the seeds for what would become our "Prejudice across America" tour.

Whitworth College is a private, residential, four-year, liberal arts college affiliated with the Presbyterian Church. We sit on the northern fringe of a city (Spokane) that sits on the eastern edge of a state (Washington) that is the northwestern border of the country. We live in what Tom Robbins has called the "spectacularly mildewed corner of the American linoleum." Whitworth enrolls approximately 2,000 students: 1,600 undergraduates and 400 graduate students.

When I first came to teach here in the fall of 1989, Whitworth's literature described us as a "selective" liberal arts institution. By "selective," the administration apparently meant "if you can fog a mirror with your breath, you will be selected." Over the past decade, however, an increasingly larger pool of regional high school graduates from which to select, coupled with an ambitious president and board of trustees, have begun to restore luster to the meaning of "selective." The average entering high school GPA of our most recent freshmen class, for example, was 3.56; their average SAT score was 1140. Whitworth has developed a strong academic reputation in the region and is regularly listed as one of the top fifteen western universities in the annual rankings of the *U.S. News and World Report.*

Like most other private liberal arts colleges, the price tag of a Whitworth education is substantial. We receive minimal support from public funds. Total costs for one academic year run upward of $20,000, although few of our students foot that entire bill. Most receive scholarships, financial aid, or "discounts" of some sort. In general, however, our student body comes from predominately middle- to upper-class backgrounds. Among our students are representatives from thirty states and twenty-five foreign countries—as far away as Japan, Israel, Ukraine, Korea, and Ghana. Despite that broad representation, the campus is essentially a racial mirror of its geographic region. Similar to other schools in our area, only ten percent of our undergraduates (about 160) are racial minorities. Of these, the vast majority (nearly one hundred) are Asian or Pacific Islanders—most from Hawaii.

From its founding in the late nineteenth century, Whitworth has prided itself on innovative curriculum design. In 1969, Whitworth was one of the first institutions in the country to adopt the four-one-four academic calendar. This calendar includes regular-length fall and spring semesters that sandwich a January semester. During the month of January, students take one intensive course. Although the number of schools using the four-one-four calendar continues to decrease, it still remains a staple of the Whitworth experience due to its flexibility and potential for innovative and short-run off-campus courses.

During our January term, many students participate in internships, independent studies, or study tours. In any given January semester, Whitworth will have students studying journalism in South Africa, the history of philosophy in Europe, sociology in Central America, education in Native Alaskan schools, cross-cultural psychology in Hawaii, or ecology and conservation in South America. My nagging pull to develop a cross-country study tour on prejudice in America had a ready outlet. All I had to do was submit a new course proposal, develop an itinerary, con-

tact speakers, arrange housing and transportation, finalize a budget, select students, and summon the will to leave my wife and family for a
month. That was all.

The faculty governance structure that supervises new course proposals
typically moves at a glacial pace. Despite that, I received approval early
in the fall of 1995 to offer the first installment of "Prejudice across
America" in January 1996. Student recruitment was challenging. There
were still too many parts of the itinerary and costs "to be determined"
and I had a difficult time communicating the vision of the course both
to interested applicants and potential speakers. Trying to find housing to
meet the strict boundaries of the proposed budget was second in difficulty only to getting Amtrak to return my calls. Despite these obstacles,
sixteen very trusting students eventually met me at the San Francisco
airport to begin our month-long journey across the nation—from San
Francisco to Los Angeles to Denver to Chicago to Memphis to New Orleans to Atlanta to Washington, D.C.

The pain and guilt I felt at leaving my wife, Patti, and two young
children (Brennan, then five and a half years old, and Hannah, nearly
three years old) during that month were incredible. On a swaying train
somewhere between Memphis and New Orleans, I swore that I would
never do the tour again. However, after reading the students' journals
and seeing the ways in which their lives had been changed, I realized
that the tour was the most significant and important thing I had done in
my role as a teacher. The tour's impact on students was concrete and
inarguable. As I followed my students' careers over the next year—
including an officer-in-training at Quantico, Virginia; a youth minister
in Phoenix, Arizona; an elementary school teacher in Missoula, Montana; and a VISTA volunteer in Portland, Oregon—I saw the results of
immersing them in an experience where they could begin to see with the
other's eyes. So, given my wife's permission and my children's grudging
understanding, I began planning for a January 1998 tour.

Much of where we would go and what we would do on the 1998 tour
was similar to the 1996 tour. However, there were many areas in which
I believed the experience could be improved. Some of the adjustments

were merely logistical—one more day here, one less day there. I found alternative lodging, where necessary, and reconfigured the budget to account for previously unforeseen costs. I eliminated Denver from the itinerary, thereby wiping out nearly fifty hours of brain-scalding train travel from Los Angeles to Chicago. I dropped the Amtrak portion of our expansive western itinerary and replaced it with more economical (in both time and money) flights. I added Birmingham and planned a stop there on the holiday designated for Martin Luther King Jr.'s birthday. (The final itinerary, with addresses and phone numbers, can be found in appendix A.)

Three other adjustments to the 1998 tour were more substantial. First, I had not adequately prepared the 1996 students for what they would see and hear on the tour. Too often, both they and I looked like deer frozen in the blinding headlights of information and questions for which we had no sufficient background to respond intelligently. For the 1998 tour, I implemented a required fall preparation course with a beefed-up reading list, out-of-class writing, research and film assignments, essay examinations, and weekly group discussion. It was this course, which is discussed in chapter 1, that would give us the vocabulary and background from which to process the experiences of the tour.

Second, I realized that the content of the 1996 tour had been too diffuse. We meandered through several forms of racial, religious, age, and gender prejudice. We spent too little time on too many things. For the 1998 tour, I decided to focus our attention on the experiences of five specific minorities in America—blacks, Asian Americans, Hispanics, Jews, and American Indians. I realize that this omits several significant racial and religious groups that have been victims of prejudice in our country. It also ignores the compelling issue of sexism. However, my conviction is that if we learn the principles behind prejudice directed at these five specific groups—and learn them well—we can apply many of the same principles to prejudice directed against other groups. I choose to sacrifice breadth for depth in hopes that depth actually provides us with a better ability to broadly apply our learning.

The final substantial adjustment to the 1998 tour related to the itinerary planning. In 1996, I had too often relied on "AAA tour book experiences." Other than Denver and Atlanta, my previous experience with each of the cities on our itinerary was minimal. I had little choice (and even less time) but to rely on industry-standard recommendations. However, because of the publicity surrounding that tour, I had now developed a substantial pool of community contacts in each city that could give us—or at least lead us to people who could give us—more authentic, "behind-the-scenes" profiles of cities and communities we would visit. It is these people, their stories, and how those stories impacted us that form the heart of this book.

A brief aside: I recognize that names and language have the power to define others and, as such, can perpetrate racism. The phrase "non-white," for instance, sets white as the norm or standard from which everyone else can only deviate. Similarly, "racial minority" can be misleading because people of color are a majority of the world's population. The names by which we refer to various racial or ethnic groups must convey respect and dignity. At the time of this writing, the most widely accepted names for the four major American racial minority groups are: African American, or *black* (although some might consider the term "black" pejorative, Gallup polls consistently show that for the vast majority of blacks it is a nonissue); *Asian American*; Hispanic American, or simply *Hispanic* (west coasters more often use "Latino" in place of the colder and more generic "Hispanic"); and *American Indian* (although often referred to as "Native Americans," there is an increasing consensus for that generic government term to be replaced by this more precise designation).

Although I have chosen to use these names throughout this book, I recognize that they are problematic for at least two reasons. First, these names are imprecise and mask some tremendous within-group diversity. For instance, unlike other countries and cultures, the United States rejects the idea of a graduated spectrum between black and white. The last use of an intermediate term (that is, "Mulattoes") was in the 1910 census. Our grossly inadequate categories of "black" and "white" ignore the complex shades of our interracial reality. Similarly, the broad category of "Asian Americans"—including Chinese, Japanese, Filipinos,

Koreans, Asiari Indians, Vietnamese, and the Hmong, among others—represents twenty-four ethnic populations who speak more than thirty major languages or dialects. The grouping of "Hispanic Americans" includes Chicanos (or Mexican Americans, the largest of the Hispanic groups in this country), Puerto Ricans, and Cuban Americans. Finally, the wide stamp of "American Indians" includes more than 550 distinct tribes each with unique cultural, genetic, and sociodemographic characteristics.

Second, given the constancy of change in the commonly accepted terms describing various racial groups in America, it is highly likely that new ones will supplant these terms as they become misused and take on offensive or racist connotations. Between 1900 and 1960, for instance, "Negroes" and "Coloreds" were largely accepted as social, scientific, and political denotations. At the height of the Civil Rights movement, the descriptor "black" was usually taken as an insult. In the past three decades, however, the connotations of "Negroes" and "Coloreds" have become offensive and the terms "blacks" and "African Americans" have replaced them. I apologize in advance for any offensive connotations that the terms used in this book may take on for future readers.

The publicity surrounding the 1996 tour made student recruitment for the 1998 tour less a matter of "recruiting" and more a matter of "selecting." In the spring of 1997, I received about seventy completed applications for twenty student openings. My undergraduate teaching assistant, Joy Crawford, and I reviewed each of the applications and personally interviewed every single applicant. Part of our selection process was based on relatively clear-cut factors—grade point average, major and minor, academic classification, letters of recommendation, previous travel experience, and reasons for interest in the study tour.

Other parts of our decision-making were more intuitive. Would this person be a good travel partner for an intense cross-country, month-long study tour? What positive things would she bring to the group dynamics? How might he detract from the group? Is this someone I would want to sleep next to on a crowded, rumbling, overnight leg on Amtrak? Most important, does this person have a teachable spirit? Is this someone willing to put himself or herself in a position to be challenged and possibly changed? Joy, who was one of the 1996 tour participants and a favorite student of mine, had uncanny insights into many of these questions and, with only a few exceptions, we confirmed each other's perceptions of an applicant's fit for the tour.

When all of the dust settled, we had selected twenty of what we hoped were Whitworth's best and brightest students. We may have unintentionally excluded some outstanding applicants and included some that we would come to regret. However, we selected what we thought would be the best *group* for this tour. On many levels, we had selected a tremendously diverse group. They were student government leaders, athletes, musicians, and campus activists. Their majors included psychology, political science, communication studies, elementary education, American studies, English literature, biology, and religion. The students' hometowns were in Washington, Oregon, California, Montana, Colorado, Idaho, Alaska, and Texas. We came from a broad array of socioeconomic and religious backgrounds. Counting Joy and myself, our group included fifteen females and seven males.

However, the broad diversity in these areas was not matched by equally broad racial diversity. In the many times I spoke about the 1996 tour, one of the most frequently asked questions had to do with the absence of racial diversity among the students on the tour. Audience members intuitively recognized, as I had learned firsthand, the value of a racial minority perspective in our group dynamics and discussions. Without such diversity, it is too easy—as I saw in 1996—for the students to retreat to the insular comfort of "the group" and pull back from facing the toughest questions of the day. For the 1998 tour, I intentionally solicited applications from our on-campus racial minority population. I spoke with our Black Student Union, Asian-American Club, Hawaiian Club, and International Student Union. I personally recruited several racial minority students to apply. Disappointingly, however, only one minority student applied for the tour and he withdrew his application when it became clear that he could not afford the costs of the tour. (I remain committed to increasing the number of minority applicants for future tours. One donor already has stepped up to sponsor a scholarship for a minority applicant for the January 2001 tour.) Given the absence of racial diversity in the group, it would remain my task to push each of us away from the comfort of our "sameness" and toward the challenge of seeing with the other's eyes.

1. THE PREPARATIONS

The best way to go into an unknown territory is to go in ignorant, ignorant as possible, with your mind wide open, as wide open as possible and not having to meet anyone else's requirement but my own.

Dorothea Lange, American photographer

It is better to know some of the questions than all of the answers.

James Thurber, American author

The essential key to our journeys of self-discovery on the tour would be the ability to frame good questions in good ways—without thinking we already had all of the answers. It was important for us to be "preparedly ignorant." If we could do that, we would position ourselves to squeeze the most out of our month-long trip across America. The fall preparation course was designed to bring us to that point of "teachableness." In other words, the answers that we *could* find on the tour, we would be in a position *to* find.

In January 1996, students worked on exams and a research paper while on the road. They then had several weeks into the following spring semester to finish the work and turn it in. Unfortunately, their focus on the academic requirements of the month diverted their attention away from the experiential side of the tour. Instead of speaking *with* people, they camped in front of museum exhibitions and meticulously jotted down minutia *about* people (most long-since dead) for their exams or paper. They did not ask good questions because they were so intent, at my urging, on finding the "right" information for an exam or paper thesis.

Therefore, for the 1998 tour, I decided to frontload all of the examinations and assignments into the fall preparation course. The students would not only be better prepared for the trip, but also would be able to focus on the human experiences of the journey. They could speak *with* people in the here-and-now rather than passively recording events, quotes, and perspectives from museum placards. Following the tour, the only remaining requirement would be a typewritten copy of their daily journal.

For the fall preparation course, we met one hour per week and, consistent with college policy, students received one academic credit. For the tour itself, they would receive three academic credits (which is equivalent to a standard, nonlaboratory, semester-length course that meets three hours per week). I warned them ahead of time that the workload would in no way correspond to the academic credits received. What I would require them to do in the fall preparation course easily would rival the work of a three- or four-credit, semester-length course. The January tour would be twenty-four hours a day for twenty-three days and, in that sense, equivalent to dozens of academic credits.

I also let the students know that the situation was no different for me. I teach seven courses per academic year. For this one study tour and preparation course, I put in more work than I do for all of my other six courses *combined*. (Hopefully, that does not say more about my other six courses than it does about the study tour and preparation course.) Regardless, I reminded the students, we will only be disappointed if we expect the amount of work required for this preparation course and tour to correspond to a "fair" number of academic credits. I assured them, however, that the amount of work and preparation *would* directly correspond with how much we would learn.

The fall preparation course included five assigned textbook readings. The main text, which served as the common thread around which the course was woven, was Ronald Takaki's *A Different Mirror: A History of Multicultural America*. Takaki, a professor in the Ethnic Studies Department at the University of California, Berkeley, is today's preeminent multiculturalism scholar. Beginning with the colonization of the "New World" and ending with the Los Angeles riots of 1992, this book recounts the history of America in the voices and from the perspective of the minority peoples themselves—American Indians, blacks, Jews, Irish Americans, Asian Americans, Hispanics, and others. Along with standard historical sources, Takaki uses folk songs, poetry, and memoirs to evoke the words and feelings of ordinary people. Because of its broad scope, *A Different*

Mirror sometimes tends to oversimplify and occasionally relies too much on familiar material. However, it is still an excellent and accessible introduction.

Because much of the tour focuses on the Civil Rights movement, students also read Harvard Sitkoff's *The Struggle for Black Equality, 1954–1992*. Sitkoff's book is a highly regarded and very readable historical account of the Civil Rights movement. I complement the Sitkoff text with a primary source reading—Martin Luther King Jr.'s *Why We Can't Wait*. King's firsthand exploration of the events and forces behind the Civil Rights movement, centered on Birmingham, will come alive as we stand by the cell where he wrote "Letter from a Birmingham Jail" and walk through the doors of the Sixteenth Street Baptist Church in which four young black girls were killed by a hate-monger's bomb in September 1963.

The tour also focuses on one specific religious prejudice—antisemitism. We get some background on the Jewish experience in America through Takaki's book. In anticipation of our visits to the Wiesenthal Museum of Tolerance in Los Angeles and the U.S. Holocaust Memorial Museum in Washington, D.C., the students also read a survivor's account of the Holocaust. For this, I selected Elie Wiesel's *Night*. Although it is a book familiar to most of the students, Wiesel's memoir remains a classic to be read and reread.

Finally, the students read photocopies of the page proofs from my *Face to Face: The Changing State of Racism across America*. In addition to the background information students would pick up on the psychology of racism, having them read the page-proofs introduced them to my way of thinking about these issues. Although that could be dangerous (I certainly did not want twenty-one students parroting back my opinions), it also had the benefit of providing a starting point from which, if I managed it well, some fruitful discussion could emerge.

In addition to the five required texts, students kept up with a potpourri of print and electronic articles and several out-of-class film assignments. I also required students to conduct background research on each of the eight cities on the itinerary. This research included finding one novel or film that would be a good introduction to the city, two "must do" things in the city (other than those on our itinerary), one unique place to eat (unique as in "reflective of area cuisine," not as in the Hard Rock Cafe), one relevant website, and a brief synopsis of the typical January weather for the city. Joy would then collate everyone's responses and distribute a summary sheet the following week. Finally, students were required to complete two out-of-class essay examinations drawing from course notes and readings as well as a list of thirteen additional resources (mostly books) placed on reserve in the college library.

I begin the course by outlining a common vocabulary that will form the basis for our future dialogue. The five terms I lay out are: (1) *stereotypes*, cognitive shortcuts that contain beliefs about the attributes of an individual because of his or her membership in a specific group; (2) *prejudice*, positive or negative attitude toward an individual because of his or her membership in a specific group; (3) *discrimination*, positive or negative behaviors toward an individual because of his or her membership in a specific group; (4) *racism*, an individual's negative prejudicial attitude or discriminatory behavior toward people of a given race, or institutional personnel, policies, practices, and structures (even if not motivated by prejudice) that subordinate people of a given race; and (5) *antisemitism*, an individual's negative prejudicial attitude or discriminatory behavior toward people of the Jewish faith, or institutional personnel, policies, practices, and structures (even if not motivated by prejudice) that subordinate people of the Jewish faith.

I then briefly review the three myths that structure my book—the myths that life is good for racial minorities, racism is declining, and America can be a color-blind society. I choose not to delve into the specific evidence I present to counter each of these myths. However, the students have read enough of the book to recognize my general argument that one can only accept these myths by ignoring compelling evidence to the contrary. I remind the students to keep these myths in mind throughout the fall course and January study tour.

The tone in our first meeting is a bit odd. The students have been looking forward to the tour for months now and they seem to think to-night should have more of an "ice-breaking" or "celebratory" mood than it does. Maybe it should. It is, after all, the first time we have been to-gether as an entire group. However, I am so overwhelmed by the logistics necessary to get this tour going that I can be nothing but task focused. In general, that is one of the most difficult things about leading these tours. I want to form and deepen relationships, be a part of every fun thing everyone does, play games, read, and sit in a coffee shop for hours and just hang out. It's not that I don't occasionally do those things. It's that the nuts-and-bolts details of the tour frequently overwhelm me—what bus to take tomorrow, what time to leave, where to store luggage. I often find myself physically present with the students, but mentally else-where. Of course, as the tour leader, it does pay for me to be task focused. However, it is a good reminder that, in addition to the logistical details, I need to be more aware of the relational experience of the course.

From this point on, the fall preparation course will unfold around four objectives: building human relations skills, increasing self-awareness of our own prejudicial attitudes and discriminatory behaviors as well as of our personal histories, building awareness of diversity, and preparing ourselves for personal interaction with diversity.

Building Human Relations Skills

At its heart, interacting with people different from us is interacting with people. The success of that interaction depends on basic human relations skills—most notably, how well we listen and disagree. These two skills will determine how teachable we are on the tour.

The art of listening is tremendously undervalued in America society. In our everyday conversations, most of us do not listen. We simply wait until the other person stops talking so we can set them straight. We nod our heads to signify our "attention," but most often our brains are whir-ring away to come up with that remarkable rebuttal that would make the Greek philosophers stand up in their sandals and applaud. Be honest. What do you really enjoy the most about conversation? Seldom is it lis-tening to what other people have to say. Rather, it is our enthusiasm in telling our own story or opinion. All of us, some more than others (particularly college professors), like to hear ourselves talk.

I encourage the students to reclaim the lost skill of listening. Can they prevent themselves from always focusing on *their* reaction in a conversation? Can they discipline themselves not to think about what *they* are going to say while someone else is talking? Can they avoid the temptation to continually frame the other's comments in *their* experiences (for example, "That reminds me of a time when I . . . ")? Better listening starts with making a sincere effort to pay attention to what is going on in someone else's thoughts, feelings, and experiences.

Listening requires a submersion of the self and an immersion in the other. When we commit to this, we open up an avenue of understanding and discovery. The Quakers have a saying to illustrate this commitment: "When we listen devoutly, the heart opens." I remind the students, and myself, that sometimes our open heart will be flooded with the pain, rage, and resentment of the person to whom we are listening. This is especially likely in cross-boundary conversation and is a situation for which we must be prepared. Catherine Meeks, a professor and director of African-American studies at Mercer University in Macon, Georgia, even contends that rage and reconciliation are two sides of the same coin: "As long as we talk about reconciliation without acknowledging our very real and legitimate rage, we are trying to have a manipulated reconciliation. . . . White people as well as black people have a responsibility to be honest about their rage."

I tell the students the story of a middle-aged black professional that spoke openly about his rage on the 1996 tour. In a room adorned with a portrait of Martin Luther King Jr. and his quote urging all of us to sit at the table of brotherhood, we asked this man about his views on the prospects for racial reconciliation. In reply, we were hit with more than forty-five minutes of pent-up rage. "Why racial reconciliation? I do not want that. All that will do is pacify white guilt. Every time whites talk about reconciliation, I look for the hook behind the worm. I'm as reconciled to whites as I want to be. Let us [blacks] have our own businesses, clubs, and theaters. I don't want any part of what whites are offering! You want to make me happy? Don't reconcile with me! Just compensate me for all that you have taken! Just give me what you owe me!" He concluded with a somber warning: "I fear for white Americans. You will reap what you have sown."

Even as I described the event to the students, I remembered that the forty-five minutes seemed like an eternity. However, that experience reminds us that a commitment to listen is a commitment to face another person's rage. In other words, our commitment to listen must be unconditional—it cannot be restricted to listening only to that with which we agree or that which we find comforting.

Over the next week, I ask the students to engage in a conversation where they are not intending to respond, but only to understand. How does it change what they hear? When they give themselves permission to not *have* to respond, do they become better listeners? Even as I speak, I realize the necessity of being a model of listening and I am sobered by my own shortcomings in this area.

In addition to facing the rage in others, I tell the students that our commitment to listen also is a commitment to disagree in ways that continue a conversation. Racism is a sensitive issue and our hesitancies to engage in conversations about it are justifiable. However, disagreements are a significant source of growth. To avoid them is to cut us off from a chance for personal development. We may be swayed by the other's argument, we may sway the other, or we may, at the least, come to more clearly know what we believe by fully understanding an opposing viewpoint. If we remain afraid of the possible tension or conflict, we will never engage in meaningful and constructive conversation about racism.

To disagree in ways that continue a conversation is an art. Parker Palmer, a sociologist and renowned teacher, has said: "Truth is an eternal conversation about things that matter. . . . And if I want my students to be in the truth, I want them to know how to be in the conversation, not just resting on conclusions. I want them to know how to hang in with a conversation that is increasingly difficult because it's increasingly diverse and it invokes much woundedness and much anger and many struggles. There are ways to stay in the conversation if you understand that that's what truth is."

Again, I realize the necessity of being a model in this area and I am discouraged to recognize my even greater shortcomings in disagreeing. Tact and subtlety are lost on me and, although I like to think it a charming eccentricity, I know that I too often disagree in ways that bring conversation to an immediate halt.

I assure the students that we will have bouts of heated disagreements. Our conversations, between ourselves and with others, will not always be easy. The challenge is to stay in conversations that are difficult and to disagree in ways that keep a conversation going. To do this, we cannot preach or be self-righteous. We must communicate, by our words and actions, that understanding (not personal victory) is the goal.

Increasing Self-Awareness

How do we become aware of our own prejudicial attitudes and discriminatory behaviors? Unless we are brutally honest with ourselves, most of us protect our self-esteem by excluding our personal stereotypes, prejudices, and discriminatory behaviors from conscious self-awareness. It is only when we actually engage in personal contact with members of different groups that we become aware of our deepest biases. As psychologist Thomas Pettigrew describes: "Many [people] have confessed to me . . . that even though in their minds they no longer feel prejudice toward blacks, they still feel squeamish when they shake hands with a black." When our contact with diverse groups is limited, we should be wary of the false comfort that comes with our belief that we have no negative stereotypes, prejudices, or discriminatory behaviors. It may be that only in the context of actual physical contact do we become aware of those thoughts and feelings.

My students will have a month of physical contact with diversity. During that time, they will have countless experiences that will allow their deepest biases to emerge. At this point, I want to increase their self-awareness on another front. I want to engage them in an approximating experience of what it is like to be on the receiving end of biased treatment.

There is a plethora of classroom assignments directed at this goal. Some are pitiful approximations that minimize or relativize the issue to a dangerous degree. Others at least stimulate discussion. I distribute an out-of-class assignment that I hope does the latter. I forget where I first ran across the assignment, but it has always intrigued me and I have yet to find the right pedagogical setting in which to use it. This may be it, it may not. Only using it will tell.

I inform the students that for the following week they are to wear a pin or label displaying an upside-down pink triangle. If asked what the pin represents, they are to say: "I am wearing this pin to commemorate the gay men and lesbians killed and persecuted during the Holocaust." No other comments (especially "it's a class assignment") are necessary. I mention that wearing the pin does not mean they are homosexual, nor does it mean they are representatives of the homosexual community or support homosexual activities. People of all sexual orientations, as many students from larger cities know, wear the symbol. It is not a secret symbol used by homosexuals to identify each other. They are simply wearing the pin to commemorate a group of people persecuted in the Holocaust. Although homosexuality is not a specific topic of the course, in the process they also will learn something about the general topic of prejudice. Next week they are to return ready to discuss people's reactions to their wearing the pink triangle as well as their own reactions to wearing it.

I hand out a short piece detailing the Nazi persecution of homosexuals, who were most often referred to in Nazi documents as "filthy queers." As the paper describes, the Nazis adopted an antihomosexual platform soon after Hitler took office on January 30, 1933. A year later, the Nazis began incarcerating homosexuals in concentration camps, where they were forced to wear a pink triangle patch, the "rosa Winkel," to identify them as homosexuals. Although the Nazis did not order their extermination as they did the Jews', thousands (estimates run between 10,000 and 220,000) of homosexuals perished through maltreatment, slave labor, and execution by firing squads solely because of their sexual orientation.

As the group disbands, the stunned look on some faces piques my curiosity about our next meeting together.

Less than twenty-four hours after distributing the assignment, I received calls from three faculty colleagues regarding the pink triangle exercise. One praised it as innovative and important. However, the other two questioned its efficacy and raised ethical concerns about *requiring* students to participate in an exercise that so clearly was at odds with their (I was not sure if it was the students' or the faculty members') personal belief systems about homosexuality. Both asked that I consider canceling the exercise immediately. By the end of the week, several other colleagues had called with similar concerns and three of the students had contacted me to let me know that they were refusing to continue with the exercise. Two simply said it made them feel too uncomfortable and the other cited personal religious beliefs that precluded him from any activity that could be construed as supporting homosexuality.

I knew the exercise was a bit of a risk. Christianity has long condemned same-sex intimacy. Psychiatrists and psychologists once labeled homosexuality as a mental disorder. It was only in 1997–1998 that the American Psychiatric Association and American Psychological Association voted to reject therapy aimed solely at turning gays and lesbians into heterosexuals. Homosexuals continue to be routinely subjected to stigma, stereotypes, cheap humor, and falsehoods that frighten or alienate many people. There was no reason to suspect that my students, cloistered as we are in our pine-cone curtain of a campus, would be immune to any of these impressions. In fact, there were a lot of reasons, including our affiliation with the Presbyterian Church and a disproportionately large number of students and faculty who would identify themselves as Christian, to suggest that the exercise might be very risky.

Despite this background, I still was not prepared for the intensity of some of the reactions. However, at least I could be prepared for the debriefing. I did not want to be defensive and lash out with a high-minded justification of why the exercise was pedagogically sound. Rather, I wanted to prepare myself to shape this into a powerful learning experience. Just recently, I exhorted the students to nurture their skills of listening and disagreeing. I now had to be prepared to model both of those skills. This promised to be a pivotal point in our group's development.

As I walk into the room, the tone is taut. We may not know each other well enough to say many of the things we would like to say tonight. Some of what we might want to say may be said in ways that put a barrier between others and ourselves that will linger through, and long past, the tour. I decide to directly acknowledge the controversy raised by the exercise. "I realize that a lot of other people, both faculty and students, have had some strong reactions to this exercise," I begin. "I want to lay aside those outside reactions and focus on your reactions. With the exercise, I simply wanted you to get a brief glimpse of what it's like to be stigmatized. I told you that wearing the pink triangle did not mean that you were homosexual, nor did it mean that you were a representative of the homosexual community or support homosexual activities. As you've found out, though, other people's reaction to your wearing of the pink triangle hinted at many of the very things I told you it did not represent. I'm sure that some of your felt stigmatized, ridiculed, stared at, misunderstood and, perhaps, even harassed."

"As uncomfortable as that was," I continued, "I also hope there were things you learned from the experience. I wish all learning could be comfortable. In truth, though, sometimes learning means provoking discomfort. In this case, I think the end of learning justifies the relatively unpleasant means used in the exercise. I may or may not be right. What do you think? Did you learn enough from the exercise to justify the discomfort it presented? Or was the exercise an inappropriate requirement to impose on you?"

There follows a long period of silence as students weigh the relative benefits of speaking out versus the costs. To my right, I notice that one student is a bit teary. She quietly begins speaking: "When I first put on the pink triangle, I assumed that I would be the 'teacher' for the week. Instead, I learned an irreplaceable lesson. When I came back to school from a weekend celebrating my Mom's birthday at home, a young woman approached me. She walked up to me and asked about my triangle. Immediately, I remembered that I was wearing it and proceeded to explain what the symbol meant. After I had finished talking about the homosexuals in the Holocaust, she asked me if I was a lesbian. I froze at that moment. Half of me was disgusted that she could find me to be a homosexual. The other half of me was ashamed that I felt so violated by a simple question. I responded as calmly as I could that 'No, I am not a lesbian.' Still flustered, I asked this woman if she was a lesbian. 'Yes,' she smiled, and looked at her feet. I tried to soothe her embarrassment and asked if it was hard to live in Spokane, a place that is not generally accepting of homosexuals. She answered, 'Yes. It's really hard to live in Spokane. It's hard to be black and a lesbian in Spokane. You know, I have a daughter.' "

She is now weeping noticeably. The group waits until she begins again: "At that moment I was completely at a loss for anything to say. I did not need to. Her eyes met mine and, as they teared up, she left and walked away. I stood in that same spot for a long time. The few words that she had spoken to me just moments before had pierced my spirit. It was almost as if I understood what this woman felt. For the first time in my life, I could identify with someone that was so different from me. But somehow I knew that we were the same. I even imagined us being friends."

As she stops, several in the room have become teary-eyed. Her willingness to deeply feel and openly share those feelings with others has touched a chord deep in each of us. There was probably much more behind her reactions than simply the exercise. Regardless, to my silent relief, she has set a tone for the hour. Of course, it is difficult to follow someone who has been so transparent about the impact this exercise left on her. It is several moments before someone else speaks up about their reactions. Over the rest of the hour, students, following her tone, speak openly about the discomfort and learning inherent in the exercise.

Many students report that they gravitated to other students in the course wearing the pink triangle or other people who knew them well enough to know that the pink triangle did not communicate anything about their sexuality. They found themselves avoiding contact with unfamiliar people out of fear that they would assume more about their sexuality than was warranted by their wearing the pink triangle. These students began to recognize the constraining influence of labels or a stigma on interpersonal interactions.

Several students reported that often other people would ask questions like "Why don't you commemorate the other groups who also died? Women and children died too, you know! What about the people who weren't homosexuals that died during the Holocaust?" As we debriefed as a group, several students realized that if they had been wearing a symbol commemorating a different group, it was very unlikely they would have been asked "What about all of the homosexuals that died during the Holocaust?" Some of this surely reflects ignorance. The persecution of homosexuals in the Holocaust is not common knowledge. However, part of this reveals underlying antigay prejudices.

I briefly wonder what my own lack of participation in this exercise reveals. Why didn't I join the students in wearing the pink triangle for a week? My justification was that my wearing the pink triangle would lend professorial legitimacy to the exercise and mellow the responses others gave to the students. But, I now wondered, could it be that I have a discomfort with the exercise that betrays some cryptic antigay prejudices of my own?

Toward the end of the hour, several students express a sense of "betrayal" at the other members of the class who did not wear the triangle or wore it in ways (excessively small or hidden under a lapel) that violated the spirit of the exercise. To this point, the students who quit the exercise have yet to speak up. The tone set by the one student's opening remarks clearly has made it a chilly climate for anyone who would speak out against the exercise. It also has become clear that gender has played a role in students' reactions. I suspect that the six males, three of whom were the only ones I know of to outright *quit* the exercise, recognize this and that the well-documented male fear of being labeled as "homophobic" makes them even more hesitant to speak up. I also know that other students, both male and female, have chaffed at an assignment that required them to put forth a different public persona than their own. One later expressed how difficult it was for her to submit to professorial authority when it required that she stand for something not of her own choosing. How can I bring these voices into a conversation dominated by other viewpoints?

Unfortunately, our time tonight has ended. However, I breathe a silent sigh of relief because I know that I was at a loss as to how to bring those voices out. I leave excited about the learning experiences and growth shared by many. As one student tells me, "Do I think the whole experience was a little taste of hell? Yes. But am I glad that I wore a pink triangle? Yes." In a course where we often concentrate on other people's prejudices, students were forced to focus more on their own knee-jerk reactions and stereotypes. However, I am also disappointed that I was not more adept at structuring a climate where *everyone* felt free to express their thoughts and reactions. I realize that the success of this course, and the tour, hinges precisely on my very ability to do that.

We now move to the second part of increasing self-awareness—becoming more self-aware of our personal histories and our racial, ethnic, and religious stories. Tonight, the students open with some good questions: Why sharpen our sense of identity by more directly connecting us with our racial, ethnic, and religious stories? Don't the costs of drawing attention to the very things that divide us outweigh the benefits of increasing self-awareness?

I acknowledge that increasing self-awareness of who *we* are may actually reinforce our perceived differences from *them*. However, I argue that there are at least three benefits that outweigh this potential cost. First, we have an opportunity to learn about the people who influenced the people who influenced the people who influenced us. The vast majority of us know little about our heritage beyond our grandparents. It was not until recently, for instance, that I could have even told you the names of my great-grandparents. In more clearly exploring our past, we come to understand the lingering influence of the past upon our present. It is a matter of education, not exclusion. We get an alternate understanding of who we are. We recognize that our identity does not begin and end with us individually. Rather, our identity is, in part, a cumulative "hand-me-down" from the past as well as a connection to the future. We hurt ourselves if we turn a blind eye to that which nurtures us in our own stories. In the words of Malcolm X, "A race of people is like an individual man; until it uses its own talent, takes pride in its own history, expresses its own culture, affirms its own selfhood, it can never fulfill itself."

Second, for most of us, an examination of our personal stories will reveal that, not too long ago, we too came from another shore. In a time where restrictive immigration legislation is frequently discussed, it is helpful for each of us to recognize that had such legislation been in place four or five generations ago, our lives today would be drastically different. It is good to be reminded that most of us came from somewhere else.

Finally, we benefit from increasing our self-awareness about our personal stories because we begin to understand why story is so important to people as a source of identity, belonging, or personal place in the large scheme of things. This is as important for whites as it is for racial minorities. We have lost our own "white" cultures and stories. We have no European-American identity. Our ancestors worked extremely hard to dismantle their European identity in favor of what they perceived to be the true "American" identity. As a result, we have become disconnected from our languages, foods, music, games, rituals, and other cultural expressions. Often, we fabricate connections by looting other traditions for our identity. In *Dakota: A Spiritual Geography*, Kathleen Norris bemoans white Americans who seek "the sacred in Native American spirituality, often appropriating it in ways that add to the already bitter experience Indians have of being overwhelmed and consumed by white culture."

Discovering our stories can be invigorating and instructive. For example, some of the students will discover for the first time that their heritage includes Swedish, German, or Irish roots. Over time, they will develop a sense of pride in and identification with these roots. Through this process, the significance of heritage to racial minorities begins to dawn on them. If it comes to mean so much to my students, how much more must it mean to groups of people for whom their identities and self-esteem have been devastated by American culture? Is it any wonder, for instance, that blacks have taken such tremendous pride in their African heritage when white America has denied them so consistently the opportunities to find identity and esteem in this country?

I tell the students that becoming more self-aware of our personal racial, ethnic, and religious stories is crucial to a truly multicultural society. Increasing self-awareness of our own stories need not imply a rejection of our membership in a larger political entity—America. The search for our stories can build bridges between racial groups and actually solidify our connection to the broader classification of "Americans." It is done as part of, not separate from, improving intergroup relations.

We are capable of knowing and understanding ourselves through two or more different groups. We can hold each group in positive, if not necessarily equal, regard. We should not have to lose our heritage to become good Americans. If we do, all of us lose. The fact that we use hyphenated names to indicate cultural and social connections to our ancestors has nothing to do with our loyalty to the United States. Short of making it an obsession, recognizing the affiliations that have traditionally helped hold America's communities together need not threaten our sense of national belonging. In Ole Rolvaag's *Giants in the Earth* trilogy, a country pastor gives a prophetic warning when addressing Norwegian farmers in Dakota: "If this process of leveling down, of making everybody alike . . . is allowed to continue, America is doomed to become the most impoverished land spiritually on the face of the earth; out of our highly praised melting pot will come a dull . . . smug complacency, barren of all creative thought. . . . Soon we will have reached the perfect democracy of barrenness. . . . Dead will be the hidden life of the heart which is nourished by tradition, the idioms of language, and our attitude to life."

Having outlined the rationale for increasing self-awareness of our personal stories, I then ask the students to break into small groups of three or four. In these groups, they are assigned an ethnic-sharing exercise I picked up at some long-forgotten academic conference. Given the moaning from some quarters, you would think I asked them to permanently tattoo a pink triangle on their forehead. The exercise is meant as a "get-to-know-you" game as well as an introduction to the importance of heritage in identity. In addition, it also should help them develop greater sensitivity to others' experiences—something we all could hone after last week's experiences.

In the group, students respond to questions such as: How do you identify yourself and what does your identity mean to you? Which type of identity do you most often emphasize—racial, ethnic, religious, economic, gender, geographic area, or sexual orientation? What is the significance of your name? Where did it come from? Describe a time when you wished you belonged to some other group or a time when you wished you were not identified with so visible a group. How did you cope with these feelings? Describe something a parent, relative, or friend said, either about another ethnic or racial group or in the presence of a friend of that ethnic or racial group that embarrassed you. How did you react?

As I move from group to group, it becomes clear that real identities, real experiences, and real feelings are being shared. However, it also becomes clear that some facades are still carefully maintained. Disclosure for every student does not come easily or often. I empathize with the students who feel threatened by an exercise such as this. I hate forced self-disclosure, especially in a "large, puffy pillow" group setting. But it is not empathy these students want. They just want to stop the stupid exercise.

I move on to the final assignment. I ask each student to outline a genealogy examining their family history. I give them copies of some materials I have downloaded from genealogy-related websites—family and home information sources, pedigree chart, and time line. I also encourage them to interview their parents and other relatives for additional information. I know that it is not long enough, as they quickly remind me, but I ask that they turn in whatever they have done on the assignment two weeks from tonight. I know they will not have time to complete it. However, at least they will have time to start it.

At the next meeting, we continue with the notion that the ideal of a multicultural society is to maintain and develop group identities in the context of the broader identity of "Americans." How does this play out? How do we draw strength from our multiple identities? How do we live in a place where two or more cultures edge each other? In this "borderland," where people of different races occupy the same territory, how do we meet on communal ground?

We develop three guiding principles. First, we must encourage the reality of a truly multicultural society. We must not force other cultural identities into a homogeneous "American" (that is, white) identity. The "melting pot" theory, which suggests that cultures who share an economic, political, or geographical space will fuse together until they are indistinguishable to form a new culture, always has been problematic. In the early part of this century, for instance, Langston Hughes recognized that there was a "mountain standing in the way of any true Negro art in America—this urge within the race toward whiteness, this desire to pour racial identity into the mold of American standardization, and to be as little Negro and as much American as possible."

Many contend that the "mold" of American standardization is even inherent in the apparently noble enterprise of integration. A black undergraduate interviewed by sociologist Joe Feagin remarked, "To integrate means simply to be white. It doesn't mean fusing the two cultures; it simply means to be white, that's all. . . . They have no reason to know our culture. But we must, in order to survive, know everything about their culture." Manning Marable, director of African-American studies at Columbia University, agrees that integration, in practice, has threatened blacks' sense of community and identity—without fulfilling the promise of improving their lives or ending racism.

Today, a "salad bowl" model that encourages groups to maintain and develop their group identities has replaced the "melting pot" theory. In this transition, we recognize a second principle for living in the borderland—we must come to appreciate the richness of America's racial diversity. We must recognize the beauty of our melange. We must see promise where we have typically seen peril.

This study tour operates on the well-established social psychological axiom that the greater our familiarity with a social group, the more we see its diversity and, as a result, the less likely we are to stereotype. The students will be exposed daily to the history, food, celebrations, contributions, sufferings, and traditions of racial minorities. As Paul Kivel writes, "When we aren't remotely familiar with the music, literature and dance of people we live with, we cannot expect to understand what they experience or what moves and guides them. We cannot honor and respect their concerns and life choices."

I don't want this to be reduced to a "culture at a distance" approach to diversity. In other words, I don't want us to just focus on the "safe" aspects of culture that gently introduce us to an appreciation of the fascinating differences between groups. Rather, I want us to complement that appreciation by directly confronting the historical, personal, and structural reasons for the disparities between groups. We need to meet head-on the existing social and political fabric that underlies racism. Only by doing that we will take a significant step toward racial reconciliation.

The third principle we discuss for living in the borderland is that we must no longer ignore the reflections of racial minorities on their own cultural experiences. We must recognize that racial minorities are experts on their own experiences and listen to those reflections. We must come to appreciate the relevance of those reflections to whom we all are. One person wrote the following statement in response to a community lecture I presented: "A major in African-American issues or studies is irrelevant! This type of major, if one can call it that, should only exist at schools with a large black population." Such a comment is a result of a social and educational system in which we have defined America too narrowly.

Carol Hampton, national field officer of the Native American Ministry of the Episcopal Church, has written: "You taught me that my history mattered not at all unless it impinged on yours and then you taught my history only from your perspective." We have to go beyond such compartmentalized thinking and realize that "their" story, as told by "them," is an important part of "our" story, as understood by "us." At times, hearing "their" story leads us to the painful realization that our image of America as a free and democratic nation must be qualified. We are forced to revisit our assumptions about our country's past, present, and future. In short, we are challenged to think outside of the narrow and traditional compartments of understanding in which most of us were educated.

Building Awareness of Diversity

Our time spent building human relations skills, coupled with an increasing self-awareness of our own prejudicial attitudes, discriminatory behaviors, and personal histories, has helped prepare us to frame questions in good ways. However, we now need to build an awareness of diversity that will help us frame *good* questions in good ways.

To that end, we spend the next several weeks digesting and discussing the information from the Takaki, Sitkoff, King, and Wiesel texts. I have already told the students that about fifty percent of the tour will focus on black experiences; about fifteen percent each on Jewish, Asian-American, and American Indian experiences; and the remaining five percent on

Hispanic experiences. It is not an ideal mixture. The emphasis on black experiences in America and the lack of emphasis on Hispanic experiences is especially disproportionate. However, the texts and discussion for the preparation course give us a chance to bring more balance to our background information. We systematically explore, in the traditional, old-school practice of text analysis and discussion, the culture, language, history, contributions, and sufferings of American Indians, Asian Americans, blacks, Hispanics, and Jews in this country. In the process, we are left with more questions than answers. To what degree have the legal successes of the Civil Rights movement been countered by the ingeniousness of contemporary white society to develop new social and economic systems to continue the legacy of racial exploitation? Does the de jure residential and educational segregation of pre-1960s America still remain as de facto segregation? Are we closer to the threshold of racial hostility than we are to that of racial reconciliation?

Years of education, reinforced by television sitcoms, have left the students trained to get all of the answers before the class is over. However, I remind them that the preparation course is about learning to ask good questions in good ways. This is exactly what they are doing. Throughout the month of January, we will look for some of the answers to these questions together.

Preparing for Personal Interaction with Diversity

The first three course objectives are the building blocks for our final objective—personal interaction with diversity. I emphasize that the application of our knowledge in the context of personal, face-to-face interaction with diversity is the keynote of the tour. It is why we are traveling cross-country, rather than staying in this classroom and interacting with ourselves. I further emphasize that, at times, this interaction will not be comfortable. Nor will it always be ego bolstering. In the long run, however, if we allow it, it will become the first step on our journey to see with the other's eyes.

I shift into preaching mode and tell the students that if it is a journey they are willing to begin, it should be a journey they are willing to see through to the end. To commit to interacting with diversity is to commit to doing it on terms outside of our comfort zones. I use an example from the 1996 tour to illustrate my point. At the end of that tour, the students and I met for a final debriefing on our last evening in Washington, D.C. Among my questions to them were: "What could I do differently next time? How can I make the next tour better?" Most of their responses centered around the issue of wanting to spend more time in personal interaction with diversity. When I pushed them for a picture of what that interaction would look like, they replied with some very noble ideas—working in a soup kitchen, building a shelter with Habitat for Humanity, or passing out blankets to the homeless. In the midst of those noble desires, though, there was hidden an unsettling truth. The truth was that my students, similar to most white Americans, were only comfortable relating to the other in specific situations of *unequal* status— situations where they were the saver and the other needed saving. They were not drawn to positions where they would have to learn from or be influenced by a minority. They wanted to do *all* of the teaching and influencing.

This "messiah complex" speaks to one of the great unspoken truths about interacting with diversity. Unless we are wholeheartedly willing to be taught and influenced, to see with the other's eyes, no amount of clever pedagogy, rhetoric, or incentive will make a difference. I praise the students for their willingness to begin this journey, while also challenging them to have the intellectual courage to follow the road where it leads.

As the final class closes, I hand out two packing lists that Joy and I constructed as a result of our 1996 experience. The students do not seem overly impressed by them. I suspect they will not even glance at the lists again until the night before the tour, when they are frantically trying to figure out how to get everything they have laid out into one portable backpack. We have not covered all that I wanted to in this preparation course. Some assignments were flops. Others needed more time for debriefing. The readings were extensive, but only touched the tip of the iceberg. Regardless, the students are better prepared than the 1996 group to ask good questions in good ways. They know the basic facts behind much of what we will encounter. Now they can appreciate more nuances of what they will see, hear, and feel. They should be more discerning and critical. I take some measure of comfort in the realization that I have done all I could to bring them to a point of "teachableness." The answers that we *can* find on the tour, we are in a position *to* find. I wish the students a happy holiday season and tell them I will see them in Los Angeles in less than three weeks.

2. LOS ANGELES: TAIKO DRUMS, BLUES, AND THE BANANA BUNGALOW

Tip the world over on its side and everything loose will land in Los Angeles.

Frank Lloyd Wright, American architect

January 5

Before it seems possible, the plane from Spokane to Los Angeles has touched down at LAX. I find most of the students at our prearranged meeting point. Joy is waiting with several others at the baggage claim. Once we are all assembled, I call a shuttle service and the trip has officially begun. We make our way toward Hollywood and our three nights at the Banana Bungalow.

The original settlement of what would become the city of Los Angeles is traced to September 4, 1781. In anticipation of that day, Felip de Neve, governor of California, had taken great pains—at the order of King Carlos III of Spain—to establish the settlement as a new pueblo. He drew up plans including a plaza, fields, pastures, and royal lands. The range of planning before the first settler arrived is ironic in light of the unfettered growth of contemporary Los Angeles.

Three-fourths of the original forty-four settlers recruited by de Neve were nonwhite. Twenty-six were of African descent and seven were American Indians. At the founding ceremonies, which were watched by the Yang-Na Indians, the Franciscan monk Junipero Serra named the new town after Saint Francis of Assisi's first church—"El Pueblo de Nuestra Señora la Reina de Los Angeles de Porciuncula," or "The Town of Our Lady the Queen of the Angels of Porciuncula." This Spanish provincial outpost neither knew nor cared that the United States had been born and would shortly begin its relentless move across the continent. The first Yankee settler in Los Angeles would not arrive until about 1820.

At the time of its 1850 official incorporation, the city of Los Angeles had a population of 1,610 and an area of twenty-eight square miles. It did not have a graded street, a sidewalk, a water system, lights, or a single public building of its own. On Saturday morning, citizens swept or cleaned the street in front of their homes. Street lighting was simple:

Owners whose house faced the street were obliged to put a light at the front door during the first two hours of darkness. Progress was validated with the release of the first Los Angeles telephone book in 1882—all three pages of it. Today, Los Angeles' phone book is a tad larger. It is the second most populous city in the United States, with a population in excess of 3.7 million people crammed within an area of 470 square miles. Los Angeles County now has nearly 9 million residents. Today there are 7,366 miles of streets and water and power are brought from mountains hundreds of miles away.

In 1960, four of five people in Los Angeles County were white. However, with LAX serving as the "new Ellis Island" for foreign immigration to this country, the Los Angeles metropolitan area is now a Third World metropolis. Area publicists boast that the Los Angeles region has the richest diversity of food, clothing, architecture, entertainment, languages, worldviews, and religions available anywhere in the world. It is often billed as the "multicultural capital of the world" and hailed as a model of living in diversity. As a city where more than one hundred languages are spoken in the public school system, members of the four major racial minority groups make up more than sixty percent of the total area population, and there is more racial mixing than in almost any other major U.S. city, Los Angeles certainly resembles its self-appointed moniker. How well it serves as a model of living in diversity, however, is open to question.

There is a strong thread of racial and ethnic polarization running through Los Angeles' past and present. For example, when America seemed to be turning a corner with the passage of the Civil Rights Act in 1964, California (similar to many other states) reacted with legislation to block the fair housing components of the act. The feeling of injustice and despair in the inner cities was especially pronounced. On August 11, 1965, a routine traffic stop in the Watts neighborhood of South Central Los Angeles provided the spark that lit the fire of those seething feelings. After eleven days of violence, the Watts riots left thirty-four dead, more than a thousand people injured, nearly four thousand arrested, and close to $40 million in property damage. A subsequent study of the riots revealed that they were symptomatic of much deeper problems—the high under- and unemployment rate in the inner city, poverty, neglect, poor access to housing and social services, police misconduct, and a failing public education system. Many of these problems only worsened when residents of South Central Los Angeles who could leave the area did, taking with them much needed professional and capital resources. Even today, several areas of the community destroyed during the 1965 riots have yet to be rebuilt.

Nearly thirty years later, Los Angeles would again erupt in racial violence. On April 29, 1992, a largely white jury in Simi Valley, California, rendered their verdicts in a controversial case involving the 1991 videotaped beating of a black man, Rodney King, by four white LAPD officers. Despite the searing image of the beating played day after day on the national airwaves, three of the four officers were acquitted of state criminal charges of assault with a deadly weapon and using unnecessary force. The jury failed to reach a verdict on the fourth officer. For the next three days, violence and mayhem ran throughout various points of the city. The hardest hit areas were South Central Los Angeles and Koreatown. Mayor Tom Bradley imposed a curfew. Schools and businesses were closed. Four thousand National Guard troops were summoned. Veterans of the Kuwaiti desert found themselves patrolling the paved streets of America's second largest city. The toll was devastating—at least fifty people dead, thousands injured and arrested, and more than $1 billion in property damage. These riots still stand as the worst civil unrest in U.S. history.

In episodes of urban unrest, there are two conflicts involved. The first is the riot itself. The second is the subsequent ideological battle as commentators, politicians, and social activists seek to impose their particular interpretations of the causes and consequences of the riots onto the national consciousness. It is in this post-riot ideological battle that we find the most striking difference between the 1965 and 1992 riots.

In general, the 1965 riots were seen as a result of social problems afflicting the black community. This liberal interpretation of social unrest argued that such riots are more or less inevitable under certain conditions. The experience of widespread discrimination, police harassment, social injustice; the inequitable distribution of resources and power; political alienation; and the inadequacy of governmental institutions contribute to the build-up of social pressures that eventually result in unrest and disorder of some kind. The widespread responses to the 1965 riots—the war on poverty, policies of infrastructure improvement—testified to dual beliefs that society must take some of the blame for the riots and that things can be put right by readjusting the social framework. In short, the 1965 riots were seen as just a violent social hiccup that could be resolved by manipulating the social architecture.

In the wake of the 1992 riots, however, a very different ideological consensus emerged. In the immediate aftermath, most felt obliged to pay some lip service to the liberal interpretations of the 1960s. However, in the ensuing months the national discussion began to be dominated by more conservative or "riff-raff" theories of civil disorder that blamed the violence on the criminality or immorality of the individuals involved, rather than addressing the social circumstances that might have given rise to such tensions and frustrations. The root causes of the riots were placed in the flawed nature of the rioters and the "dependency culture" engendered by welfare programs, rather than in any problems with the way that society treats those at the bottom. Rather than being a *catalyst* for the riots, the King verdict was seen as merely a *pretext* to be exploited by criminals, hoodlums, and the other low-life of Los Angeles. Thus, the 1992 riots were not a response to social problems *afflicting* the urban communities, they arose from problems *within* those communities themselves.

Kofi Buenor Hadjor, who teaches African studies at the University of California, Santa Barbara, argues that the 1992 riots led liberals to be taken in by this traditionally conservative theory of civil disorder. The resulting convergence has led to a postliberal consensus in American politics that blames the poorest and least powerful members of American society not only for their own plight, but for many of the problems facing the nation as a whole—from crime to budget deficits. This represents a major shift in the political and social climate in America from that surrounding the riots of the 1960s. Analysts continue to track the

implications this shift will have for governmental policy on race relations, welfare spending and police strategies.

What is the state of race relations in post–Rodney King Los Angeles? The
answer depends on whether you see the glass as half full or half empty.
Half-full advocates argue that Angelenos have put the riots behind them.
They see undeniable progress in post-riot recovery—in both physical and
relational terms. They point to polls showing that an increasing number
of Angelenos are satisfied with their communities, with the city as a
whole, and with the LAPD. Six months after the riots, eighty-two percent
of Angelenos said race relations in their city were poor. A year later,
seventy-nine percent still held that view. In 1997, "only" sixty-six percent of poll respondents believed that race relations in Los Angeles were
poor.

Of course, the half-empty advocates have a heyday with the quixotic
implication that a city where two-thirds of the citizens still believe that
race relations are poor is anything close to a healed city. They argue that
there are still signs of underlying negativity and division. Earl Ofari
Hutchinson, a black sociologist and author, says: "Despite unprecedented, citywide soul-searching and the promise from national and even
global attention [after the riots], Los Angeles is still a Balkanized city of
separate, unequal societies. Despite some superficial changes, . . . I would
venture to say this city is in many ways more divided into whites,
blacks, Latinos, Asians than in 1992."

Hutchinson's view is supported by the fact that there is little in the
way of a human relations infrastructure in the Los Angeles area. What
does exist in this area is poorly funded and has little or no decision-
making power or authority to develop and implement policy. Most insid-
ers believe that the postliberal consensus has left no room for serious
consideration of the problems of urban impoverishment that were the
basis of both the 1965 and 1992 riots. Instead, society has absolved itself
of the blame by focusing on the "problem" posed by the urban poor
themselves—their immoral behavior, their dependency culture, their
criminal and drug habits. This self-absolution led to inaction. For instance, the organization that was to be the centerpiece of riot recovery,

known as Rebuild L.A., failed to attract needed corporate interest and, as a result, was torn apart by mismanagement, infighting, and overexpectations. Entrepreneur Peter Ueberroth left Rebuild L.A. in 1994, and it was downsized to a research group that closed its doors early in 1997.

However, we must not allow a tendency toward self-absolution to deafen us to what the riots yell about urban impoverishment and racial and ethnic relations in Los Angeles. There are at least four important lessons to be learned from the riots.

First, the 1992 riots reflected more than simply minorities' long-held suspicion and distrust of the justice system. They also were symptomatic of the perpetually unaddressed economic and social problems underlying the 1965 riots. As Krashaun Scott, a former member of the Los Angeles Crips gang, says: "South Central Los Angeles is a Third World country. What we got is inadequate housing and inferior education. I wish someone would tell me the difference between Guatemala and South Central." The sobering reality is that there would not be much to tell. For example, the unemployment rate in South Central Los Angeles remains at fifty percent—much higher than the national rate during the Great Depression. Even for those who find employment, racial disparities in Los Angeles can still be measured in dollars and cents. The mean yearly income for whites in the Los Angeles area is $29,755 compared to $20,299 for blacks and $13,267 for Hispanics. Undocumented immigrants earn an average of $7,904, which is still more than blacks that lack a high school diploma. Even the usually conservative *Business Week* recognized the economic spark to the 1992 riots: "Racism surely explains some of the carnage in Los Angeles. But the day-to-day living conditions with which many of America's urban poor must contend is an equally compelling story—a tale of economic injustice."

Second, the 1992 riots revealed other underlying racial and ethnic torrents that divide. Sociologists Albert Bergesen and Max Herman of the University of Arizona even suggest that the "desegregation" of black neighborhoods in South Central Los Angeles by the recent influx of Hispanics and Asians was the *primary* precipitator of the unrest. Bergesen and Herman see the riots as defensive backlash violence from majority blacks in response to the rapid demographic shift in their neighborhoods. In their understanding, it is the physical racial transformation of the neighborhood itself—rather than poverty, police harassment, social injustice, bad schools—that fuels the propensity for riot violence. Moreover, it is not just the changing proportion of racial groups, but the *rate* of change that triggers racial violence. In Bergesen and Herman's model, the ethnic transformation that occurred in South Central Los Angeles resulted in a rising temperature ready to boil. The Rodney King verdict was the catalyst for the temperature to spike and send this city into seizure.

Although Bergesen and Herman dangerously minimize other important aspects of the social context, they do remind us that the riots revealed deep racial divisions that did not adhere to our literal black-and-white understanding of racial tension. As social critic Richard Rodriguez reflects, "The Rodney King riots were appropriately multiracial in this multicultural capital of America. We cannot settle for black and white conclusions when one of the most important conflicts the riots revealed was the tension between Koreans and African-Americans. . . . Here was a race riot that had no border, a race riot without nationality. And, for the first time, everyone in the city realized—if only in fear—that they were related to one another." As Rodriguez asserts, the deepest of the racial divisions was that between blacks and Koreans.

Between 1970 and 1990, Los Angeles' Korean population swelled dramatically to become the largest Korean community outside of Asia. Most of these immigrants came to America with little money. Because of the need to invest in low-capital-interest businesses that provided for a quick return on investments, Korean immigrants often opened businesses in neighborhoods nearly devoid of large corporate-owned grocery chains. Most of these neighborhoods were in areas of urban impoverishment left vacant by Jewish business owners after the 1965 riots. In 1975, there were 615 Korean-owned businesses in Los Angeles; by 1985, there were more than 2,300, most of them in historically black neighborhoods.

At the time of the 1992 riots, Koreans ran the bulk of South Central Los Angeles' grocery and liquor stores. The poignant images of these Koreans ferociously guarding their businesses from looting and fire still linger. Paul M. Ong, chair of the Department of Urban Planning at the

University of California Los Angeles, reports that 2,073 Korean stores were burned, looted, or damaged in the 1992 riots, accounting for losses of $359 million. These losses represented more than one-third of the total damage sustained within Los Angeles. Recognizing the prevailing direction of the hostilities, some non-Korean owners even hung signs outside their buildings saying "Chinese-owned" or "Latino-owned" to divert the mob.

Many of the Korean businesses damaged during the riots did not have the insurance necessary to rebuild. A large number of Korean retailers moved to Seattle, San Francisco, Denver, or back to Seoul. For those who did rebuild in Los Angeles, city politics often made the process as difficult as possible. Recognizing the strained relations, several black-Korean friendship societies formed after the riots. Most no longer exist today. If levels of animosity between blacks and Koreans in Los Angeles are lower today, it is only due to an exodus that has dropped the number of Korean-owned businesses in South Central Los Angeles by close to fifty percent.

The post-riot prognosis for relations between Koreans and Hispanics, however, is more hopeful. During the 1994 riots, Hispanic reactions were most intense in Koreatown. Koreatown—which is bordered on the north by Sunset Boulevard, on the west by Crenshaw Boulevard, on the south by the Santa Monica Freeway, and on the east by Hoover Avenue—is dominated by Korean businesses. However, seventy percent of the residents are Hispanic. The riots were an opportunity for some Hispanics to vent their anger and frustration about the disrespectful treatment and exploitation to which they were often subjected as customers and employees in Korean-owned businesses. Since the riots, however, these two communities have forged a new understanding rooted in commonalties in immigrant status, enthusiasm for small businesses, and even an odd linguistic connection (more than 20,000 of Los Angeles' Koreans come from Latin America and speak Spanish as their second language). Koreatown now stands as a community learning to live and prosper in the tensions of racial diversity.

The third lesson learned from the unrest is that the legacies of the riots have left a deep mark on our future—the children. For example, Jo Ann Farver, a researcher at the University of Southern California, compared inner-city preschool children in Los Angeles to children of similar age in low-income areas of San Jose, California; Detroit, Michigan; and Newark, New Jersey. In stories they were asked to make up, the children from Los Angeles invented more unfriendly characters that displayed significantly more aggressive behavior.

Fourth, academics assessing the employment impacts of the 1992 riots also suggest that racial divisions have deepened. It is estimated that nearly 100,000 jobs were lost because of the riots. Job losses for Hispanics and blacks accounted for seventy percent of all jobs lost. Because Asians did not benefit at all from efforts to create jobs in the aftermath of the riots, they also were affected adversely—although not as much as Hispanics and blacks.

Only 26,000 jobs have been created in the rebuilding efforts, thus resulting in a net loss of 74,000 jobs. Research reveals that Los Angeles' restoration projects targeting the job losses suffered during the riots have disproportionately benefited whites. Job losses for whites amounted to only fifteen percent of the total job losses after the riots. However, whites have obtained sixty percent of the jobs generated by restoration projects. Minorities, which make up the remaining eighty-five percent of job losses, have seen relatively few employment benefits. The poorly named "restoration" projects reveal how little Los Angeles learned from the riots and are now among the many factors contributing to the growing racial and ethnic divisions in Los Angeles.

After we have set up our bunks at the Banana Bungalow, we meet outside for a brief informational session. I remind the students to practice the utmost courtesy with their roommates. It is a long trip and I tell them that nothing can ruin it more than discourteous early-morning people, long-lasting-shower folks, or late-night bongo players. I then ask the students to pair off with a partner that they will keep for the entire month. Each set of partners then pairs off with another set. A colleague suggested this as a more efficient alternative to counting heads several times a day. Now, I will simply yell "check" and have each person check their partner and each set of partners check their other set. It sounds good in theory and I think it will work. I also divide the students into two groups—red and black, after our school colors. In each city, one group will be assigned to me and the other to Joy. When we cannot all get on the same bus or go on the same tour, we will have two ready-made groups that can alternate.

I close by encouraging the students to do a few things. First, I encourage them, if possible, to lower their expectations of the trip. They have been anticipating this trip for well over a year now. It simply will not live up to their inflated expectations. So I ask them to relax a bit and take each experience for what it offers. Second, I encourage them to have a teachable attitude every day. We will all benefit by putting on our "What can I learn today" hats, rather than our more comfortable "I know everything I need to know" hats. Finally, I remind them of the importance of being on time. We will have a lot of "hurry up and waiting," but that is a lot better than the alternative—missing a scheduled event on the itinerary.

January 6

I froze to death last night. I wore several layers of clothes, a wool stocking cap, and my gloves. However, I thought that maybe my blood was just getting thinner as I aged. I take a perverse comfort in hearing that each of the students also spent last night shivering under a single bed sheet. The Banana Bungalow is obviously no better prepared for this cold snap in Los Angeles than we are. The bungalows have no heaters and the few blankets that are available were readily gobbled up by the staff. One student, who got up for a late-night walk to get his frozen blood flowing, reports that last night's low reached thirty-four degrees—as measured by a thermometer *inside* one of the bungalows. We cannot assume that the thermometer was actually working. Not much else at this place does and I don't see why the thermometer should be any different. Regardless, I cannot image the reading was that far off.

Some of us brave the showers. Although they did not empty and some unusual creatures floated up from the drain, they at least provide a brief respite of warmth. Very clearly, others chose not to shower. After a pseudo-breakfast (two pieces of toast free, extra pieces at 25¢ each), we board a city bus for our trip to downtown Los Angeles and Little Tokyo.

On our way to Little Tokyo, we pass city hall. The Los Angeles political scene is a microcosm of the city's triumphs and struggles with racial and ethnic diversity. Blacks, for instance, have long exercised a degree of power in Los Angeles out of all proportion to their numbers. They make up about ten percent of the county's population, but hold about twenty-five percent of the jobs in city government and about thirty-three percent of those in county government. Blacks have held three seats on the fifteen-person city council since the 1960s. Three of the region's representatives in the U.S. Congress are black, including Maxine Waters, the chairperson of the congressional Black Caucus. Perhaps most notably, Tom Bradley served as mayor of Los Angeles from 1973 to 1993.

Today, however, the golden age of black power in Los Angeles politics is fast fading. Bradley's successor as mayor is a rich, white Republican, Richard Riordan. Bradley's carefully constructed coalition of South Los Angeles blacks and Westside Jews has collapsed, first strained by the popularity of a black antisemite, Louis Farrakhan; further strained by the O. J. Simpson trial; and then broken by the 1992 riots. In addition, demographic changes have conspired to limit black political influence. Both the Hispanic and the Asian populations in Los Angeles have more than doubled over the past two decades. The number of Hispanic- and Asian-owned businesses in Los Angeles County has increased from 70,000 to 220,000 since the early 1980s, while the number of black-owned businesses has remained static at 20,000. Watts (which is now more than sixty percent Hispanic) and South Central, once synonymous with black America, are now being racially demographically annexed to Hispanic East Los Angeles.

Unfortunately, the demographic gains for the Hispanic and Asian communities have not led to corresponding political gains. The biggest reason for their lack of political voice is that the number of Hispanic and Asian registered voters is not even remotely proportionate to their share of the population. In the thirty-seventh congressional district, for example, blacks make up thirty-two percent of the population, but fifty-five percent of registered voters. Hispanics make up forty-five percent of that district's population, but only sixteen percent of registered voters. Some of this discrepancy is due to age, citizenship status, and education level.

Entry to political life for Hispanics and Asians remains problematic. For instance, it took a voting-rights suit in 1991 to get Gloria Molina elected to the lowest rung of the political ladder, the school board. There even are charges that some established black politicians, who learned too well from their white predecessors, are deliberately using their power to slam doors rather than build bridges for newcomers to the political machinery.

Hispanic activists in Compton, for instance, routinely accuse black politicians of being interested only in preserving their own positions in the face of changing demographics. Although Hispanics now make up more than half of Compton's 93,500 residents, blacks control the mayor's office, the city council, all but one school board seat, and four of five municipal jobs in Compton. Whereas political leaders have generally turned a deaf ear, some black clergy in Compton have been outspoken in support of the Hispanics' criticisms. As one minister said, "We are today the entrenched group trying to keep out intruders, just as whites were once the entrenched group and we were the intruders." A Hispanic scholar noted that "some of the things black councilmen say about the Hispanic population sound like the kinds of things southern whites would have said about blacks in the 50s: 'We were here first. We're being pushed out. These are our jobs. How dare you [try to] take them away?' "

However, there are signs that Hispanics and Asians are ready to take the reins of political power. The use of deracialized electoral strategies to capture offices in diverse jurisdictions has led to the emergence of successful political candidates such as Mike Hernandez, Richard Alarcon, and J. Kim. This has, in turn, led to substantial increases in registered and participatory Hispanic and Asian voters.

Hispanics were particularly politicized by Proposition 187, which tried to restrict public education and health and social services to undocumented illegal immigrants. Endorsed by a margin of fifty-nine to forty-one percent in the November 1994 elections, the proposition is currently in litigation (and may be for years to come). Ironically enough, the controversy surrounding Proposition 187 actually aroused a docile Hispanic electorate and sowed the seeds for a revitalized Hispanic political voice. In the April 1997 mayoral election, for example, the Hispanic turnout nearly doubled to fifteen percent of the vote. Many political analysts expect Hispanics (long described as the "sleeping giant" of the political scene) to become the dominant constituency in Los Angeles.

As I walk past city hall, I am again struck that Tom Bradley's principle of defusing the polarizing effects of race by building winning cross-racial coalitions still has a lot to teach all of us about living in diversity.

Our first stop today is a guided tour of Little Tokyo and our opening interaction with Asian-American experiences. From the fall preparation course, we know that Asian Americans have immigrated from more than twenty countries and have been in America for more than 150 years. Following the abolition of slavery, large numbers of Chinese were recruited by American businesses to come and work in this country. Shortly afterward, however, their presence became highly contested. They were often persecuted not for their vices, but for their virtues of discipline and hard work—virtues that made them temptingly employable in times when jobs were increasingly scarce. In 1882, the Chinese Exclusion Act became the first law to prohibit the entry of immigrants on the basis of nationality. In the next decades, more than six hundred pieces of anti-Asian legislation limiting or excluding persons of Asian ancestry from citizenship were passed. Until the 1965 Hart-Cellar Act, Asian immigration remained either illegal or so sharply limited as to be virtually nonexistent.

Our morning tour is presented by the Little Tokyo Business Association in conjunction with the Japanese-American Cultural and Community Center. Our tour guide, a very soft-spoken elderly woman whose name we never really do catch, tells us that the first Japanese immigrants (the *Issei*) set foot in Southern California more than one hundred years ago. "They were sustained," she continues, "by their pride in the centuries-old culture of Japan. It enabled them to believe in themselves as somebodies, even though they were often treated as nobodies, because they were the inheritors of an ancient culture going back more than two thousand years." Little Tokyo, which is now in the midst of redevelopment, was one of their sustaining influences.

The tour is brief and unimpressive. Understandably, our tour guide is more intent on getting out of the biting cold rather than answering a lot of questions about the role of Little Tokyo in preserving her cultural heritage. In forty-five minutes, we whirl by a one-hundred-year-old grapefruit tree in the Japanese-American Cultural and Community Center Plaza, the James Irvine Garden, several displays of public art, and the New Otani Hotel and Garden. Perhaps it is because most of the businesses have not yet opened for the day, or it is simply the unusual cold, or it is a testimony to a marked degree of assimilation, but we all are struck by the relative sense of desertion we feel throughout Little Tokyo. Had someone not told us, we would never have suspected we were in a distinct racial enclave within Los Angeles. As we wait for a crossing light to change, I tell the students to save these impressions for contrast to Chinatown in San Francisco.

At my request, at the end of the tour our guide has made arrangements for us to visit the Jodoshu North American Buddhist Mission. Cultural diversity has many different facets. One of these is religion. Throughout the tour, I will ask all of the students—whether or not they themselves are religious—to examine the influence of religious beliefs and practices on culture. Given the dominant influence of Buddhism in the Japanese culture, this seems to be the perfect place to start.

Buddhists, regardless of which of the thousands of strands you are discussing, are incredibly intentional in the attention given to details and symbols in their religious practices. The Jodoshu building, which was completed in 1992, is a radical departure from the traditional design of most Buddhist temples. The general design of the building reflects the concepts of peace and harmony inherent in both Japanese and American Buddhism. We enter through a gate that is sustained by three pillars and has a triangular roof. We later learn that this gate refers to the basic religious minds that Jodoshu members should possess: first, a sincere mind; second, a deep mind; and third, a mind aspiring for birth in the Pure Land. In testimony to Buddhist efficiency, it also refers to the three ways in which one can attain enlightenment: wisdom, compassion, and truth. The apex of the triangular roof points toward the west, the traditional home of the Amida Buddha. The path between the gate and the entrance to the temple is bordered by representations of two basic elements of the Buddhist world, fire and water.

We are met at the entrance by a young monk. His English is halting and he is clearly intimidated by our presence. However, he is just as clearly eager for the opportunity to share his religion with a group of interested others. As we enter, he points out that the front view of the building consists of two rectangular shapes on either side of the main entry leading into the sanctuary and altar. They are symbolic of two hands embracing the sanctuary. The roof, which is made up of three imposing arcs, represents both clouds floating in the blue sky and the temple rising toward the Pure Land, a place where all Jodoshu Buddhists aspire to be. Above us, in the wide entryway, are twenty-five soft lights hanging from the ceiling. Each light, he informs us, represents one of the twenty-five Bodhisattvas (beings who, having reached the brink of nirvana, voluntarily renounce that prize and return to the world to make nirvana available to others). In general, the building communicates a sense of freedom and open-mindedness, both of which are basic teachings of Buddhism.

As we enter the sanctuary, we are greeted by the unmistakable smell of incense. A very high ceiling gives us the sense of having entered another world. On the ceiling panels, where one would typically expect to see traditional flowers found in Buddhist temples, are painted instead the flowers of the fifty states. Our host tells us that these were chosen to indicate Buddhism's close tie with the United States. However, our attention is most drawn to the altar at the front of the sanctuary. The image of the Amida Buddha, the Buddha of Infinite Light and Life, is enshrined in the center of the altar. He is flanked by Zendo (613–681 c.e.), the Chinese monk who was the founder of the Jodoshu school in China, and Honen Shonin (1133–1212 c.e.), the founder of Jodoshu Buddhism in Japan. Gold encases the artifacts on the altar and beautifully represents the eternal light that emanates from the Amida Buddha. In this ultramodern building, the very traditional altar is a striking call to the distant past.

I am intrigued at the way in which our host has introduced us to his religion. He could have simply listed the basic beliefs, described the Ten

Transgressions and Five Grave Offenses, related the Original Vows of Amida Buddha, and been done with it. Instead he has chosen to teach us through the physical structure of the building. To use the corporeal to teach the spiritual is nothing new, but he has done it in an incredibly engaging manner.

I also get the strong sense that the monk is not looking to evangelize potential converts. He simply wants to share an important part of who he is with us. His open-mindedness is a direct reflection of Buddhist teachings and is reinforced as he patiently explains the traditional Buddhist belief that there are many different paths to get to the top of the mountain. Such tolerance flies in the face of most Western religious traditions and I see more than a few of the students flinch at his comments. Such tolerance, however, is one of the many factors at the heart of the exploding popularity of Buddhism in America. It would be a mistake to reduce the appeal of Buddhism to the latest religious fad of the Richard Geres, Phil Jacksons, Tina Turners, Herbie Hancocks, Courtney Loves, and Steven Segals. Today, there are more than 100,000 American-born Buddhists and their number increases daily. There is clearly something about the do-it-yourself philosophy and daily spiritual interconnectedness of Buddhism that is touching a chord deep within many Americans.

We conclude our time at the mission in a narrow meditation room. Here, one comes to recite the Nembutsu and meditate as a way of cleansing the mind. As further illustration of his religion's open-mindedness, the monk asks one of our students to come forward, kneel on the mat, strike a wooden drum with an intricately carved stick, and chant the Nembutsu with him. Again, the practices of many religious worldviews are so sacred that only a privileged few can participate. Here, however, there is no fear that a "nonbeliever" will taint a sacred space or object. One of our students steps forward to participate. Our host is impressed enough with her recitation of the Nembutsu to assure her of a place in the Pure Land.

We leave the mission feeling as if we have found a new friend. Although the student who recited the Nembutsu seems smugly excited about her new place in the Pure Land, I doubt that there will be a rush of students from a small Presbyterian school in the Pacific Northwest flocking to convert to Buddhism. What a valuable experience, though, to hear about the religion from a young Jodoshu monk and get a glimpse of what it means to his cultural identity.

We split up for lunch among the dozens of options found in Little Tokyo. Afterwards, we rendezvous at the Japanese-American National Museum. The museum, a private, nonprofit institution founded in 1985, was the first in the United States dedicated to sharing the experience of Americans of Japanese ancestry. Since 1992, it has been housed in a unique 1925 building that has a quirky mix of Italian, Babylonian, Egyptian, and traditional Buddhist elements. As we enter the building, we notice the extensive construction to our right that will eventually triple the size of the museum.

We begin our time at the museum in a debriefing with two of our volunteer docents—Hal Keimi and Mas Masumoto. Both are elderly men who seem incredibly excited to share their individual and collective cultural stories with us. They are part of the *Nisei* generation, children of the first generation *(Issei)* of Japanese immigrants. Although their parents were never permitted citizenship status, both of our hosts—having been born in the United States—were citizens from birth. However, their citizenship status did not spare them from what the American Civil Liberties Union has called the worst single wholesale violation of civil rights of American citizens in our history. In the wake of Pearl Harbor, Keimi and Masumoto were among the 120,000 Japanese Americans, two-thirds of them U.S. citizens, taken from their homes and locked up, without trial or hearings, simply because of their Japanese ancestry. Rather than determining individual commitments of loyalty, the United States government proceeded on the basis that this entire racial group was disloyal, whereas people of German or Italian ancestry were not subject to similar treatment. (Although, as Chief Justice William H. Rehnquist has noted, people of German and Italian ancestry were far more spread out in the general population and, thus, less likely to be viewed as a threat.) The perceived prevalence of military danger, coupled with an extensive history of anti-Japanese prejudice, made public acceptance of the Japanese menace—and the need for internment camps—an easy sell to most

Americans. Judicial justification followed as the internment camps were approved by the Supreme Court as a legitimate exercise of the war powers of the president.

The ten primary internment camps were located in isolated areas of Utah, Arizona, Colorado, Wyoming, Arkansas, Idaho, and California. Although conditions and experiences varied greatly, as both Keimi and Masumoto related, there was typically no physical brutality in the internment camps. Camp communities were set up to resemble normal communities to the greatest extent possible. Each of the camps had schools and hospitals, a newspaper, some degree of democratic self-government, and many leisure activities. However, there were certainly severe hardships—removal from their homes, the forced sale of houses and liquidation of businesses at less than market value, and the harsh living conditions of the camps themselves. Perhaps harshest in Masumoto's experience was the loss of dignity, pride, and respect that dramatically altered family dynamics. One six-year-old, thinking the camps were in a foreign country, poignantly kept asking his mother to "take him back to America."

It was not until the beginning of 1945, as it was clear the United States was winning the war, that most of those who were still interned were released "back to America." Starting on the bottom rungs of organizational and occupational ladders, the Japanese then began the long process of rebuilding their lives and communities. For many, however, the stolen opportunities never would be regained. At the famous Pike Place Market in Seattle, for instance, two-thirds of the 1941 stall vendors were Japanese Americans. Today, none are. It was not until the Civil Liberties Act of 1988 that the U.S. government issued an official apology for the internment. Along with this apology, redress payments of $20,000 were provided to all living inmates of the internment camps. On October 9, 1990, the Reverend Mamoru Eto of Los Angeles was the first to receive a check.

As we file out of the upstairs conference room, I overhear a couple of students commenting on the lack of bitterness reflected by Keimi, Masumoto, and the general tone of the museum. One student is especially perturbed: "The history of the revoking of the rights of American citizens simply on the grounds of their skin color should anger every person, should scare every person. It should create a resolve to never let it happen again, because it very well could and might. I feel that the museum does not send a strong enough message." Although most do not feel as strongly, we do wonder how *Nisei* have found a river of forgiveness in the desert of their internment experience. Have they adopted a broad cultural norm of resignation to misfortune and simply moved on? Or does an abiding bitterness linger beneath a veneer of comfortable assimilation? As the two groups follow their respective docents, Masumoto feels the questions in the air and says to his group: "Some people don't understand how we've found such peace in America after the war years. Though some may disagree, I think we've chosen a noble task—to focus our energy on assimilation more than bitterness. To hold fast to our heritage and be as fully American as we can be. It may not be a perfect solution, but it's been our solution. We cannot, though, lower our guard and pretend that something like that may never happen again. We must always keep our eyes open."

Masumoto leads our group through the exhibit "An Artist's View of the Japanese-American Internment," which allows us to view a portion of the work of Kenjiro Nomura. On April 30, 1942, Nomura, his wife, and son were forcibly removed from their home in Seattle and transported to the Puyallup Assembly Center. Eventually they were incarcerated, along with nearly 10,000 other Japanese Americans, in the Minidoka (Idaho) internment camp. Nomura produced a gripping visual record of his experience with whatever materials he could find, often using industrial paints and government-issued paper. He left us many compelling images of camp life, including landscapes and portraits of daily rituals. His stark and concrete work gives a face to all that we have read and heard at the museum.

By now, our group is the only remaining one in the museum. Keimi and Masumoto, enjoying the ready audience they have found in the students, invite us to the lower level of the museum where they teach us some basics of origami. The men's nibble and adept fingers are tough to keep up with, but most of us manage to produce at least one thing that passes as an identifiable object—a shirt, bow tie, or kimono.

Keimi then introduces us to his favorite avocation—the art of taiko drumming—and invites two students to participate in a call-and-response drumming. They both acquit themselves admirably and one's "this girl's got rhythm" pose takes the day. As Keimi asks for one more volunteer, most eyes settle on me, and I hesitantly approach the drum. I have a classifiable rhythm disorder that is only exacerbated by crowds. Especially crowds of college students waiting for a good laugh. I stay with Keimi through a few patterns, but quickly lose him as they increase in sophistication. Undeterred (at least he was), he continues to teach the unteachable. Finally, he literally collapses in laughter, joined by the students, and the moment is past.

As we shake hands and leave the museum, we have smiles on our faces. Part of the smiles was put there by my taiko drumming talents. But the biggest part comes from having spent three wonderful hours with people interested in sharing their history and identity with us. As one student writes: "I felt like I was being met with open arms, and by people who were truly excited that I was interested in them and their heritage, and want to show me the important things and events of their community." We all feel like we have bridged a gap in "our" understanding of who "they" are.

Ironically, however, part of their history and identity spun around an injustice that "we" perpetrated to "them" more than fifty years ago. As we make our way back to the bus, I wonder if our amazement at their lack of bitterness was not something else. Maybe it was really relief at the sense that Keimi and Masumoto let us off of the hook for our ancestors' transgressions against them. Had they been a bit more bitter and angry, I doubt we would be leaving with the same reactions. Is it a false sense of joy that we feel? Or, if we are honest, isn't it at least mingled with a strong measure of relief?

There is no debriefing meeting tonight. I take stock of how the group has decided to cope with another night of near-freezing temperatures. The manager has graciously rented some space heaters for each bungalow.

However, he informs us that only two heaters at a time can be turned on. Any more than that will blow out a fuse and we will all be in the cold. So, we arrange a rotating system of artificial warmth for the night. Some students augment this with body warmth and pile on top of each other into one bed. One goes for the "street look" and patches together every piece of clothing he has in a magnificent pattern of hope. Another bungalow discovers a roommate's interesting quirk—she cannot sleep while wearing socks—and brainstorms about possible solutions. I have neither a heater nor a blanket, but I *can* sleep with socks on, so I head off to my bungalow. The anxious tension of the first "official" day of the tour, coupled with six hours of waiting for and riding on Los Angeles' public transit, has taken its toll. I fall asleep to the rhythmic sound of my chattering teeth.

January 7

The heaters, body warmth, and general exhaustion seem to have led to a better night's sleep than our first. City buses are running late this morning. Two actually pass by our stop and, although only half-full, keep moving when they see the size of our group. By the time we finally catch a bus down Santa Monica Boulevard, jump off at Century City, and take a brisk walk to this morning's appointment, we are twenty minutes late.

The Museum of Tolerance houses the Simon Wiesenthal Center. The center, which is named after the famous Nazi-hunter, has emerged as one of the leading human rights organizations in the world since its inception in 1977. It now claims to be the largest Jewish organization in the world, reaching a peak of 402,000 members early in 1994. The well-publicized Museum of Tolerance, which was founded in 1993, is a glitzy, high-tech, interactive museum that appeals to the MTV generation. It focuses on two themes through unique multimedia exhibits—the dynamics of racism and prejudice in America and the history of the Holocaust.

The desk clerk is perturbed that we are late. "The museum is heavily booked," she reminds us, "and when one group is late it throws off the whole day." Her frustration with us is heightened when she sees that each of us carries a small backpack or book bag. "You're supposed to leave those on the bus." I explained that we rode on city buses, not chartered buses. She seems somewhat placated, ushers us through the security gate, and directs us to a small closet where we can leave our bags. Joy and I raise our eyebrows at each other. It was such a tone that led the 1996 group to dub this the "Museum of *In*tolerance."

To reach the first segment of our tour, we walk down a corridor with a display entitled "We the People." At the end of the corridor, we must enter the exhibit through one of two doors—one marked "prejudiced" and the other "unprejudiced." One of the high school students attached to our group tries to open the "unprejudiced" door, but finds it permanently locked. We all go through the "prejudiced" door, clearly being identified with the perpetrators, and enter the Tolerancenter. Seeking to reach an audience that is primarily not Jewish, this area has several hands-on exhibits related to the major issues of intolerance that are part of daily life. The exhibits, which are aimed primarily at junior- and senior-high schoolers, have been described by critics both as "creative and engaging" and "offensive and ineffective." Unfortunately, we have little time to make any judgement for ourselves. Docents push us from all angles to hurry up and move on to the next area. I can see the frustration beginning to build in the students' faces.

I wish I could tell them that this is unusual or would ease up in a few minutes. Unfortunately, my several previous experiences at the museum—both with groups and as an individual—had the same modus operandi. You feel as if you are on a high-speed carnival ride, and you wonder why you weren't handed goggles at the entrance. This museum experience offers a wealth of information that whizzes by you like cars on a busy freeway. There is no time or place for reflection. I know the museum has to service a lot of people every day. During the school year, for instance, at least one thousand elementary, junior, and high school students visit the museum each day. Many of these students are "at-risk" kids from disadvantaged neighborhoods whose entrance fees are subsidized by museum members and supporters. However, I wonder if it might be better to restrict the number of daily patrons and offer a greater opportunity for experiencing, processing, and reflecting.

After a brief rest in front of a synchronized sixteen-screen video wall detailing the struggle for civil rights in America, we are ushered into the Holocaust section. Here we move step-by-step through dioramas with taped scripts. This section carries more power as we are forced to immerse ourselves in the chronology of the Holocaust. At the end, we find ourselves in a replica of a gas chamber. This is the inevitable end that we all knew would come, but that is powerful nonetheless. This culminating moment is the reason I return to the museum. As we sit on cold, stone benches (the only places to sit in the entire museum), we watch videos of death, piles of bodies, mothers discussing the loss of their children. I remember that this is where my wife Patti began to weep when we last came here together. I hear weeping around me and notice a lump in my throat as I think of my children, Brennan, Hannah, and Noah. It is not cheap emotional manipulation. It is simply that the barrage of information thrown at us finally has a chance to sink in and wash over us.

We then sweep through the multimedia learning center on the second level. The databanks in this center include more than 50,000 photos and maps, 6,000 encyclopedic entries, and fourteen hours of historic film footage and video testimonies. However, we are most drawn to the room of artifacts and documents on this level. Housed here are original letters of Anne Frank, artifacts from Auschwitz, artwork from Theresienstadt, a bunk bed from the Majdanek death camp, and a flag sewn by Mauthausen inmates for their American liberators. Unfortunately, the room is packed with people. When we do finally get it, we have all of two minutes to stand next to history. The mounting frustration that had dissipated somewhat through the Holocaust section now returns in full force.

We have now been in the museum for nearly two and a half hours. I know our collective blood sugar is low, but I push the students to stay for one more program. On most afternoons, the museum has Holocaust survivors speak. I tell the students that the opportunity to hear firsthand from a survivor is a rare one. They are one of the last generations to have this opportunity and it is one I do not want them to miss. Over the next forty-five minutes, we join a group of junior-high students from the Los Angeles Unified School District in an auditorium.

We hear from Elaine Geller, a Polish woman. During the war years, her parents had arranged for a Christian family to take her in. However, as her father was taking her to that house, he saw that other Christian families were turning such children over to Nazi authorities for reward. He fled and Geller ended up being incarcerated in a concentration camp from four until eight years of age. She lost her mother and a sister during that time. Two of her uncles were shot for hiding jewelry in bread. She survived with an aunt, and much of her testimony comes from long conversations with her father and brother.

During the question-and-answer period, one of our students asks Geller if she believes the Nazi perpetrators were inherently evil. Our students are aware of my work in this area and know my argument that, by and large, the Nazi perpetrators were ordinary people like you and me who became enmeshed in an extraordinary situation that led to their commission of extraordinary evil. I, of course, was never directly victimized by that evil. It is a good question to ask of someone who was. Geller's response catches us off-guard. "Yes! I think they liked what they were doing! There's even some research to support that!" Her anger, which was barely beneath the surface throughout her testimony, now rises in full force. "These were not ordinary people! They were monsters! They cannot be forgiven or forgotten!"

We have been at the museum for nearly four hours, so I quickly hustle the students to Century Square for a late lunch. After lunch, I tell them that our debriefing meeting is at 9:00 P.M. tonight at the Banana Bungalow. The rest of the afternoon and evening are free. Some choose to see a movie, others browse bookstores, and some, including me, head back to wash clothes and prepare for our final night of near-freezing sleep.

On the way back, a few students and I end up chewing on a question raised by our visit to the Museum of Tolerance: "What lesson should a Holocaust museum teach?" As Jon Wiener, a professor of history at the University of California, Irvine, points out, the Museum of Tolerance is predicated on the premise that Jewish suffering in the Holocaust was not unique. By placing the Tolerancenter first, the museum begins with a message of universalism. The exhibits in the Tolerancenter call attention to the past and present victimization of many other peoples in ways that have much in common with the Jewish experience. By acknowledging and emphasizing other groups' victimization, the museum connects the Jews' story to that of others. As we went through the Holocaust section, however, it was easy to develop a sense that the problems and suffering of other groups are trivial. By the end of our visit, the initial message of universalism had been superseded by the message of the uniqueness of the Holocaust.

Perhaps this is as it should be. Perhaps the Holocaust *was* so incredibly unique that it should stand apart from other cases of human suffering. On the other hand, doesn't the Holocaust impose on all of us an obligation to fight against all forms of hatred and exclusion? If so, shouldn't it be connected to the larger narrative of our inhumanity to each other? After all, as Michael Lerner writes, "'Never Again' means not only never again to the Jews, but never again to anyone, to any people, to any culture." Scholars in genocide studies certainly are split on the issue. Regardless, the premise of the Museum of Tolerance seemed contrary to its actual design and emphases. We look forward to the comparison promised by our visit to the U.S. Holocaust Memorial Museum in Washington, D.C.

The first part of our debriefing is spent going over the logistics of tomorrow's itinerary and departure. We then begin discussing two days of experiences. As we talk, I realize that I should be more insistent about nightly debriefings. Our experiences have already begun to jumble and students have to work hard to recall some of their reactions to yesterday's events.

Immediately, however, students are drawn to the contrast between the testimonies of Keimi and Masumoto and that of Geller. I warn them that these are two cases that defy comparison. As egregious as was the internment of Japanese Americans during World War II, it was not a government-sponsored plan of total extermination. Although the internment camps involved a loss of dignity, pride, and respect, they were absent of the physical brutality that was commonplace in the concentration camps of the Holocaust.

Regardless, students remain struck by the prevalence of anger in Geller's testimony relative to the lack of anger in Keime's and Masumoto's. We do not know enough about their stories or either of their cultures to reach any clear conclusions. I push the students on why Geller's anger so jolts our ideal that passivity and friendliness go hand in hand with tolerance. I argue that this ideal is ill-founded. Part of the mythology surrounding Martin Luther King Jr., for instance, has been built on down-playing his moments of anger and bitterness. The King we think we know is very different from the one revealed on a critical examination. I challenge the students to be more aware of his anger as we continue on the tour. King's genius was not to ignore those emotions. Rather, his genius was to subvert those emotions to a higher calling of tolerance and reconciliation. When we do not recognize that, we are unfairly critical of those who still express anger and bitterness at their victimization. One of the students even remarks that Geller's anger removed her credibility. I wonder why we do not allow anger to coexist with a desire for reconciliation. Why can't we stand the ambiguity of it all?

We then transition to our time at the Jodoshu mission. As I suspected, several students' experiences were colored by the monk's claim that there are several paths to redemption and enlightenment. For these students steeped in the Western Christian tradition, religious pluralism is not a virtue. As the conversation continues, some become clearly defensive about their belief that there is only one way to eternal redemption. Others become irritated at what they see as a close-minded arrogance among some in the group. We will not answer the question tonight or through this month. However, I do encourage the students to remain open to comments that make them uncomfortable. It is in that zone of discomfort that learning will take place.

When I ask about any unique experiences that the group has not shared, several students talk about their excursion into downtown Los Angeles following yesterday's time at the Japanese-American National Museum. They were struck by how "foreign" they felt at the Grand Central Market, where almost half of the signs were in Spanish and Spanish was the language spoken by almost everyone. Some were honest enough to admit that they were concerned about their safety in this area. Others expressed their annoyance at that fear and wondered why being in a different place with different people has to automatically engender fear.

As the debriefing closes, a small group of students remains behind to continue the conversation. Among this group are some students who I know struggle with the issue of religious diversity and, to some extent, even struggle with overemphasizing the victimization endured by racial, gender, and religious minorities. It is with this group that I must continue to find ways to bring them into the conversation. Many of their thoughts will challenge the thinking of the rest of the group—including mine. It is vital for their growth, as well as ours, that they find a space to be heard in our experiences.

One of these students writes in his journal that evening: "How much pain does prejudice actually cause? I really can't imagine it causing the kind of pain that death causes, with the obvious exception of when prejudice takes the form of physical violence and murder. The modern-day racism that we face takes the form of subtle attitudes that tear a person's self-confidence apart if they are not able to transcend that. And it takes the form of a lack of opportunities. But we all have our lot in life. All of us face things that destroy our self-confidence, we all face pain, and we all have certain disadvantages. Some of us get paralyzed and have to deal with the loss of our legs and/or arms. Others face divorce and the subsequent pain of that. Others have a total lack of confidence in themselves because of circumstances in their upbringing. Others are never able to fit in socially. Others have learning disabilities and can't compete in our society that values a certain type of intelligence. And still others suffer from chronic depression. And all of us eventually face the inevitable pain of tragic events."

"What I'm getting at," he continues, "is that racism is still bad, but I don't see it as worse than what we all face. Maybe this is because I don't relate. People who struggle with shame because they're economically lower class is something that tears me apart. People who aren't accepted and sought after in social circles really affect me. I hate seeing the depression and self-doubt in people who just aren't socially skilled. It's not fair. Does racism fit in that same category? I, personally, wouldn't care very much if the majority of people saw me as inferior for no good reason. I don't think I would care too much if me and 'my kind' were all put together in an internment camp. It would draw us closer together. Sure, it would be tough. But no worse than the estrangement that I feel for reasons totally unrelated to race. Racism seems horrible to me at the same level that a lot of evils in our world are. . . . Why do I feel guilty because I'm not as concerned with creating a racially unbiased society as I am with people who face economic struggles and the people in my dorm who are lonely in the midst of all the community of Whitworth College?"

These are great questions that reveal a depth of honesty and self-insight that are laudable. Unfortunately, the student sharing them in his journal entry never felt comfortable sharing them in our group setting. It was only after returning from the tour and reading his journal that I found these questions. It was a loss for all of us that I did not find ways to bring this voice into our discussions more often.

January 8

Having been bothered by our lateness to the Museum of Tolerance yesterday, we start today bright and early. We are scheduled for a 10:00 A.M. program at the House of Blues on Sunset Boulevard and arrive at 9:00 A.M. Not acknowledging the muttered comments about "I could have had an extra hour to sleep," I encourage the students to use the hour for journal writing and a warm cup of "jo" at a nearby Starbucks.

The House of Blues is a chain of multidimensional restaurants that combine Delta-inspired cuisine and live music. Part of founder Isaac Tigrett's vision was to use the House of Blues to promote racial harmony through cultural education and preservation. The House of Blues Schoolhouse Program in Los Angeles fulfills this vision by providing a unique opportunity for area grade school children to learn about African-American history and contributions. Our 1996 time at the House of Blues left me with no doubt that my students would be challenged by a program directed at grade school children. My students are products of an educational system with a selective memory regarding the contributions of various racial and ethnic groups to American life. I knew this program would be a highlight of the tour.

We begin with a brief tour of the House of Blues. We learn that portions of the roof are covered with rusted tin from old buildings at the junction of Highways 61 and 49 in the Mississippi Delta. Blues mythology has it that at this crossroad Robert Johnson sold his soul to the devil to play the meanest blues guitar in the region. If you ever listen to his music, you will suspect that Johnson, King of the Delta Blues, may have gotten the best of that deal. He later died in agony after being fed lye by a jealous girlfriend. Or perhaps Johnson was stabbed in a juke joint by a jealous husband. Or, if you prefer another version, he was killed by a jealous husband who gave him tainted liquor, the seal on the bottle of which was broken. At any rate, we do know Robert Johnson died hard and young in 1938, leaving a musical legacy that led directly to rock-and-roll.

The interior of the House of Blues, like its franchised descendants across the nation, is festooned with incredible folk art on its walls, ceilings, and floors—beer bottle caps in ingenious designs, soulful paintings and poetry (much of it from children), plaster-cast relief portraits of countless blues legends, and breathtaking pottery and masks from Africa. It's like waking up to find yourself in your grandmother's favorite junk drawer.

We take our seats around the fifth-grade children on the floor of the concert area. We then sit enthralled as two black actresses dramatize the history of Africans in America. One begins with a powerful portrayal of a young African girl captured by slave traders. The other enters, our eyes immediately drawn her way, laden with chains and tells the story of the Middle Passage. For nearly an hour, they continue through slavery, the Civil War, the Great Migration of 1910–1920, the Black Renaissance, and the Civil Rights movement. As they go, we learn of the many contributions made by blacks that our teachers and textbooks had neglected—their important roles in the creation or patent of the baby stroller, air conditioner, refrigerator, elevator, and roller coaster.

The actresses' presentation is followed by the house band that takes us through the history of the blues. Along the way, they point out that several important features of the blues, including its characteristic tonal shadings, call-and-response structure, repeated refrains, and use of the falsetto voice, derive from African musical tradition. Using their incredible musical gifts, they trace the powerful and elemental influence of blues on rock-and-roll, pop music, jazz, soul, country, reggae, and rap. The band's engaging presentation touches a part of us that has yet to be touched. "I believe there is something very special and significant about a culture's music," one student writes. "It is one of the most powerful forms of expression. I find that through music I can understand and speak and learn and feel. It is a personal avenue of release to satisfy deep emotions, and getting in touch with another culture's music is a good way for me to listen to their souls and feelings." Another agrees, "This music really reveals what it means to be human for these people." Toward the end of their presentation, the band invite several audience members up to sing the blues. Two students join in. As expected, they both give similar renditions of the "Banana Bungalow Blues." As we all laugh, another student later reminds us of the deeper lesson, "The blues, as any art, is about issues that matter to you. It doesn't have to be perfect, just meaningful."

The band closes with a rousing rendition of Jimi Hendrix's "Purple Rain"—a very popular choice for our Seattle-area students. As I look out, I see fifth-grade children moving to music they have probably never even heard, their eyes and smiles wide. As I look closer, I see even bigger eyes and smiles—most of our group is dancing as well. As the program closes, the emcee comes out and has the students yell out four affirmations: "I am somebody! I am unique! I am special! I believe in myself!" Just as I am smugly thinking of the cuteness of these trite sayings, I realize that my students and I are yelling even more loudly than the fifth graders.

As we leave the House of Blues, we take one glance back at its motto, "Unity in Diversity," and feel grateful to have seen that motto in action.

As we wait in LAX for our fog-delayed short flight to San Francisco, we reflect on Los Angeles' billing as the "multicultural capital of the world." Its demographic diversity is unquestioned. By the middle of the next century, our nation as a whole will look much like Los Angeles does now. However, the current state of racial and ethnic polarization in Los Angeles is open to debate. In the words of California historian Kevin

Starr, "On the cusp of the 21st century, Los Angeles has been probing two possibilities for the rest of urban America. The city as a cutting edge of culture—say, a new Athens or Alexandria—or the city of the dreadful night." As the nation's premier laboratory for multiculturalism, has Los Angeles become the prototype of living with diversity or is it an apocalyptic dystopia? There is certainly a lot of evidence to support a portrayal of a city that remains torn and divided. But there is also some compelling evidence of a rainbow on the horizon that promises hope.

I think back to Roosevelt High School in East Los Angeles. A sprawling urban campus of more than five thousand students, Roosevelt serves a Hispanic community that borders neighboring Asian-American communities in Monterey Park and Little Tokyo. In 1995, Roosevelt students discovered that their neighborhood had not always been monocultural. While flipping through a 1941–1942 yearbook, some students found a picture of a tranquil Japanese garden on campus as well as the faces of four hundred Japanese-American students then attending Roosevelt. Just one year later, both the garden and the students were eerily absent from the yearbook's pages. The garden was destroyed and the students and their families were interned in Manzanar.

Motivated to redress a past injustice, Roosevelt's younger generation of students pledged to rebuild the garden to dovetail with the fiftieth reunion celebration of the classes of 1942–1945. With the support of the Japanese-American National Museum, Roosevelt's Hispanic students pieced together what the garden looked like from the old yearbook photographs and graduates' recollections, mobilized community support to implement their design, and recruited local landscape architects, contractors, and suppliers to donate services and materials. Finally, in 1996, the six-hundred-square-foot traditional Japanese garden was completed. It is a good deal smaller than the original one and its trees and shrubberies have not had the time to grow lush. But it stands as an emblem of the school's multicultural heritage and a reminder that where seeds of understanding are sown, empathy and reconciliation can take root.

3. SAN FRANCISCO: THE GOODNESS OF UNCLE GUY

When you get tired of walking around San Francisco, you can
always lean against it.

Unknown

After the quick up-and-down flight to San Francisco, we head for our hostel at Fort Mason in the Golden Gate National Recreation Area. At 31,000 acres, this is one of the world's largest metropolitan parks. It is beautifully situated on the bay that includes the historic Presidio of San Francisco and the Marin Headlands. The hostel itself, which was opened in 1980, is housed in a renovated, historic, Civil War–era building. We arrive late in the evening. From the front of the hostel looking south, we are treated to the scenic lights of San Francisco. Tomorrow, we will wake up to a fresh morning and enjoy breakfast on a bluff overlooking the San Francisco Bay and Golden Gate Bridge.

San Francisco and Alameda Counties are among the five most racially diverse counties in the United States. Surprisingly, San Francisco County is second only to New York's Queens borough in racial diversity. In many ways, the story of how the Bay Area came to such diversity is similar to the stories of other large American cities. The pushes and pulls of labor and industry, coupled with the ebb and flow of legislative dictums, account for much of the contemporary face of San Francisco. However, that is not the entire story. The vagaries of history, chance, and the forces of nature also mark the evolution of racial diversity in the San Francisco Bay Area. As a mirror of who we were and are, it forms one of the most intriguing stories in American history.

European discovery and exploration of the San Francisco Bay Area and its islands began in 1542 and culminated with the mapping of the bay in 1775. Prior to that time, more than 10,000 indigenous people, in forty or so native tribes, lived in the coastal area between Point Sur and the San Francisco Bay. These people were later to be called collectively the "Ohlone," a Miwok word meaning "western people." The world of all of the Ohlone tribes would drastically change with the arrival of the missions and military posts at Monterey and San Francisco. Of the approximately

20,000 Ohlone-speaking people who inhabited the San Francisco and Monterey Bay regions in 1769, less than 2,000 were left by 1810.

The world first took notice of the Bay Area during the gold rush of 1849. During the previous year, nuggets of gold were discovered in the American River at the site of a sawmill being built near the town of Coloma, about 150 miles northeast of San Francisco. The next several years saw riches accumulated and lost, dreams attained and dashed. When the gold dried up in the late 1850s, San Francisco was well on its way to becoming a financial metropolis renowned for its grand hotels and sumptuous restaurants.

However, the impact of the gold rush went far beyond the wallet. A new community was born as San Francisco changed from a sleepy western village into a frontier boomtown. San Francisco's population exploded from about 800 in 1848 to 35,000 in 1852. Many of the erstwhile fortune-seekers, dubbed the "Forty-niners," planted roots and became farmers and shopkeepers. Prospectors from Mexico, Peru, and Chile broadened even more the racial and ethnic diversity of the area. But the greatest change to the face of San Francisco came from the thousands of Chinese laborers recruited to build railroads, work the gold mines, and tend the fields in the 1840s and 1850s. Added to the influx of nonnative prospectors and laborers was the arrival of hundreds of thousands of Irish immigrants fleeing their homeland's potato blight and economic depression during those same years. The end result was a city of astounding racial and ethnic diversity. By 1880, there were 75,000 Chinese in California, with the largest Chinese community in San Francisco. By 1900, more than twenty-five percent of San Franciscans were of Irish descent.

The Bay Area's expanding face of diversity continued as thousands of East Indians came to work on the Western Pacific Railroad between 1908 and 1910. In the following decade, special rules permitted temporary Mexican farm workers, railroad laborers, and miners to enter the United States due to the expanding economy. Many of these people also found their way to the Bay Area. World War II, like the gold rush, again brought dramatic racial and ethnic changes. Blacks from the South and Hispanics from Nicaragua and El Salvador were recruited to work in Bay Area shipyards. In 1942, thousands of Mexicans arrived to work on agricultural and railroad jobs under the Bracero Program. By 1951, that program was formalized to allow about 350,000 Mexican *braceros* ("pair of arms") into the United States each year until 1964. A new wave of Asian immigration resulted from the abolition of quotas by national origin as dictated by the Federal Immigration Act of 1965. By 1970, nearly half the population of San Francisco had grown up speaking a language other than English. A decade later, at least sixty-seven races and nationalities resided in the Bay Area.

Today, this region verges on becoming a place where no single racial group is a majority. As of 1997, American Indians, Asian Americans, blacks, and Hispanics accounted for forty-six percent of the population in the nine-county region. Despite this tremendous diversity, or perhaps because of it, the history of race relations in San Francisco is much less calamitous than that of Los Angeles. Somehow, this large, urban community has avoided major racial conflagrations in the past decades. Although tension does exist, San Francisco is not a community likely to explode in the racial violence and riots seen in so many other urban cities.

Why? I asked this question of a city official on our 1996 tour. She cited the unusual economic and educational demographics of the region as the most prevalent factors. Marin County has the highest annual per capita income of any U.S. county. Economic disparity does exist within the county, but not, in her opinion, along the racial lines one typically sees in other areas. In addition, thirty-five percent of San Franciscans have earned at least a bachelor's degree—the third highest percentage among U.S. cities after Raleigh and Seattle. In the official's opinion, this high level of educational attainment leads to greater tolerance and, coupled with the relative affluence of the region, makes San Francisco less likely to be a tinderbox of racial violence.

January 9

Unfortunately, history's marginalization of American Indians is mirrored in our itinerary. Of all the racial minority groups, the plight of the American Indians is the least documented, least discussed, and least cared about. The plethora of museums, exhibits, and memorials about the experiences of other racial groups in America stands in stark contrast to an appalling relative absence of memorialization of the American Indian experience. In mainstream American society, Indians remain the stock caricature set up by Hollywood decades ago. However, today the students and I have a chance to visit the infamous Alcatraz Island, the 1969–1971 occupation of which many proclaim to be the genesis of the American Indian activist movement.

Dr. Troy Johnson, currently on the faculty of the American Indian Studies Program and History Department at California State University at Long Beach, is the preeminent historian of the Indian occupation of Alcatraz. As he points out, thousands of American Indians see Alcatraz Island as a powerful symbol and a rallying point for unified Indian political activities. The nineteen-month occupation of Alcatraz Island was the catalyst for a rise of American Indian activism that began in 1969 and continued well into the late 1970s. The answer to why *this* place and *this* event were so pivotal to American Indian consciousness lies in the wretched history of white and American Indian relations.

American Indians did not share in the immigrant experience of other groups. However, their resident status did not prevent them from becoming aliens in their native land. The fact that the nation's frontier was another's homeland was conveniently overlooked. The Naturalization Act of 1790 excluded American Indians from citizenship. They were regarded as domestic subjects, analogous to children of foreign diplomats born here. Ultimately, however, American Indians were not accorded the courtesies typically given domestic subjects. The fulfillment of the nation's "manifest destiny" by westward expansion and government removal efforts in the 1800s made clear the American Indians' true standing—"savage dogs." They were thought so little of that American soldiers made bridle reins from strips of skin taken from their corpses, tobacco pouches from their severed testicles.

The demographic impact of our "manifest destiny" was particularly noticeable in California. Just as diverse faces of color were appearing in increasing numbers throughout that state, one significant face of color was steadily disappearing. In the early 1800s, an estimated 360,000

American Indians lived in California. In 1830, the non-Indian population living in California was only 4,256. By 1851, disease and removal had dropped the number of Indians living in California down to fewer than 100,000. Conversely, the state's non-Indian population had risen to roughly 250,000. At the turn of the twentieth century, only 16,000 Indians remained in all of the burgeoning California population—an incredible decline of more than 344,000 persons in *one* century.

In the final decades of the nineteenth century, the assimilation of Indians into mainstream society became the goal of those bent on further westward expansion as well as those who considered themselves supporters of the Indian people. In 1879, for instance, boarding schools for American Indian children became national policy. They were run by well-intentioned "liberals" of the time who were devoted to "saving the savages." With the motto "Kill the Indian and save the man," the boarding school was a place where children were stripped of their past, their family, their spirituality, their culture—a place where they were trained to be "American." Even after World War II, though no longer national policy, many American Indians saw the boarding schools as the only option for formal education and willingly sent their children. The repercussions of these experiences are still being felt in the fragmentation of American Indian families and communities.

By the 1950s, thousands of American Indians had migrated into urban life through boarding school placement and railroad, military, and defense-industry jobs. In 1953, with House Resolution 108, Congress unanimously passed a ruling that ultimately led to the displacement of 11,466 American Indians. Now, thousands more were forced to relocate to urban areas distant—in both physical and psychological terms—from their sparsely populated rural areas. In their relocation efforts, the government promised vocational training, financial assistance, job placement programs, and adequate housing for American Indians who would move to certain large cities.

San Francisco was one of those cities. However, the promises of assistance were hollow. Most American Indians who relocated found themselves trapped in unfamiliar urban environments with no marketable skills and often very little English. Many gravitated toward poverty-level housing and welfare. Some returned to their reservations and continued to wrestle with substandard medical care, sanitation, and housing and an educational system Congress called "a national disgrace." Among those who remained in the cities, disillusionment, resentment, and distrust were high. By the mid 1960s, an estimated 40,000 American Indians from one hundred tribal groups lived in the Bay Area, most of them employed in menial jobs at low pay.

It was out of this atmosphere, in concert with the national consciousness of the 1960s, that alliances and grass-root organizations devoted to unifying American Indians in the Bay Area grew. Many of these groups were stridently vocal in their complaints against their treatment. They wanted the right to control their own lives independent of the federal government. They wanted Indians' futures to be determined by Indian acts and Indian decisions. They wanted assurance that Indian people would not be separated involuntarily from their tribal groups. At times, some of these groups took a militant stance. One late 1960s article in *Warpath*, the first militant pan-Indian newspaper in the United States, summed up much of the sentiment brewing in the American Indian Bay Area community: "The 'Stoic, Silent Redman' of the past who turned the other cheek to white injustice is dead. (He died of frustration and heartbreak.) And in his place is an angry group of Indians who dare to speak up and voice their dissatisfaction at the world around them. Hate and despair have taken their toll and only action can quiet this smoldering anger that has fused this new Indian movement into being."

Signals of rising Indian activism in the Bay Area were everywhere. In March 1969, Indians picketed the federal office building in San Francisco to protest the lack of educational opportunities and to accuse the Bureau of Indian Affairs of perpetrating ignorance among American Indians. In April 1969, a press conference was called to object to police racism and brutality toward American Indians. That same month, at a public forum held by the National Council on Indian Opportunity, American Indians in the Bay Area spoke out against racism, educational deficits, inferior healthcare, unemployment, and poor housing. Sounding a prophetic note, Richard McKenzie, a Sioux, said he believed that kneel-ins, sit-ins, sleep-ins, eat-ins, pray-ins "wouldn't help us. We would have to occupy government buildings before things would change."

The first occupation of Alcatraz Island by American Indian activists came in 1964, the year after the island had been vacated by the federal penitentiary system. That occupation lasted for only four hours and was carried out by five Sioux, led by Richard McKenzie. The occupiers claimed the island under an 1868 Sioux treaty that entitled them to take possession of surplus land. In ensuing court petitions, the Sioux offered to pay 47¢ per acre for the land, the price the government had offered for 65 million acres taken from California American Indians under the Indian Claims Commission Act of 1946. At the same time, the American Indian Foundation submitted a proposal calling for the island to be the site of an Indian cultural center and university. The government's deaf ear to both the petitions and the proposal left Alcatraz Island as an icon to the Bay Area Indian people—a representation of the many broken treaties and arrogant disdain for their goals or needs.

Over the next several years, American Indian leaders tried to spin the iconic representation of the island into something powerful enough to unify the Indian community. They defined practical, historical, and political reasons for the island to be turned over to Indian people and began to draw explicit plans for its use. Before they could submit a formal application, however, the San Francisco Board of Supervisors endorsed oil baron Lamar Hunt's bid for commercial redevelopment of Alcatraz Island on September 29, 1969. The ensuing public outcry was so great that a final decision was delayed until federal recreational uses for the site could be explored.

In was in this brief delay that committed activist American Indians, primarily students, saw an opportunity to draw the nation's attention to their plight by occupying Alcatraz Island. On November 9, 1969, Richard Oakes, a Mohawk Indian who would quickly emerge as the charismatic leader of the occupation, and a group of fifty Indian supporters set out on a chartered boat to claim the island for the Indian people. The original agreement with the owner of the chartered boat was that they would circle the island rather than risk an attempt to dock. Not content to simply make a symbolic claim, however, Oakes and four other men jumped overboard and swam 250 yards to the island. They claimed the island by right of discovery. After a brief time, the Coast Guard transported the five men back to the mainland.

In meetings following the November 9 occupation, Oakes realized that a prolonged occupation, with young Indian people who could tolerate hardship conditions on a cold and isolated island, was possible. He immediately began recruiting American Indian students from UCLA. Before dawn on November 20, 1969, a landing force of seventy-nine American Indians—men, women, and children—again sailed to Alcatraz Island. Despite an attempted blockade by the Coast Guard and in full view of media helicopters, the Indians landed successfully. Not simply an ordinary trespass, the landing soon came to be seen for what it really was—a full-fledged occupation of a vacant federal government facility.

As days and weeks passed, it became obvious that the Indian occupiers would resist removal. They clearly and consistently made their demands known—they wanted the deed to the island and funding sufficient to establish an Indian university, a cultural center, and a museum. It became equally clear that the occupation was a public-relations nightmare for the Nixon presidency, a presidency already besieged by the My Lai massacre and soon to be confronted with the political hurricane of the May 1970 Kent State shootings. The will of the occupiers, coupled with the government's emerging policy of noninterference, forewarned a long and drawn-out occupation. The federal government was playing a waiting game, hoping that support for the occupation would subside and those on the island would elect to end the occupation.

As time went on, the government's waiting game won out. Indian organization on the island began to fall into disarray. Some Indian students returned to school. Those who left were replaced by others who had not been involved in the initial occupation and, worse yet, were often unwilling to learn about the original motives for the occupation. Additionally, many non-Indians, often from the San Francisco hippie and drug culture, began taking up residency on the island. In January 1970, Oakes's thirteen-year-old stepdaughter, Yvonne, fell three floors down a stairwell to her death. Oakes and his family, convinced the death was not accidental, left the island shortly thereafter and two competing groups maneuvered back and forth for subsequent leadership. The strong spirit of egalitarianism originally found in the occupation began to erode into a struggle for individual power and money. By early 1971, the press—which had been largely sympathetic to this point—also turned against the occupiers and began publishing stories of alleged beatings and assaults on the island. Public opinion had clearly shifted. Finally, on June 11, 1971, armed federal marshals, FBI agents, and special-forces police stormed the island and removed the remaining fifteen occupiers. The occupation that had lasted nineteen months and nine days was over in less than thirty minutes.

The occupation of Alcatraz Island remains the longest prolonged occupation of a federal facility by Indian people. What was its impact? Ultimately, it should not be judged by whether the demands of the occupiers were met. Rather, final accounting should acknowledge the underlying goals of the Indians on Alcatraz Island—to awaken the American, and international, public to the reality of the plight of the first Americans and to assert the need for Indian self-determination. As a result of the occupation, directly or indirectly, U.S. government policy became more sensitive to both of those goals. Government officials ended the termination of Indian tribes and began to support tribal self-rule, economic development on reservations, and cultural survival as a distinct people. In 1970, the administration introduced twenty-two legislative proposals on behalf of American Indians. Six were passed into law that year and forty-six the following year.

Perhaps more important, the occupation at Alcatraz Island gave birth to a new era of American Indian politics that continues today. It was the beginning of the pan-Indian movement in the United States. In the words of Wilma Mankiller, former principal chief of the Cherokee Nation, the occupation of Alcatraz "relit [the] flame, and out of the fire, all these people spread in different directions to do incredible work." On Thanksgiving Day of each year, Indian people still gather on Alcatraz Island to honor those who participated in the occupation and those who today are carrying on the struggle for Indian rights.

Grace Thorpe, a Sac and Fox, takes the impact of the occupation beyond the political: "It helped produce . . . the revival of our languages, the revival of our old Indian ways, of our traditions." Edward Willie, a Paiute-Pomo, agrees, "Before Alcatraz, I had no idea what an Indian was. People would ask me, 'Are you Indian?' 'Yeah, I'm a full-blooded Indian.' But I had no idea what that meant."

I am interested to see how the group responds to Alcatraz Island and the story it tells. I am especially interested in the multimedia exhibit that opened in the summer of 1997 entitled "We Hold the Rock." The exhibit is the first full-scale attempt by the Golden Gate National Parks Association to tell the story of the Indian occupation of 1969–1971. It is a story that needs to be told well. During the previous times I have visited Alcatraz, the Indian occupation has only been mentioned briefly in the introductory spiel by the park ranger. When it was mentioned, it was almost always cast in the ignoble sense of "the Indians occupied the island, wrote a lot of graffiti, and destroyed a lot of the buildings." The park had neglected the fact that a large group of people felt so unheard that they saw the taking of federal property as the only option to be heard.

We should pay extra for what the misty, cool morning rain adds to the atmosphere of our ferry ride to Alcatraz Island. After the brief introductory film about the history of Alcatraz Island, which is almost exclusively focused on its years as a federal penitentiary, we make our way to the "We Hold the Rock" exhibit. The exhibit is not well marked and is certainly not well publicized. As a matter of fact, nine of ten tourists go immediately to the prison tour and most will leave the island without even knowing this exhibit exists. My initial reaction to the exhibit is disappointment. It is literally located in a hole-in-the-wall immediately behind the larger main theater rooms. The room has a couple of television monitors, a readerboard or two with some very basic information and quotes, and bench seating for just a few people. It clearly falls a distant second to the "real" purpose of Alcatraz Island—catering to tourists' fascination with the prison. As one student says later, "I expected this part of the island's history to be a more prominent display. Well, I guess I really didn't expect it, but I wish that I could have expected it."

Regardless, the story told by the exhibit and the interviews comprising the bulk of the videotape are captivating. Students are especially struck by the resignation apparent in many of the video testimonies. "The people in the video," writes one student, "didn't seem very bitter about how the occupation ended. But they also didn't seem to have very much hope. I can see why this may not be present in their community, as everything they hope and invest their lives and self in seems to be eventually taken away. I would also lose some ambition. I wonder if this is why many Indians live the life they do today—because of their lack of hope." Another student remarks that the Alcatraz occupation seems a poignant metaphor for the American Indian resistance movement: "It is so interesting to me that the American Indian stand and the beginning of their unified struggle against the larger American political system was initially started on a tiny, isolated island filled with concrete and iron. It is as if the American Indian resistance was caged in from the beginning. Their movement appears to be isolated today just like their initial resistance in 1969." Students also struggle with the role of public property and who should define its purpose and use. "It is too bad," one later writes, "that the land is used to allow people to gloat about the good old days of prisons and prisoners like Capone, when it could be used for a museum about American Indians or some other thing for the enhancement and enrichment of the American Indian community."

The group takes its time weaving through the rest of the story of Alcatraz Island. After a few hours, three students and I make our way back to the mainland on the ferry. On the way, we discuss the legacy of the Indian occupation of Alcatraz Island. As we know, it had an immediate impact on politicizing American Indians. We wonder, though, how much of that impact is left today. For instance, the Muwekma Ohlone Indian Tribe, the aboriginal inhabitants of San Francisco, remains embroiled in a fight for their ancestral homeland in the Presidio. They argue that the Presidio's standing as a national park is not justified because their tribe was not given their right of first refusal when the U.S. Army abandoned the land. Their petition takes on special urgency because there are now plans to rent portions of the Presidio to corporate interests for millions of dollars. In addition, the National Park Service and National Park Association also have plans to build a playground over the sacred grave mounds of the Muwekma Ohlone elders at a part of the Presidio called Crissy Field.

The matter is complicated further because the Muwekma Ohlone are no longer a federally recognized tribe. They claim that, in 1927, a local agent of the Bureau of Indian Affairs arbitrarily and unjustly decertified them. Rectifying that event is their immediate priority. Their website indicates that the Department of the Interior stands ready to reestablish their tribal recognition. However, the workings of government are painfully slow and we cannot help but wonder if the snail's pace says something about the waning political influence of American Indians as we enter the twenty-first century.

January 10

Chinatown is a neighborhood where the old country still lives inside the new one. The roughly twenty-four square blocks of Chinatown is home to the largest Chinese community outside of Asia. Its maze of Chinese neon signs and tiered pagoda roofs stand in stark contrast to the city's ultramodern downtown skyscrapers. Today a popular tourist destination, the history of Chinatown betrays a legacy of discrimination and repression.

In the mid 1840s, following defeat by Britain in the first Opium War, a series of natural disasters occurred across China that resulted in famine, peasant uprisings, and rebellions. When the news of gold and opportunity in *Gam Saan* ("Golden Mountain," the Chinese name for America) reached China, many seized the opportunity to seek their fortune. Soon, ship after ship bearing Chinese immigrants sailed into San Francisco. Most of the Chinese ended up performing menial labor in prospecting or building the railroad lines. As the gold rush died out and the railroad lines were completed, 20,000 Chinese were suddenly out of work. The industrious Chinese labor force became a threat to mainstream society. In a state where almost one-fourth of the labor force was unemployed in 1877, the Chinese were seen as unwelcome competition in the struggling economy of San Francisco.

By 1870, Chinese were increasingly becoming the targets of racial discrimination and repressive legislation. In the following decade, more than thirty anti-Chinese pieces of legislation were enacted at both the state and local levels. They were prohibited by law to testify in court, to own property, to vote, to have families join them, to marry non-Chinese, and to work in institutional agencies. Culmination of this discriminatory legislation was the Chinese Exclusion Act of 1882. This act, which was the first law to prohibit immigrants on the basis of nationality, suspended the immigration of Chinese "laborers" for ten years and denied naturalized citizenship to the Chinese already here. The Chinese Exclusion Act was renewed in 1892 and extended indefinitely in 1902.

It was in this climate that "Little Canton," later to be dubbed "Chinatown" by the local media, took shape in the 1880s. At that time, 22,000 people were packed into twelve blocks of wooden and brick houses, businesses (including 7,500 laundries), temples, family associations, rooming houses for the bachelor majority (the ratio of men to women was twenty to one), opium dens, and gambling halls. In this exotic neighborhood, Chinese immigrants found the security and solidarity to survive the racial and economic oppression of greater San Francisco.

A dramatic change to the faces of Chinatown and San Francisco, in both physical and demographic terms, followed the April 18, 1906 earthquake. Perhaps more destructive than the quake itself was the subsequent fire. Ignited by gas leaking from ruptured mains and fanned by high winds, the fire swallowed the predominantly wooden buildings, destroyed much of the city, and leveled Chinatown. The totality of the destruction was extraordinary. In the final toll, hundreds of people died and some 28,000 buildings were destroyed.

The 1906 earthquake was disastrous—in more ways than one. Since that time, no other major American city has endured a catastrophe that so starkly and thoroughly divided its history into "before" and "after." In Ronald Takaki's words, the earthquake was "a natural disaster . . . that changed the course of Chinese-American history." The fire destroyed most municipal records in San Francisco. Chinese immigrant laborers, who were forbid by an 1884 federal court ruling to bring their wives and families to America, could now claim they were born in America and, as citizens, held the right to bring their wives and families to this country. As a result, between 1910 and 1924 about 10,000 Chinese women came to America. These women constituted one in four Chinese immigrants, compared to just one in twenty in the 1800s. Legally, all children of U.S. citizens were automatically citizens, regardless of their place of birth. This influx of "paper sons and paper daughters"— instant citizens—insured almost overnight a corrective balance to the demographics of Chinatown's "bachelor society."

The physical landscape of the area changed as well. San Francisco became a city of brick and stone buildings. Chinatown also remade itself. A wealthy businessman named Look Tin Eli obtained a loan from Hong Kong. Hoping to stave off San Franciscans who would not allow Chinatown to be rebuilt in its old neighborhood, Eli designed a new Chinatown to be rebuilt in its original location in the city center. Eli's plans called for the new Chinatown to be emphatically "Oriental" to draw tourists. The goal was to create a neighborhood so appealing and idiosyncratic that no one would want to dismantle it. Eli did not let himself be constrained by realism in achieving this goal. For instance, what is commonly perceived as traditionally Chinese about the area's architecture (for example, golden, curled eaves on the corners of buildings) was, in fact, an invention to please outsiders. In the words of one longtime Chinatown resident, Mr. Philip Choy, it is "pseudo-Chinese." This synthetic Chinatown—dreamed up by an American-born Chinese man, built by white architects, and looking like a back-lot movie stage set—continues to give millions of tourists the illusion that they have visited a small piece of China.

Professional guides, who include a quick romp through this neighborhood as part of a larger San Francisco tour, lead most groups who tour Chinatown. Typically, such tours focus on the area's quaintness. Often, the ultimate goal is to make sure that everyone has a chance to buy a bag of fresh fortune cookies. The history of Chinatown as a sanctuary from racial discrimination, and its present role in San Franciscan society are seldom mentioned. However, it is exactly those stories that I want our group to hear. To ensure that we do, I have asked the Chinese Cultural Center to arrange a walking tour of Chinatown. I have also specifically asked the center to schedule Mr. Guy Young as our docent for the day. A longtime resident of Chinatown, Mr. Young was a highlight of the 1996 tour and I know this year's group will enjoy him just as much.

The fact that I requested him, though, makes me rethink my philosophy about the tour. I have said that the tour is about stretching us out of our comfort zones. We need to meet people who challenge us and make us confront our role in perpetuating prejudice and discrimination. We should be seeking out people who make us uncomfortable as they force that mirror of self-reflection in our faces. "Uncle Guy" will not do any of this. He is a quiet, unassuming man who engagingly introduces you to his culture, community, and ethnic history. Similar to the docents at the Japanese-American museum in Los Angeles, I know that we will leave him feeling much better about ourselves and our place in the world than we should. It will be good to make another friend, but is this the best thing?

As I wrestle with these questions, Uncle Guy walks in and meets us at the Chinese Cultural Center. After a brief introductory lecture, we begin our walking tour of Chinatown. The relentless cold rain that greeted our morning walk from the hostel to the center has subsided only slightly. As we meander through the streets and alleys of Chinatown, we pass aromatic produce stands overflowing with bok choy, oranges, apples, cabbage, ginger root, watercress, celery, carrots. Along the way, Uncle Guy points out the value of family, respect, and education in the Chinese community. He explains how the definition of family really means community. For instance, there are few homeless people in Chinatown. Those who have fallen on hard times are provided for by benevolent community associations. Even as Uncle Guy says this, I notice that the one homeless person we have seen in Chinatown is very different from those you see just several blocks away in Union Square. Rather than sitting idly, singing, or playing a musical instrument, he is bowing on his knees, forehead to the ground, holding a cup between his prayerful hands. It is as if he knows that the community will respond if he shows need. It is not necessary to dance or make a spectacle of himself to receive charity. As a member of the community, his needs will be met—not by federal, state, or city bureaucracies, but by his community.

Simply walking with Uncle Guy is a lesson in the value of respect in the Chinese community. In mainstream America, respect for a person directly corresponds with the amount of their contributions to society. Those who contribute much, receive much respect; those who contribute little, receive little respect. One unfortunate implication is that elderly people, whose contributions to society typically have lessened (or, at the very least, changed from what we consider "important"), receive far less respect than they deserve. In Chinese society, however, respect accorded others bears little or no relation to what they have or have not contributed to society. Respect is not earned, it is simply given. This is especially true with the elderly, whose role in Chinese society is truly valued and to whom members of the community show tremendous respect. We see this in the residents' reaction to Uncle Guy as well as in his reaction to them. In one instance, an older Chinese man had run out of coins for a parking meter. Without hesitation and with no fanfare whatsoever, Uncle Guy reached into his pocket and deposited the necessary coins in the meter. It was an act of respect, community, and civility that, I suspect, would have been duplicated exactly had the situation been reversed.

Uncle Guy is especially vocal about the value of education in the Chinese-American community. He tells us that most children in Chinatown attend a "normal" public school, take a few hours off to help with the family business, and then return to "Chinese" school, where they study the Chinese language, culture, and tradition. Uncle Guy believes strongly that education is the key to opportunity. As he describes the educational attainments of his own children, his glowing pride in what they have accomplished speaks volumes.

One can make the argument that no other minority population in the United States is viewed more favorably than Asian Americans. The values they place on family, respect, and education mirror those of the Norman Rockwell American ideal. Using indicators such as educational achievement, occupational status, and income, social scientists and journalists have proclaimed the "success" of Asian Americans in achieving the "American Dream." This "model-minority" stereotype has been reinforced through statistic-heavy articles depicting Asian Americans as an exceptionally accomplished and industrious minority group. Their phenomenal success is still held up as an example of what can be accomplished by minorities who are willing to claim their given birthright in this land of opportunity.

However, the model-minority stereotype is, at best, a double-edged sword. For instance, it tends to disparage those minorities who still suffer significant economic and educational deprivation. Often, Asian Americans are the unwitting victims of backlash from other racial minority groups who, themselves buying into the stereotype, tire of the cross-racial comparisons. More insidiously, the model-minority stereotype is wielded by those who wish to bring an end to entitlement programs and educational reform as well as those who wish to deny that racism exists. Wendy Walker-Moffat, a social welfare professor at the University of California at Berkeley, writes: "It is in the vested interests of those who want to avoid the costs of educational reform to maintain the 'success' of Asian-Americans as evidence that ethnic minorities can succeed in existing schools without affirmative action, in-service teacher education, or special program support. Particularly in times of economic recession, the costs and benefits of educating special groups with particular need, such as immigrants, become a political issue."

In addition, the model-minority stereotype distorts the reality of the Asian-American experience by exaggerating their "success." Clearly, there are Asian Americans who are very successful, many even in the stereotypical fields of science and technology. Asian Americans also have a higher average income than other minorities and a lower divorce rate. However, the statistical data trumpeting these achievements is often used the same way a drunk uses a lamppost—for support rather than illumination. Economic indicators, for example, neglect the fact that most Asian Americans reside in states with higher costs of living than the national average (for example, California, New York). Furthermore, higher family incomes often simply reveal the presence of more workers in each family rather than higher individual incomes. Even data on educational attainment is subject to qualification. For example, six percent of adult Asian Americans have not completed elementary school—three times the rate for whites.

It must also be noted that the Asian-American population is incredibly diverse in terms of geographic, linguistic, religious, and class background. As a result, there is tremendous variation in educational attainments of immigrants from rural China, ethnic Chinese from Vietnam, and American-born Chinese from middle- to upper-class urban backgrounds. Cultural subgroups within the Asian-American population, including Asian Indians, Cambodians, Chinese, Filipinos, Japanese, Koreans, Laotians, and Vietnamese, have a level of need similar to any member of a racial minority in America. This tremendous within-group variation is masked by the broad brush-strokes of the model-minority stereotype.

This new kind of racial stereotyping, disguised as flattery, blocks greater awareness of the diversity of Asian-American experiences and the complex pressures faced by Asian Americans in daily life. It obscures the psychological and social needs of Asian Americans to the point that some people are now calling this population the "invisible minority." People and institutions that buy into the stereotype perpetrate—wittingly or unwittingly—a form of discrimination. Daya Sandhu, chair and associate professor in the Department of Educational and Counseling Psychology at the University of Louisville, writes: "The myth of Asians as a model minority, based on the success image of a few elite individuals, has a very negative and debilitating effect on the general population of Asian-Americans. . . . Both social and psychological forces to conform to the model minority stereotype place an inordinate amount of pressure on Asian-Americans." The attitude that there is no need to worry about Asian Americans because they are doing better than everyone else is divisive and destructive. In an era anxious about the growing minority underclass, the Asian-American model-minority stereotype is merely a consoling fiction.

As the walking tour comes to a drenching end, one of the students asks Uncle Guy about his personal experience with discrimination as a Chinese American. Although too reserved to share intimately, he does say that the catastrophic events of World War II opened up many doors for Chinese Americans. Labor shortages opened jobs previously closed to

Chinese. More significantly, the 1941 Japanese attack on Pearl Harbor became a vehicle of opportunity for Chinese Americans. China became an ally in the war against Japan and public sentiment in favor of Chinese Americans began to shift. Mr. Young most vividly remembers December 17, 1943—the day that President Roosevelt signed the repeal of the sixty-one-year-old Chinese Exclusion Act. Although, in reality, the repeal led to just a tiny trickle of Chinese immigrants and a relatively small increase in naturalized citizenship, Mr. Young still warmly recollects the feeling that "they" were finally accepted by "us." After helping build America, he and his family could now seek political membership, own property, and build a home in their adopted country.

We close our time with Uncle Guy with a dim sum lunch at Ryumon on Washington Street, near the Chinese Cultural Center. I once read that "dim sum" literally means "bits of heart" or "tiny morsels that are eaten to please one's heart." Uncle Guy tells us that it really means "point here," and that it simply refers to how you select food from the endless carts of meat, vegetables, and seafood that are wheeled out from the kitchen. I think he is speaking tongue-in-cheek, but as a notoriously picky and cowardly eater, I am pretty sure "dim sum" will translate as "swallow quickly and think of a quarter pounder with cheese" for me. I had expected a particular thematic taste, but dim sum foods can be sweet, salty, spicy, or sour. The one thing that they do have in common is that they tend to be gelatinous. At the other table, I overhear Joy describing one item as a "breast implant." As the carts keep parading by, though, I find myself actually enjoying the food—once I have Joy's bizarre image out of mind.

The conversation at our table with Uncle Guy centers on the issues facing Chinatown today. It is clear that the neighborhood, similar to Fisherman's Wharf, has become homogenized into an all-purpose visitors' bazaar with t-shirts, trinkets, and baubles. In some ways, relentless tourism has threatened to level the neighborhood in the same way that the 1906 earthquake did. Uncle Guy recognizes the tension between preserving the past and responding to the present. Over the past two decades, for instance, there have been several attempts to declare

Chinatown a historic district. All of these attempts have failed. In large part, they have failed because many merchants, property owners, and developers worry about building restrictions and other rules that would impede profitability.

Today, groups like the Chinatown Community Development Center continue to search for a balance between historic preservation and contemporary adaptation. Over the next few years, for example, thirty-one alleys in Chinatown are scheduled to get facelifts with $2.9 million of city money. These renovations will restore a historic network of commercial passageways and, by including historical lessons, give a nod to the interests of tourists.

However, in Uncle Guy's opinion, the immediate crisis facing Chinatown is the graying of its population. He points out that the core of Chinatown itself, limited by its capacity to grow, no longer serves as the major residential area for the Chinese of San Francisco. Although many older Chinese, like himself, still choose to live there, most younger Chinese have moved out of crowded Chinatown to the Richmond and Sunset Districts. Today, about 370,000 Chinese people live in the Bay Area, up from 55,700 in 1960. There are an estimated 15,000 residents of Chinatown, about eighty-five percent of whom are Chinese. He wonders what his great-grandchildren will know of Chinatown. Will they know its history and role in the preservation of Chinese culture on the West Coast? Or will they simply know it as a sell-out to the tourist industry and a gross caricature of a proud culture?

I open our Saturday night debriefing by asking for the students' general impressions of their time in San Francisco. For the next several minutes, I am flooded with a torrent of comparisons to Los Angeles. It is clear that the students feel a sense of safety and security in San Francisco that they did not feel in Los Angeles. They find San Franciscans to be more talkative, friendly, and spirited than their relatively reclusive and lifeless counterparts in Los Angeles. One student says, "This is a beautiful city. I feel safe here, where in Los Angeles it felt dark and dangerous. I guess I felt that way in L.A. because I was more clearly the 'minority.' I felt that I was being watched constantly." Another student says, "The people in

Los Angeles seemed very detached. There was little care for what was happening around them. They were concerned with their personal destination and little else. There seemed to be no joy or pride in their jobs or lives. It was a city of dead souls. San Francisco has a fervor for life that inspires me. The people are alive, alert, friendly and have a general sense of joy surrounding them."

We process these perceptions as a group. Is it something about the relative affluence, prosperity, education, and romanticism of San Francisco that places it more easily within our comfort zone? Is it that we have spent no time on public transit here (except for the cable cars) compared to the hours spent on buses in Los Angeles? Or is it simply that we are sleeping and eating much better? Regardless of the reason, it is a good reminder that feeling too comfortable in a given place or at a given point in our life can be a red flag to check our perceptions.

By canceling the previous night's debriefing, I lost the opportunity for intensive discussion about Alcatraz and the American Indian occupation. I thought we could pick it up tonight, but—as I should have expected—the rest of our conversation centers on the most recent event, Chinatown. Several students mention how impressed they were by the values placed on family, respect, and education in the Chinese culture. One student imagines what would happen if we instilled this Chinese emphasis on education in our non-Chinese families, taught respect and community in our public schools, and demonstrated the Chinese family and community on television in an honest portrayal instead of a stereotype. A few students are especially caught by the role of titles in respect. When one student asked what he preferred to be called, our docent said, "Mr. Young or Uncle Guy is most respectful. Guy is too familiar." When the assistant curator of the Chinese Cultural Center joined us at lunch, a recent immigrant from Hong Kong, he introduced himself as "James" and Uncle Guy immediately corrected him to say "Mister" or "Uncle" before his name.

I shift the conversation by asking the students if our interactions with Uncle Guy were *too* comfortable to be a valuable learning experience. Did I make a mistake by not having a docent who would have really pushed us on the prejudice and discrimination perpetrated by whites against Chinese Americans? A few nod their heads, but, interestingly, most argue that this was a great experience. One student is especially adamant: "Uncle Guy respected us and explained his culture without force or any blame toward our ancestors. He paid for our meal. His generosity was so loving that I could not help but feel overwhelmed. I did not deserve to be part of his world. I was so thankful for our visit. I think I made a connection with him, and I felt like we could be friends if we lived closer. I think about reconciliation and I am encouraged. This man made an effort to be made known to us. That's the best gift I could receive. Isn't that what this tour's supposed to be about?" She's right. I need to remember that the tension of separateness and exclusion needs to be peppered with the hope of reconciliation and inclusion.

January 11

As we wait for our flight to Chicago, I join several students for breakfast. In reality, this is a cover for another agenda—watching the Denver Broncos play the Pittsburgh Steelers in the AFC championship game. In the first half, Kordell Stewart, the Steelers' quarterback, throws an interception in the end zone. Bill Romanowski, the Broncos' volatile linebacker, gets in Stewart's face and begins banging his palm on his own forehead, shouting "Stupid, stupid, stupid!" Even the most die-hard Bronco fans in our group are embarrassed. It quickly brings us to a discussion of Romanowski's previous outburst, just weeks before, against the San Francisco Forty-niners. In that game, Romanowski—in full view of a national television audience—spat in the face of J.J. Stokes, a San Francisco receiver. The penalty handed down for this detestable act? Seventy-five hundred dollars. Seventy-five hundred dollars to a man making millions for hitting other people with as much ferocity as he can muster.

Of most interest in our discussion, though, are both the racial undertones of Romanowski's penalty and the public reaction to his behavior. Romanowski is a white man. Many suggest, myself included, that had he been black, both his penalty and the public reaction would have been much more severe. For instance, Bryan Cox is a black linebacker, the same position as Romanowski, with a similar penchant for detestable behavior on the field. In 1993, Cox was fined $10,000 for giving the finger to Buffalo fans. In 1995, he spit in the direction of Buffalo fans—not on them, but at them—and was fined $7,500. As columnist Bob Kravitz pointed out, it would seem that either inflation or the fact that Romanowski actually spit *on* somebody would have mandated a fine greater than $7,500. And what about public reaction? In the days following his spitting incident, Romanowski was most often described as "just a guy who plays hard, a real throwback, like Nitschke or Butkus." For similar behavior, Cox was vilified as the angry, young, black gangster thug who threatens all that is wholesome and pure about American society and sport.

Is Romanowski racist? Probably no more so than any of the rest of us. The fact that Stokes is black was incidental. Romanowski might well have spat on his mother in the same situation. However, the penalty levied against him and the public reaction to his behavior betray the depths of institutional and public racism that still pervade American society. Each of us are again reminded that race colors every aspect of our life—even something as innocent as a sporting event.

4. CHICAGO: ARVIS TELLS IT LIKE IT IS

It is wonderful to be here in the great state of Chicago.

Dan Quayle, former U.S. vice president

Most tour books and many residents of Chicago trace the city's beginnings to 1802 and the building of Fort Dearborn by U.S. federal troops. In truth, however, the birth of Chicago goes back to 1772. In that year, a black fur trader from Haiti, Jean Baptiste Pointe DuSable (1745–1818), founded the settlement Eschikagou on the northern bank of the Chicago River. Some say DuSable was the son of a French nobleman, others say he was a runaway slave. Regardless, his settlement marked the true dawn of Chicago and DuSable stands as the first Chicagoan. DuSable's home, which is located near the present-day Wrigley Building, was the site of the city's first wedding, first recorded birth, first election, and first court. As is the case with many cities across the country, however, early historians contrived to erase minority pioneers from their city's founding. In Chicago's case, it was not until 1968 that DuSable was properly recognized as the city's founder. At that time, official confirmation finally came of Zebina Eastman's 1886 proclamation of DuSable as "the Black root from which all our glory has sprung."

Soon after its founding, Chicago attracted settlers from around the globe. As a result, today's Chicago is home to more than 2.8 million residents and more than one hundred ethnic groups. One resident in seven is foreign born. School children speak some 110 languages and can find bilingual-education teachers in twenty schools. Each ethnic group has stamped the city with its unique contributions of food, custom, language, and tradition. This rich heritage is celebrated with more than eighty neighborhood festivals. Chicagoans, never at a loss for a reason to celebrate, can carouse at a German-American Fest, be enchanted by the Chinatown Autumn Moon Festival, march in the Mexican Independence Day Parade, sway to a Latin Music Festival, and enjoy the Taste of Ireland Festival—all without leaving the city limits.

Although a few neighborhoods have become highly integrated, the early residents of Chicago established a patchwork of separate neighborhoods that still exists today. The expanse of the city, which is twenty-five miles long and ten miles wide, gives every ethnic group its own streets and corners. The city administration officially divides the town into seventy-seven defined neighborhoods such as Greektown, Chinatown, Bronzeville, and Little Italy—although there are probably a hundred more unofficial neighborhoods. These areas give Chicago the intimacy of a small town amid the clamor of a metropolis. Where else but in Chicago can you find the largest Polish population this side of Warsaw *and* a South Asian community where you can have a traditional Pakistani meal or buy a sari and exotic spices from a local international market? Old-time apothecaries continue to do strong business in German-influenced Lincoln Square and street signs in the Ukrainian Village are still in the Cyrillic alphabet.

Although charming to tourists, Chicago's residential segregation also reinforces stubborn social, economic, racial, and ethnic boundaries within the city. Chicago's publicity materials tout it as the quintessential "melting pot," but closer examination reveals that a more apt description would be an "egg carton" with rigidly formed compartments. Most Chicagoans think of whole neighborhoods as "our people" or "their people." Blocks and blocks of gray area are left as if they belong to no one. In short, Chicago is as ethnically Balkanized and racially segregated as many other cities in the country.

Fortunately, at least for social scientists, the rigidity of the "egg carton" can be quantified. In its housing statistics, the U.S. Census Bureau tracks a factor called "residential segregation." The various measures of residential segregation can tell us many things. Among the most informative are: *dissimilarity*, the distribution of a minority group within a population; *interaction* or *isolation*, the degree of potential contact or possibility of interaction between minority and majority group members; *concentration*, the relative amount of physical space occupied by a minority group in the metropolitan area; *centralization*, the degree to which the minority group is located near the center of an urban area; and *clustering*, the extent to which minority group members adjoin one another, or cluster, in space. Statistics like these and their interpretations can dull the senses. However, they also can provide a quantitative reflection of how the minority lives in the midst of the majority.

I will not use each of these statistics for every racial minority group in every city. However, for Chicago some of them convey a clear picture of what the city looks like. For example, only Detroit, Michigan, and Gary, Indiana, have a higher measure of dissimilarity (that is, segregation) of blacks than does Chicago. With 1.0 being maximum segregation and a national average of 0.686, Gary weighs in at 0.899, Detroit at 0.876, and Chicago at 0.855. Of Chicago's 854 census tracts, 345 tracts (forty percent) were at least ninety-eight percent black in the 1990 census. Interaction indexes reveal that only blacks in Gary have fewer interactions with majority members in their community. With 1.0 indicating the maximum isolation and a national average of 0.624 for blacks (the highest of any minority group), Gary scores 0.842 and Chicago 0.839. Nearly eighty-six percent of metropolitan Chicago's black population would have to be moved for each of Chicago's neighborhoods to reflect the city's overall racial makeup.

Why such black-white segregation? There are dozens of contributing factors, but one seldom-recognized part of the explanation may lie in the mortgage-lending practices of banks. A 1998 study of lending practices in Columbus, Ohio, for instance, found that blacks have a much higher rate of house-loan denials in all-white neighborhoods than in black neighborhoods, especially for applicants making large loan requests. White applicants for small loans had a higher denial rate in black census tracts than in all-white areas. Another 1999 study released by the Association of Community Organizations for Reform Now found that blacks were twice as likely as whites and Hispanics were one and a half times as likely to be denied a conventional, thirty-year home loan.

But is racial discrimination the reason for these disparities? Apparently so. In 1999, the Urban Institute, a nonpartisan research organization, dispatched pairs of white and minority group members—each pair with the same incomes, assets, jobs, credit histories, and neighborhoods—to seek mortgages from lenders throughout the nation. "Overall," the study concluded, "minorities were less likely to receive information about loan products, received less time and information from loan officers, and were quoted higher interest rates in most of the cities where tests were conducted." Dan Immergluck of the Woodstock Institute of Chicago believes that it is precisely this discriminatory pattern that characterizes the mortgage-lending practices of many Chicago banks.

Similar, although not as striking, trends of higher-than-national-average segregation are found for American Indian, Asian, and Hispanic communities in Chicago. Does such segregation arise by choice? Or is it a result of social and institutional racism? Is it the future of how a diverse society lives? Or should it be the past?

Richard Conniff writes that, "No city in America has a stronger notion of itself, a fiercer sense of its own identity, or a better literature to keep it alive" than Chicago. However, despite its wonder, for some Chicago remains a gritty, foreboding place. Among the more serious challenges are a shrinking population, partly caused by an exodus of the middle class to the suburbs; poor public schools, housing, and vital services; erosion of the tax base; and the disappearance of thousands of high-paying manufacturing jobs. Chicago's public schools are not measurably better than in 1987, when then Secretary of Education William Bennett called them "the worst in the nation." With a citywide high-school-dropout rate of more than forty percent, it is little wonder that one adult in three is functionally illiterate. Seventy percent of the city's remaining high school students read below the national average for their grade level.

Chicago lost 370,000 jobs between 1960 and 1990, with manufacturing employment shrinking sixty percent. Today, manufacturing accounts for only one job in five. Many of Chicago's remaining factory jobs are comparatively low paying and those whose lack of education would once have restricted them to factory work must now resort to jobs in less lucrative service industries. Seventeen percent of Chicagoans remain dependent on welfare. In addition, Chicago still lags behind peer U.S. cities in attracting international visitors, who are said to be cowed by the city's reputation. Even executive recruiters sometimes lament that attracting newcomers to Chicago can be difficult. Of course, they also joke that it is their second most difficult job. The toughest is getting people to move away from Chicago.

January 12

Our day begins with a tour of Chicago's South Side with two community activists, Arvis Averette and Donald Crumbley. It is my turn with the red group and they join me in a van to pick up Averette. Joy heads out with the black group to meet Crumbley. All of us are looking forward to today. The South Side of Chicago is the largest black community in America and we will have a unique opportunity to see it from an insider's eyes.

During the Great Migration of 1915 to 1970, about five million rural, southern blacks migrated to the northern industrialized cities in search of an acceptable status in America. It was one of the largest peacetime internal movements in history. The conditions leading to the Great Migration were created after the Civil War, when blacks were not given "forty acres and a mule," the means of economic survival at that time. Rather, blacks became enslaved in economic bondage by being forced to become sharecroppers. Sharecropping usually meant a cycle of endless debt. As a result, the only substantial difference between sharecropping and slavery was the relative freedom to move—from field to field, from field to factory. Intensifying their deprivation was the system of legal segregation that emerged throughout the South after the 1896 *Plessy v. Ferguson* Supreme Court decision. Legalized segregation aborted the freeing effects of the Emancipation Proclamation and the passage of the Thirteenth, Fourteenth, and Fifteenth Amendments. Clearly, the future for blacks was not to be found in the South.

One of the major lights in the Great Migration was the "Black Metropolis" of Chicago. In Emmett J. Scott's words, Chicago was "the mouth of the stream of Negroes from the South." Part of the pull to Chicago was logistical. It was the terminus of the Illinois Central Railroad, which had rail lines connected to the small towns of Mississippi, Arkansas, and Louisiana. Another part of the pull was economic. Chicago was a dynamic industrial center that spawned jobs and inspired dreams. World War I had virtually cut off the flow of European immigrants, and Chicago factory managers, faced with tremendous labor shortages, were active in recruiting from the South. However, the biggest pull to Chicago was that it was not in the South.

In 1900, Chicago had a black population of only 30,000. Only one ward in the entire city was twenty-five percent black, while nineteen of thirty-five wards were less than one percent black. By 1920, however, the black population had jumped to 109,400, primarily concentrated in the predominately black neighborhoods of the South Side. It was here that a strong and vibrant community began to reinvent itself. As Richard Wright recalls, "I went to Chicago as a migrant from Mississippi. And there in that great iron city, that impersonal, mechanical city, amid the steam, the smoke . . . there in that self-conscious city, that city so deadly dramatic and stimulating, we caught whispers of the meanings that life could have."

However, the whispers were not always welcoming. As chronicled by Ronald Takaki, this incredible migration sparked an explosion of white resistance. Conflicts over housing, schools, and labor became common. World War I generated a sharp demand for labor and opened unique opportunities for blacks in industries. By 1920, the majority of black men were employed in factories rather than in domestic and personal services. Black women also were making similar transitions from maids to industry workers. Racial competition in the workplace added fuel to social antagonisms in the neighborhoods. In the "Red Summer" of 1919, race riots erupted throughout the nation. From May 10 to September 30, more than twenty-five riots rocked cities in states from Texas to Illinois, Nebraska to Georgia. The bloodiest was in Chicago. Over the course of a week, 23 blacks and 15 whites were killed and 342 blacks and 178 whites were injured.

Some antagonisms were not easily divided among black and white lines. Many northern blacks also looked down on the mainly poor, uncultured, illiterate, and backward southern blacks who crowded their cities. They keenly felt the threat of competition for jobs and houses in a marketplace that had only recently opened up to them. Despite the tensions, southern blacks wove their way into the fabric of the South

Side of Chicago. They came bearing gifts of a new culture—their churches, religion, food, and music, especially a new kind of music called jazz.

The black community in the South Side of Chicago responded to their growing pains through a focus on black solidarity and financial enterprise. The old, southern racial etiquette of deference and subordination was lost as a new generation of blacks came of age. Black leaders encouraged blacks to establish their own banks, insurance companies, stores, churches, and communities. In the words of one leader, "Why should these dollars be spent with white men? . . . If white men are so determined that Negroes must live separate and apart, why not beat them at their own game?"

Over the next several decades, the South Side of Chicago did just that. This community blossomed into a closeted society of cutting-edge art, literature, music, drama, and athletics. Home to a variety of teams in the Negro Leagues, South Siders reveled in the exploits of players such as Satchel Paige, Josh Gibson, Cool Papa Bell, and John Henry Lloyd. On Saturday nights (derisively called "nigger nights" by other Chicago residents), blacks on the South Side flocked to the Regal Theater just south of Forty-seventh street. There they saw such legendary performers as Louis Armstrong, Lena Horne, Count Basie, Duke Ellington, Ethel Waters, Josephine Baker, and Cab Calloway. A young man named Nat King Cole began his rise to stardom via an amateur night performance at the Regal. The cultural achievements were financed from within as South Side residents found economic independence in a wide variety of black-owned businesses. The *Chicago Defender* became one of the leading black newspapers in the nation and was a clarion of movement to the "Promised Land" during the Great Migration.

Still today, it is relatively easy to find older blacks in Chicago who pine for the good old days of the South Side. Like any retrospective, their views are highly romanticized. However, their memories do speak of that elusive utopia where blacks' opportunities and achievements were not limited by whites. Unfortunately, the South Side of their memories is faded and passed. What we expect to see today on our tour of the South Side is light-years away from their reminiscences.

My group begins its tour at Dearborn Homes, a public-housing project on South State Street. At Dearborn Homes, we walk from the frigid, nineteen-degree outside air into the stale, fetid air of the first floor. Can it be even colder in here? The interior is poorly lit and cheerless. We snake our way down an ice-cave of a hall and enter an obscenely warm management office. After a brief wait, a large black man ushers us into a side office. His size and bearing are intimidating. I see similar apprehension mirrored on the faces of the students. I am again reminded of how strongly race and gender influence our reactions to others. Would we perceive as much threat if he were white? Or female? Not likely. In the back of my mind, I recall a psychological study where the same videotaped shove that looked "playful" to most white people when done by a white man much more often looked "violent" when done by a black man. Such misperceptions, which spring from deep-seated racial stereotypes and fears, are one of the many factors that hinder our pursuit of racial reconciliation.

Before we can sit down, we are bombarded with a barrage of questions from the man. "How big is Chicago? How many blacks live here? Whites? Hispanics? What percentage of blacks live in public housing? What percentage of blacks are in gangs? What percentage of the poor in Chicago are blacks?" Not given a chance to respond, our host offers his own interpretation: "Oh, I guess I got the dumb group." He then rattles off the answers and scribbles them with a black marker on a large piece of paper. It is clear that this is a man who loves numbers and percentages almost as much as he loves catching people off-guard. "Chicago has a population of 2.7 million. Forty-one percent of that population is black. That's 1.1 million for you non-math types. Forty percent are white—about one million. Seventeen percent are Hispanic—about half a million. You think all of those blacks live in public housing. You think that they're all in gangs, too. Well, less than ten percent of blacks in Chicago live in public housing. Less than one percent are active in gangs. Of all the poor people in the city of Chicago, less than thirty percent are black." There's a brief, and somehow even more uncomfortable, pause. "Let's go. You're just wasting my time here. Let's go show you all of the things your mamas warned you about." As we leave his office, he turns and, to no one in particular, says, "By the way, my name is Arvis Averette."

Arvis Averette is the president and CEO of the Dearborn Homes Resident Management Corporation. In this role, Averette supervises a community-based organization that is responsible for developing resources (for example, credit union, supply company, coffee company) to be controlled by the public-housing residents. Of the sixty employees of the corporation, fifty actually live in Dearborn Homes. Averette holds a master's degree in social work from the University of Chicago and chairs the economics department at a local college. He is an abrasive, outrageous, and headstrong man. Listening to him is like taking a sip of water out of a gushing fire hydrant.

However, there is something in him that draws you. You find yourself attracted to the heat of his passion. His impatience with subtleties is refreshing. You feel respected by his brutal honesty. Not everyone in our group feels the same draw. Some are so alienated by his brusque manner that the only draw they feel is to the underside of the nearest rock. The unspoken fear initially provoked by his race, gender, and physical presence is augmented by an intimidating interpersonal tone that leaves each of us unnerved. However, every one of us will be challenged by our morning with him.

As we climb into the van, our tour begins with Averette turning and saying: "Do you know that seventy percent of all crack users are white and only thirty percent are black?" The group is still too stunned to know if they should nod in agreement, challenge the suspiciously round percentages, sarcastically question if *only* whites and blacks use crack, or simply sit and curse themselves for not sitting farther back in the van. We bump along the back streets of the South Side and wonder how long three hours really are. After several minutes, he turns again and continues "and that ninety-eight percent of people serving time for crack in prison are black and only two percent are white?"

Leaving Dearborn Homes, we pass by a deserted park and playground. Averette puts on his activist hat. "See that park? Beautiful, isn't it? Nice swings, good hoops, even a damned teeter-totter. What else do you notice? No people! Know why? The Chicago Housing Authority built the damn thing on the turf between two warring gangs. No one wants to play out here because they might get shot. Come here any time of day, any day of the week, and you'll see the same thing—nothing! The residents could have told you this before it was built. But the all-mighty CHA knows more than the residents do. Shows you that the CHA has its head up its ass."

We continue down an uninterrupted four-mile stretch of public housing on the South Side. These areas stand in ironic contrast to Chicago's city motto, "Urbs in Horto," which translates to "City in a Garden." The Robert Taylor Homes are the hallmark of this corridor—a clump of twenty-eight sixteen-story buildings, identical except for the color of their brick and their spatial orientation. Chicago has dozens of such cookie-cutter, high-rise complexes that were built in the 1950s and 1960s. Some are large enough to house 1,600 people. For one student, fresh off a trip to Eastern Europe, the complexes evoke an interesting comparison and contrast. "I tried to wipe the fog off the window of the van so that I could see all the way to the top, but the thing I see the best is the ground, which has no grass and is still frosty from last night's bitter cold. This public housing stands straight in the air and looks remarkably similar to the Stalin-Lenin-era apartment buildings I saw in Lithuania. The largest difference is the profile of the residents. Here, on the South Side of Chicago, the occupants of these structures are nearly one hundred percent black. Once again, they find themselves trapped in the bondage of what we had once called the South. I guess the fact that the compass points down to indicate this direction is not entirely benign."

When the slums were exchanged for high rises, it was thought that the problems of slum living would dissipate. As Crumbley tells his group, however, "It doesn't change the character of any person to move him from the ground to the fifteenth floor of public housing." The high rises have simply become a more intense breeding ground for the same problems. Some buildings in the Robert Taylor Homes, for example, house the sale of more than $50,000 a day in drugs. Gangs control certain elevators, and people on higher floors—including the elderly and children—often are forced to navigate several floors of poorly lit and rancid stairs. During some periods, gang violence is so intense that postal service is discontinued. "Our motto says to deliver mail in rain, sleet, and snow, but it doesn't say anything about dodging bullets," Chicago's postmaster, Rufus Porter, explains. During such times, parents fear for their children's safety while walking to their nearby elementary school and attendance drops by as much as fifty percent.

Even when the children *can* get to school, they find themselves on the short end of a huge disparity in the quality of public education. For example, the annual per pupil expenditure in some Chicago-area suburban schools exceeds $15,000. Many city school districts spend less than $5,000 per student. Whereas more than one-third of suburban students exceed state averages on standardized tests, only one percent of city students surpass those averages. Indeed, it can be argued that the present gap in education between city and suburban schools is wider than before the landmark 1954 *Brown v. Board of Education* Supreme Court decision that overturned segregated schooling.

In July 1998, the slaying of an eleven-year-old girl, Ryan Harris, in a South Side neighborhood led to the accusation of two of the youngest murder suspects in our nation's history—two boys age seven and eight. In September 1998, the murder charges were dropped when prosecutors revealed that laboratory tests had found semen, medically impossible for two prepubescent boys to produce, on the victim's underwear. In April 1999, a twenty-nine-year-old convicted sex offender, Floyd Durr, was officially charged with the slaying of Harris. Mayor Richard Daley offered a public apology to the two young boys. Residents of the neighborhood were not so easily placated by Daley's apology. Incredulous from the beginning, they abided by their conviction that had the murder happened in a wealthy suburb, no one would have been so cynical as to believe a seven- and an eight-year-old could have been responsible.

In the Harris case, the frustration of the South Side community rose from the police department's and public's quick willingness to believe that two young black children could have been guilty of such a heinous crime. In other cases, frustration has risen from the lack of attention and resources devoted to black victims of crime. On January 9, 1997, for instance, neighbors found a nine-year-old black girl unconscious in a seventh-floor stairwell at Chicago's Cabrini Green housing project. She had been poisoned with gasoline, viciously assaulted, raped, and her belly was scrawled with ink-stained gang signs. Despite the brutality of the attack, it was only after sustained pressure from the *Chicago Defender*, the city's black newspaper, and the *Chicago Sun-Times* that the tragedy of "Girl X" became widely known. Why? Primarily because the media was still in a frenzy over the December 26, 1996, JonBenet Ramsey murder case. The crimes were not perfectly analogous and, surely, class played a role in media and public reaction as well as race. Regardless, columnist Lee Bey of the *Chicago Sun-Times* voiced the beliefs of many when he wrote: "The Cabrini Green rape would be widely known had the victim been white. Then it would have been news."

In the face of such realities, the innocence of childhood is a fast casualty. Connecting with the thing she knows best, her own childhood experience, one student wonders, "I think of the children often as we drive by vacant concrete playgrounds with only a few chain links left for swings and high rise mortuaries of brick and steel. Where do they go to be children? Where do they laugh or smile or play with caterpillars in the grass? Do they know grass and the peace of lying in it, rolling down a hill of it, searching for a lucky four-leaf clover?"

In addition to the strident social problems, public housing in Chicago continues to become increasingly isolated. Each year, public transit stops on the South Side are cut and residents find it increasingly difficult to travel to jobs and schools. The similarity of this "isolate-and-contain" policy of public housing to our historical treatment of American Indians is not lost on one student. "These buildings symbolize to me how our nation has dealt with its race problem—remove it, isolate it, and control the threat in projects or reservations."

As the tour continues, our group takes turns stepping up to be slapped down by Averette. In the back seat, someone has scribbled a target design on a piece of paper that we each pass on to the next person who must ask a question. One of us asks what racism looks like in 1998 America. Turning brusquely, Arvis snaps "Like your campus!" I ask his opinion of a recent book on race relations and he growls "What is that—a trick question? I don't play those games that academics do." Someone else asks if any whites live in this area. Averette points to a set of golden arches and says, "The only white person you'll ever see at that McDonald's is Ronald McDonald himself!" We then pass a section of black-owned businesses that display a black nationalist flag. Another student, who still has some measure of courage, asks, "How would blacks feel if whites displayed a white nationalist flag?" Without hesitation, Arvis points to an American flag on the street and says, "There is your white nationalist flag! The Stars and Stripes! That's the flag that was on the ship when they hauled my ancestors' asses over here."

So far this morning, Averette has confirmed our preexisting image of the South Side of Chicago—forlorn high-rises, dire poverty, and bleakness. For the next hour of the tour, however, Averette relieves us of this stereotypical notion. It is true that mostly blacks populate the South Side of Chicago. According to Averette, 800,000 of the 1.1 million blacks in Chicago live in the South Side. However, it is not true that most of those blacks live in public housing. Although blacks make up ninety-seven percent of families in public housing, the total portion of Chicago's blacks living in public housing, Averette reminds us, is less than ten percent. Traveling past the South Side homes of Louis Farrakhan, Jesse Jackson, and Muhammad Ali, Averette shows us the "American Dream" end of the South Side economic picture. Between these two extremes lie large and vibrant middle and upper classes on the South Side.

As we pass by the new Comiskey Park and into the mostly white neighborhood of Bridgeport, we are reminded that the economic and racial lines of community are well drawn in Chicago. Averette also reminds us that the consequences of crossing these lines can be life-threatening. In March 1997, Lenard Clark, a thirteen-year-old black child, and a friend crossed the bridge spanning the Dan Ryan Expressway that connected their world of crumbling high-rise housing projects with the tidy blue-collar homes of Bridgeport. Three older, white teens, vowing to "take care of the niggers in the neighborhood," attacked Clark. The teens beat him so fiercely that he went into a coma, from which he only began to emerge one week later.

Averette, who grew up with repeated warnings not to go near Bridgeport, sees Clark's beating as just another sign of the unresolved racial tensions running through Chicago. Not slow to make comparisons, Averette believes that no other city in America deals with the depth of racial antagonism that exists in Chicago. Others, like James Grossman, coeditor of the forthcoming *Encyclopedia of Chicago History*, counter that the racial conflicts in the city are not necessarily all that different from what you would find in many other cities. Regardless, in a city where lines are so starkly drawn and where people so clearly know where they are and are not wanted, the work of reconciliation is long and difficult.

Although Joy's black group sees much of the same landscape that we have, Crumbley includes one stop that leaves quite an impression on the students. Wanting to give the students a glimpse of the daily realities of living poor in America, Crumbley stops by the public welfare office. He instructs the students to enter the office in groups of three or four and act nonchalant, like they were there to apply for public aid. Unfortunately, there is nothing nonchalant about four young white people walking into a public welfare office full of black people. The woman at the reception desk notices this immediately and yells, "You are not permitted to come here and just look!" The sense of humiliation the students feel, Crumbley reminds them, is a small taste of what those dependent on public welfare feel every day.

When I later hear about Crumbley's exercise, I am ambivalent. In his mind, the end—glimpsing the daily reality of economic dependence—justified the means—making teaching objects of people in a public welfare office. I am not so sure of this. Throughout the tour, I have attentively avoided depicting the other as "museum artifact" or "object lesson." However, as we debrief it becomes clear that the students picked up an even larger, more valuable lesson than that intended by Crumbley. They learned, again, that there is a definite limit to how much they can immerse themselves in the experiences of minorities in America. As noble as their intentions might be and as much effort as they might make, my students can still only get a gauzy approximation of what it is like to live as a minority in this country.

They are further reminded that even a gauzy approximation is only attainable by entering into real-life relationships that enable them to see with the other's eyes. Only by shedding their clinical detachment and rolling up their shirt sleeves can they get intimately involved in the hard work of racial reconciliation. As one student reflects, "Her words hit me straight in the gut because I was discovered. This trip is about looking, gawking in ignorance at what we can barely comprehend. I want to tell her about how important it is for us to see, for us to learn, and yet now nothing is more valuable than her words. I am not permitted to just look any longer."

After a lunch of sweet-potato fries and turkey chili at B.J.'s Market and Bakery (whose slogan is "Food for the Soul"), we hustle to an afternoon briefing with Wanda White, director of development initiatives for the Chicago Housing Authority (CHA). When the students originally saw the itinerary, this briefing did not get the same enthusiasm (except from our political science majors) as the other listings. Following this morning's events, however, all of us are excited to hear what White has to say. Both Averette and Crumbley are unimpressed with the CHA's management of public housing. Although they both believe the CHA to be well intentioned, they also maintain that the CHA works too unilaterally—it does not solicit or value resident input. We are excited because this is how education should work—hear one side, hear the other, and then begin to make up your own mind.

The original mission of the CHA, which was incorporated in 1937, was to build and operate "decent, safe, and sanitary" housing for persons who could not afford it. However, over time the CHA, which is the third largest provider of subsidized housing in the nation, evolved into a tool of slum clearance. During the 1950s, the CHA cleared 642 acres of slums and relocated more than 10,000 families into new high-rise housing built on the cleared land. Instead of dispersing low-income families, they were reconcentrated in densely populated pockets of inner-city communities. The building of the majority of Chicago's public housing in impoverished, segregated areas led to a discrimination lawsuit, *Gautreaux v. Chicago Housing Authority,* in 1968. By that time, more than ninety-nine percent of all high-rise family buildings in Chicago had already been built. The last one was completed in 1970.

Wanda White is a sharp, middle-aged black woman. She knows that we have spent the morning with Averette and Crumbley and she also knows what we have heard. Right off the bat, she addresses the role of resident participation in CHA policies. She explains that all residents have formal representation through elected local advisory councils and a central advisory council. These councils advise and assist in all aspects of public-housing administration. For instance, they advise the CHA on issues of occupancy, general management, maintenance, security, resident training, resident employment, and social service and modernization priorities. While openly acknowledging that some kinks still exist in the channels of communication, White affirms that today's CHA is committed to the philosophy that residents play an essential role in the transformation of public housing.

White also is open about the public perception of the CHA. Historically, the CHA has been an agency plagued by mismanagement, negative public sentiment, and hostile resident opinion. It has long been considered the country's worst public-housing agency. In 1995, however, then federal housing secretary Henry Cisneros stepped in and took over the agency. Among his reasons, Cisneros cited the fact that two boys, aged ten and eleven, had recently dropped a five-year-old out of the fourteenth-floor window of a CHA building. He gave the job of rescuing the agency to Joseph Shuldiner, who had run both the New York City and the Los Angeles housing authorities. Since that time, White maintains that improved internal control, fiscal responsibility, and tougher operational standards have taken the CHA in a new direction. For the first time in its history, the CHA's budget is balanced, management conducts critical self-evaluations, and contractors are routinely audited. White is honest enough to recognize, however, that sixty-year-old perceptions die hard and that the nature of public housing will always draw critics.

White concludes by giving official affirmation to what we all suspect—the concentration of low-income families in densely populated high-rise buildings is a failed national policy. Chicago's developments, like many across the nation, are most often characterized as "severely distressed." However, if possible, there is something "hyperdistressed" about Chicago's public housing. For example, ninety-five percent of CHA residents are on some kind of public assistance, compared with roughly twenty-five percent in New York City. The isolation, concentration, and size of Chicago's public housing has led to an epidemic of crime, an exodus of local businesses, and the destruction of families.

In White's opinion, however, the CHA is now at the cutting edge of transforming public housing nationwide. Its new mission, which was prompted by the 1980 settlement of the Gautreaux case, is to move people out of isolated, decrepit high-rise buildings into mixed-income developments and private housing. In contrast to the "isolate-and-contain" policy of the 1950s, the CHA is committed to providing housing scattered throughout the city in an effort to create communities where low-income residents will live side by side with their non-public-housing neighbors in properties that are indistinguishable from those in the surrounding community. By doing so, the CHA plans to raze 11,000 decrepit apartments, nearly forty percent of its public housing for families, over the next fifteen years.

The model of this new plan is Cabrini Green, which sits near some of the city's most valuable property. The CHA is planning a development of which fifty percent will be private housing, twenty percent "affordable housing" (for families with between eighty and one hundred percent of the median income), and thirty percent homes for those poor enough to qualify for full public-housing assistance. The city already has contributed fifty acres for the Cabrini Green redevelopment. The CHA also is responsible for another assistance program in which the rent burden of some low-income individuals is alleviated by subsidizing their rent in the private market.

Unfortunately, as White acknowledges, it is difficult to achieve the ideal of mixed-income communities. Community acceptance of low-income families is marginal: property values drop and non-public-housing residents often move away or, if they stay, may even respond violently. Others worry that private-housing vouchers merely move the poor around and, coupled with demolishing buildings, diminish the total housing stock. Cynics and conspiracy theorists even suggest that the CHA has begun to demolish buildings because the land beneath them has become increasingly valuable to commercial developers.

However, as White contends, the creation of viable, mixed-income communities holds promise for revitalized neighborhoods in which crime is reduced, businesses thrive, and families prosper. In this transformation, public housing is no longer seen as a specific community with a specific location (for example, *the* Ida B. Wells Homes). Rather, public housing simply becomes another form of affordable housing. Inherent is the notion that housing is a right, and presupposed in that right is the right of low-income households not to be relegated to America's equivalent of a leper colony—densely populated, isolated, and dilapidated high-rises.

During that night's debriefing in the lobby of the International House, it becomes clear that the red group still suffers from post-Averette traumatic disorder. At different turns, we feel challenged, chastised, informed, and idiotic. We cannot see the rainbow for the rain. Did Averette become a friend or did we become another in the long list of ignorant whites with which he must deal?

Trying to place our emotional reactions aside for a moment, I ask, "What did we learn from Averette?" In the ensuing discussion, it became clear that he, like a master teacher, had led us to two important insights. First, we had learned, if only for a few hours, what it felt like to be a victim of presumptions, misinterpretations, and stereotypes. Averette pegged us early and would not let us go. We were white, middle-class, Presbyterian, Pacific Northwesterners (he could never quite remember if we were from Oregon or Washington), and he was not going to let us forget it. Try as we might, we were not going to get out of those pigeonholes.

In our time with Averette, we had what sociologists Tiffany Hogan and Julie Netzer call an "approximating experience." To this point on the tour, we had *borrowed* approximations by listening to stories and personal accounts that minorities tell of their own experiences. Today we were given an *overlapping* approximation. As temporary prisoners of unfair and overgeneralized stereotypes, we had the opportunity to see with the other's eyes. If we have truly learned, we will draw on this experience to partially glimpse the experiences of racial minorities in America.

Second, Averette gave a healthy dose of reality to a group of well-meaning whites that prize racial reconciliation. What is the reality? For some minorities, the hurt, anger, and bitterness engendered by exclusion runs so deep that racial reconciliation is simply not at the top of their lists. "Give me," Averette said, "my own country clubs, swimming pools, schools, businesses, and so on, and I'd be much happier." We are so steeped in the aura of Martin Luther King Jr. that we are shocked when we meet minorities who have no interest in making reservations at the table of brother- and sisterhood. Given the vast racial inequities still existing in country, why are we shocked? We probably should be shocked that *more* racial minorities do not share this view. We are again reminded that the road to racial reconciliation is more difficult than most of us realize.

As our trip rolls on, we become acutely aware of what Peggy McIntosh of the Center for Research on Women at Wellesley College has called "white privilege." In short, it pays to be white. We can take a job with an affirmative action employer without having our coworkers suspect that we got it because of our race; we can do well in a challenging situation without being called a credit to our race; we are seldom asked to speak for all people of our racial group; we can easily buy posters, postcards, books, greeting cards, dolls, toys, and children's magazines featuring people of our race; we can generally count on police protection rather than harassment; we will earn more in our lifetime than people of color with similar qualifications; we are usually given more attention, respect, and status in conversations than people of color.

Most whites are as unaware of this privilege as they are of the air that they breathe. We take it for granted. Even those who are aware of it often ignore what it means. For whites made sensitive to the reality of their unearned privilege, however, there are emotional consequences. We may feel uncomfortable about being white or guilty for the fact that racism exists and that we have benefited from it. We may feel defensive, ashamed, angry, powerless, frustrated, and sad.

Our morning with Averette and Crumbley brought many of these emotions to the surface. One student states, "I guess today I just felt ashamed to be white. It is hard to be white when at times you really do not want to be. I have so much, and there is so much more that I take for granted—like the disproportionate power and benefits that come from being born white." Another's reaction was similar: "I never felt as white or ignorant and naive as I did today." "Today, I really resented being white," another wrote, "I hated associating myself with a people who seems to have done nothing but hurt other people. I hated walking on the bus feeling like the black woman next to me didn't look at me or talk to me because I was white. I wonder if she hated me."

For another student, the shame went beyond just being white. "Today was the first day that I felt ashamed to be an American. What do you tell a kid to dream for if everything he ever sees tells him he can't reach across the street, much less for the stars? How can a teacher teach students who don't come to school for fear of being shot? What can make a high-rise a home? How do you pledge allegiance to the flag of a country that sees you only as a statistic—except election years, when you're seen as a necessary vote—and tells you to be grateful you have this piece of crap high-rise to cover your head? Who is in charge of all this bullshit that is never seen on television or talked about in the State of the Union address or even mentioned by someone like Oprah Winfrey who grew up in it? How can we be this ignorant of what it's like to live where such a large percentage of the population lives?"

Another student's honesty and self-reflection are an insightful summary of what many of us feel: "All I felt when we left was emptiness and discouragement. I didn't know how to respond to someone who honestly didn't care about anyone else but his own people. I know that is how all minorities have been treated by whites throughout history. But I don't want that to be me. That is not me. I'm trying to understand and change. I don't know how to help or even where to start. I want to help. I'm tired of feeling like a jerk who has so much to learn and do. I'm tired of feeling helpless. I'm tired of feeling like I have nothing to offer this man or others different from me. I hate feeling as though I want to change racism in this country and yet there are those who don't want to have anything to do with me because of my skin color and ancestors. How do I change? How do I respect someone who hates me because I am white?" In the midst of the despair, one student recognizes the broader value of our time with Averette: "In a three-hour period of time, he challenged my beliefs about racism, charity, equality, integration, unity, and love more than anyone else ever has. For that I thank him."

After the debriefing, Joy wryly remarks, "We sure get our money's worth in Chicago!" She is referring to the fact that our time in Chicago in 1996 was as eventful and insightful as today. In 1996, we arrived at the Amtrak station in downtown Chicago on a Saturday night at about 7:00 P.M. Somewhere in my notes, I had bus directions directly to the University of Chicago, but I decided that, rather than wait for the bus, we could take the subway to a stop near campus and then walk to the International House.

Without question, the students followed me into the subway. From Garfield Boulevard, we would take what appeared to be a pleasant little walk through Washington Park and then directly onto the beautiful University of Chicago campus. We arrived and began our trek through the Saturday night of the South Side of Chicago. Within minutes, a white sanitation worker stopped to ask, "Where the hell are you going?" I pulled out my trusty map to show him our route. He looked at the six-teen white backpack-laden students behind me and laughed. He said, "You can walk that way, but you'll never make it." Undeterred, we continued for another ten minutes or so. In that time, six other cars, each with black drivers and passengers, stopped to warn us of the neighborhood we were in.

By this point, the students' fear and anxiety were palpable. However, it was only a shadow of my own fear and anxiety. We were in a part of Chicago in which I had never been. My emotional reactions were compounded by the responsibility reflected in sixteen pairs of pleading eyes. I was in over my head. I herded the students around a check-cashing store at the corner of Garfield and Indiana. The area was in a busy, exclusively black neighborhood. I called the local taxi service and requested four cabs. With the help of the attendant, I gave clear directions of where to pick us up. One hour, then two passed without the taxis' arrival. In that time, several more people stopped to ask if they could help. Finally, after explaining to one person that I had called cabs, she looked at me and said, "Honey, ain't no cabs coming to this part of the city at this time of night on a Saturday!"

I was at the end of my rope. The store would close soon, and I didn't know where to turn. Finally, the attendant, whose patience with our jittery presence was surely wearing thin, made the gracious gesture of calling a friend who ran a livery service. Minutes later, four cars—not yellow cabs, but cars nonetheless—picked us up and drove us the short distance to the University of Chicago campus.

That night and the next morning the students and I discussed our reactions. Some expressed their anger at me for getting them in that situation, others their appreciation for getting them out. However, all expressed their strong sense of fear and life-endangerment. For most, they had never been more afraid in their lives. Some opted out of the next day's activities because of the physical drain of the previous night and the possibility of finding themselves in a similar situation again.

I pushed them a bit about their fear—partly to save some face and partly to better understand my own fear. Why were we so afraid? The consensus was that our fear was rational and stemmed from being in one of the highest crime sections of the city. We exemplified what University of Southern California law professor Jody David Armour calls "intelligent Bayesians," people who practice "rational discrimination" on the basis of statistical probabilities. Given statistics demonstrating blacks' disproportionate engagement in crime, we constructed a rational defense to justify our perception of a greater threat from someone black than someone white. As much as we might regret it, we believed we were right to react fearfully in this situation because it was logical to do so. Our fear was reinforced by the other "intelligent Bayesians," both black and white, who stopped to warn us of the potential danger.

Unfortunately, "intelligent Bayesians" often turn out to be not so intelligent. Although few of us keep copies of crime statistics by our bedsides, we should note that blacks arrested for violent crimes comprised less than one percent of the black population in 1994 and just less than two percent of the black male population. This is still *much* greater than the actual probability that a black male will assault a stranger, because the violent crimes statistic also includes arrests for such things as domestic violence and altercations between friends and acquaintances. In fact, the majority of those arrested for violent offenses are white. Even in cases where we see significant race differences (for example, the rate of robbery arrests among blacks is approximately twelve times the rate among nonblacks), we cannot justify the judgement that any particular black presents a sufficiently high risk of robbery to be deemed "suspicious." As Armour points out, twelve times a very small fraction is still a very small fraction—even more so when we recognize that biases in the criminal justice system undermine the reliability of the statistics themselves.

In our case, we did not respect the personal autonomy of others because we were too busy seeing them as walking statistics. The boundaries of our rationality were not limited to our poor statistical inferences. How rational was it to assume that a pack of seventeen whites would so easily fall victim to predators? Why didn't any of us, myself included, realize that our race, social status, and size as a group made us the most unlikely of victims? How rational was it to hold on to that fear even in the face of our contradictory experiences? More than a dozen people stopped to say something to us. Of those, not a single person said anything threatening, intimidating, or mean-spirited. Every comment was supportive, helpful, and well intentioned. Surely, we could begin to see that our fear was rationally unfounded and recognize it for what it was—an illogical manifestation of our racist stereotypes.

For most of us, however, the fear ran so deep that all of the reason or contradictory experiences in the world could not have challenged it. It was as if the irrationality and very acts of kindness somehow oddly reinforced the appropriateness of our fear. Where does such fear come from? The easiest answer is to label it a product of bias learned from television and the media. But does it run deeper? Andrew Hacker maintains that fear of racial minorities is really fear of those aspects of ourselves we would prefer not to confront. This is why, he argues, whites devised the word "nigger" and gave it so charged a meaning. In *The Fire Next Time,*

James Baldwin agreed that whites need the "nigger" because it is the "nigger" within themselves that they cannot tolerate. So, minorities become movie screens for the projection of all the negative images with which whites are afraid to be marred—laziness, hypersexuality, stupidity, violence. In a tragic cycle, these negative images that whites throw on minorities then become the basis for the fears that keep us separated.

January 13

It dawns even colder and windier than yesterday. As Chicagoans are overly fond of saying, "The Hawk is definitely out today." One student, trying to put the best spin on the weather and always looking for a bargain, finds one underappreciated silver lining: "Buying coffee in Chicago is a double bonus. You buy it hot, and by the time you walk to where you are going, it's iced."

We arrive with iced coffees at the first stop on today's itinerary, the DuSable Museum of African-American History. Dr. Margaret T. Burroughs founded the museum in 1961. Burroughs was a true Renaissance woman: She taught in the Chicago public schools for forty years, has authored books and written poetry, is a well-respected social activist and cultural leader, and was recognized in 1980 by President Jimmy Carter as one of the ten outstanding African-American artists in the country. She is perhaps best known for her poem "What Shall I Tell My Children Who Are Black?" which is recited at countless school programs throughout the world. Her museum is the nation's oldest, nonprofit institution devoted to the collection, preservation, interpretation, and dissemination of African and African-American history and culture. The museum's collection of paintings, drawings, and sculpture by African-American artists has been said to be among the ten most notable collections of such works in the country.

With all of the hoopla surrounding the release of Spielberg's *"Amistad,"* we are most looking forward to the new *Amistad* exhibit at the DuSable. The students are fairly well aware of the basic story line. The *Amistad* incident began off the coast of Cuba in 1839 with a shipboard rebellion by fifty-three Africans, under the leadership of a young man named Cinque, who had been illegally enslaved. The revolt resulted in the killing of all but two crew members, who were spared to sail the vessel. Wandering up the Atlantic Coast, the ship eventually was seized by a U.S. revenue cutter off the coast of Long Island and towed into New London Harbor, where the Africans were initially imprisoned. Slavery had been outlawed by the British, so the status of whether the Africans were legitimately free or legally slaves became a *cause célèbre* that created a legal controversy at the highest levels of the U.S. government as well as the royal court of Spain. The men were tried for murder in Connecticut, but eventually won their freedom and return to Sierra Leone after John Quincy Adams argued their case in the U.S. Supreme Court. The fact that Cinque and his fellow countrymen, who could not speak English, persevered in their diligent pursuit of freedom in the American legal system is the basis for this amazing story.

I am excited for the students to see a scholarly historical exhibit dedicated to the story of the *Amistad*. They have been Oliver-Stoned out of a true historical consciousness. Glitz has outrun the truth. Gossip and innuendo have outpaced documentation and fact. Postmodernism argues that the history we thought we knew was just constructed by textbook writers with specific agendas and worldviews. The "creative historical license" of "cinematic historians" has run amok and only exacerbated the problem. As we tour the *Amistad* exhibit, however, we recognize that Spielberg's treatment of the *Amistad* story, as he did with "Empire of the Sun" and "Schindler's List," is relatively true to the facts and embellished only in areas that are of little consequence.

Still, several of us wonder about some of the more subtle depictions in Spielberg's movie. For example, we recall that in *LA Weekly* Ella Taylor questions yet another story line in which power resides in the white protagonist. Almost formulaic in nature, the black slave Cinque triumphs through the good offices of a white codger, Adams, who has a gift for oratory. All too often, Taylor argues, the heroism of Cinque is lost in the whites of his wild eyes and a wordless noble-savage demeanor, whereas Adams stands out as a fountain of elegant polemic. In addition, Spielberg's attempt to give blacks a mainstream representation in the movie comes from the creation of a fictitious black abolitionist named Theodore Joadson (played by Morgan Freeman). Unfortunately, Joadson is a one-dimensional character with marginal relevance to the main story line. In the end, though, Taylor acknowledges that Spielberg does reach earnestly for the slaves' point of view and ultimately does a masterful job of telling an important story.

The museum exhibit gives a deeper substance to the story with its impressive collection of maps, images, trial records, new accounts, biographical sketches, and other *Amistad*-related materials. A few students are disappointed that the actual people didn't look much like Matthew McConaughey or Morgan Freeman, but such is the price of historical realism.

After the *Amistad* exhibit, the students disperse and find other areas of the museum that fit their interests. One student who spent a semester in South Africa is especially caught by an exhibition of photographs of black South African life during the 1940s as seen through the camera of the late Leon Levson, a German refugee who emigrated to South Africa on the eve of the outbreak of World War II. The collection, which has not been on exhibit since 1948 in Johannesburg, represents fifteen years of work in which Levson traveled and took pictures of the surrounding lands, its people, and their folkways.

I also find a group of students in an exhibit entitled "Distorted Images: Made in the U.S.A." This exhibition consists of symbolic artifacts, figurines, utensils, toy packages, and an almost endless array of made-for-the-trade products that serve as barometers of the tenor of racist attitudes of the American past. One student stands slack-jawed at the case of Little Black Sambo games, cards, and figurines. Another flinches at the exhibit featuring the evolution of Aunt Jemimah: "Some of the stuff is so derogatory. I can't believe that it was printed and that thousands of people bought this stuff for their homes. It makes me realize how deep these stereotypical beliefs must run if people can look at these images and not see that they are wrong. I wonder about the many things that are now present in our society, which also are like these ads, at which my children will be astonished that I just glanced past and didn't notice. I saw this pencil that I remember playing with as a little girl at my grandmother's house. It was of an alligator and had a little black head inside of its mouth. For the first time on the trip, I feel as if my family has been part of the problem. I am no longer able to place the blame on someone else. I feel more connected and convicted by how our society deals with race."

Things on the tour have not always gone perfectly. As I listen to this student, however, I am struck by a teacher's purest joy—the door of education has been opened a crack and she has just kicked it in.

After we leave the DuSable Museum, we catch public transit and head for the Pilsen neighborhood of Chicago. Before World War II, the ethnic enclave of Pilsen was home to the nation's biggest Bohemian-American settlement. In fact, Pilsen derives its name from a city in Bohemia. Eventually, Mexican immigrants replaced the Bohemians, and the area is now alive with festive and colorful murals on local buildings, authentic Mexican restaurants, and the Mexican Fine Arts Center Museum—the largest of its kind in the nation.

In the 1990s, the Hispanic population in Chicago expanded an incredible 17.2 percent. Of the cities we visit on our tour, however, the Hispanic community in Chicago remains the most segregated, with a 0.632 measure of dissimilarity, compared to a national average of 0.507. In addition, Hispanics in Chicago have the second highest (only exceeded by Los Angeles) index of isolation at 0.513. An unbelievably high index of clustering (3.574, compared to national average of 0.811) confirms that Hispanics in Chicago display significantly greater clustering than the majority population. One of the most predominant sites of Hispanic clustering in greater Chicago is Pilsen.

There are some striking differences between Hispanic experiences and those of other groups we have discussed. For instance, the historical legacy of Hispanics is not one of abduction or slavery. Rather, many were victims of colonization by American forces seeking new territories to provide markets for American goods. Hispanics were initially enclosed by America's expanding border following the 1846–1848 war against Mexico in which Mexico ceded all of California, New Mexico, Nevada, and parts of Colorado, Arizona, and Utah—a total of more than one million square miles. Since that time, groups of Hispanics have been uprooted, exiled, or forced to migrate. Others have come to America seeking asylum and economic opportunity.

The Hispanic population numbered 22.8 million in 1993, comprising about nine percent of the U.S. population. Due to high birth rates and increasing immigration, the Hispanic population is growing rapidly. According to U.S. Census Bureau projections, by the year 2010 Hispanics will surpass Blacks as the largest racial minority group in this country—a compelling reason to reshape future itineraries for these study tours. By the year 2050, 22.7 percent of the U.S. population is projected to be Hispanic, with disproportionate concentrations in California, Texas, and New York. Already in California and Texas, the most popular baby boy's name is no longer John or James, Michael or David. It is José.

Hispanics continue to struggle against social exclusion, persecution, and extensive employment discrimination—a struggle not always recognized by society. In the 1992 Los Angeles uprising, for example, the Latino community suffered the greatest number of people killed and had the greatest amount of property damage—facts lost in much of the reporting and conversation.

We hastily devour our lunch at Neuvo Leon Restaurant. Our host in Pilsen is José Guerrero, a handsome, unassuming Hispanic artist and muralist. Guerrero was introduced to mural art in the early 1970s. One of his first apprenticeships found him assisting on the well-known mural "Solidarity" at the United Electrical Workers Union Hall. From that time on, Guerrero was hooked on mural art. After working a few years with the Chicago Mural Group, Guerrero moved on to his own independent mural projects in Pilsen, greater Chicago, and Mexico. After yesterday's tempest of Averette and Crumbley, the students instantly are drawn to Guerrero's quiet manner and soft-spoken nature.

As we begin our tour of Pilsen's murals, Guerrero stresses the value of murals in recording the everyday life and needs of a community. He encourages the participation of community members on every level—from the initial planning to the final conception and execution of a mural. Our first stop is at the Rudy Lozano Branch Library, the site of three artworks commissioned through the City of Chicago Percent for Art Program. This innovative program, which was implemented in 1978, stipulates that a percentage of the cost of constructing or renovating municipal buildings be set aside for the commission or purchase of artworks for those buildings. As a result of the Percent for Art Program, Chicago has built one of the finest collections of contemporary public art in the world.

In addition to stained glass panels by Nereyda Garcia-Ferraz and a large oil painting by Filemon Santiago, a collaborative mosaic mural by Hector Duarte and Cynthia Weiss especially strikes us. The mural incorporates Venetian glass tiles, cement, and colored grouts. These are set directly on the interior brick wall of the library. Guerrero explains that the title of the mosaic mural, "Chic-Chac," is a reference to Chac Mool, a figure that originated in the ancient Toltec culture of Mexico. "Originally," Guerrero explains, "these figures were located in front of ancient pyramids and were used to receive sacrificial hearts. The muralists substituted the sacrificial aspect of the Chac Mool for a book." Guerrero further explains that this transformed icon and the accompanying Mayan symbols celebrate the transforming power of books and draws a connection between the ancient icons and the contemporary community's library.

We bundle up and head outside for our walking tour of Pilsen's incredible murals. The murals are striking in their appearance and size. Their colors are bold and brilliant. Some occupy small spaces, others large. Some are commissioned works by professional muralists, others wonderfully crafted mosaics by school children. The value placed on these murals by the community is evident in the fact that all are free of graffiti and appear as if they were painted just yesterday. Some incorporate the architecture of the building, such as a window ledge, into their canvas. Most of the murals place a sociopolitical focus within a larger artistic context. Each of them reflects the unique nature of Hispanic experiences in America. They are the blood and pulse of the Pilsen community—a fact unfortunately lost on the occasional insensitive developer who purchases a building and callously paints over the murals.

Just south of Eighteenth Street, we see the most recent mural by Hector Duarte. It occupies a brick wall approximately forty feet long and fifteen feet high. The mural is framed on one end by the face of Caesar Chavez and on the other by Emiliano Zapata. Without words, Duarte reflects an incredible range of the everyday life and needs of Pilsen as well as those of Hispanics across America. The mural depicts solidarity, diversity, migration, rebellion, and family. The fears of poverty, rising taxes, and possible gentrification are palpable. However, you also see the hope and inspiration for a brighter tomorrow reflected in the huddled family in the middle of the mural. As we leave Duarte's mural, and Pilsen, I ask one student about her impressions. She says, "It is a beautiful concrete neighborhood full of life donated by imagination." Amen, amen.

That night's debriefing is short and spiritless. Sometime after nine, we will be leaving for an "alternative" poetry reading at a small local theater. The students, who are emotionally and intellectually worn, are not terribly attracted by the thought of venturing out again into the late-night cold. The tone becomes even more dismal as we remember the dozens of homeless people sitting in a Pilsen Catholic Church seeking warmth—physical not spiritual. In the midst of our selfish concerns about comfort, we are reminded that somewhere in this vast city someone will freeze to death tonight. We bundle up and head out into the cold.

January 14

We begin our last day in Chicago with Reverend Donald L. Sharp of Faith Tabernacle Baptist Church. He is the gregarious, disarming, sixty-year-old Southern Baptist pastor of one of the most active black churches in Chicago. Reverend Sharp is not your typical Southern Baptist. He is a pro-choice advocate and an unabashed fan of Louis Farrakhan's principles of empowerment. He decries the 1996 Southern Baptist resolution proclaiming the goal of evangelizing Jews in America—not well received by Jews who, it just so happens, believe just as strongly that their religion is right and do not need evangelizing. (In September 1999, the Southern Baptists International Mission Board launched another aggressive campaign aimed at converting Jews to Christianity. A corresponding booklet, described as offensive and condescending by Jewish leaders, offers tips on how to evangelize Jews during their ten holy Days of Awe, when they are sensitized to spiritual matters.) In direct contrast, Reverend Sharp's church has developed a program with a local synagogue where eighth graders participate in educational exchange programs. This is no high-minded evangelism, just letting two groups of markedly different teenagers—in color and religious beliefs—meet and sow the seeds of friendship and understanding.

Our rambling discourse with Reverend Sharp leaves profound impressions on the students. In a gentler manner than Averette or Crumbley, he communicates a similar sense of pessimism and exclusion. "Every day I wake up," he begins, "I look in the mirror and am reminded that I am black. That simple fact—my blackness—will literally color every interaction I have that day." He is stridently vocal in his call for black empowerment—specifically economic empowerment. Although black churches are one source of empowerment, Reverend Sharp believes that a people's worldly destiny lies in their economic leverage. If you have that hammer, you have respect and opportunity. If you don't, you don't.

Reverend Sharp's belief in the importance of economics in issues of race also is reflected in his insistence that whites have yet to understand the continuing economic consequences of slavery. I am reminded of the reaction to a recent bill, forwarded by representative Tony Hall (a white Democrat from Ohio), proposing a national apology for slavery. This bill, which Hall believes would correct a glaring omission, might have redemptive consequences for the American conscience. As columnist Leonard Pitts Jr. points out, however, it might also lead to "a post-apology scenario in which whites declare race matters resolved and become unreceptive to substantive measures to improve the lot of blacks." Pitts adds, "I'm still trying to figure out how, exactly, that scenario differs from the one we already face."

Being aware of religion's historical and contemporary role in perpetrating exclusion, we are especially challenged by the fundamental principle of Reverend Sharp's church: "We open our arms to everyone." He asks, "If white churches cannot accept unwed mothers or men with earrings or long hair or homosexuals, then what sort of chance, as a black man, do I have to be accepted and loved at such a church? . . . How do I stand a chance when my 'bad trait'—my skin color—is so obvious and unchangeable?" These are poignant questions, like so many others on this trip, to which we do not have answers. We do know that too many contemporary churches judge and condemn rather than love and protect. They focus on doctrine and theory rather than application and practice. Until that changes, the church will remain a part of the problem rather than the solution.

Reverend Sharp's biggest challenge to us, however, was to remind us that too many whites talk about wanting reconciliation and equality, but do not take any steps to implement these changes. In his mind, whites are the only ones with power and, although that power has been used to oppress, it must now be used to liberate both blacks and whites from the tyranny of racism. "The ball's in your court," he concluded.

The ball *is* in our court. Although it is nice to be reminded, we do not really need to be told that. But the lingering question remains, "What in the hell do we do about it?" Reverend Sharp senses that question in the air and says: "You know, dismantling racism is like eating a five-hundred-pound elephant. How do you do it? One bite at a time." From this point on, we adopt the phrase "It's time to start eating a little elephant" to tell ourselves that every day, in some way, there is something each of us can do to dismantle racism. It reminds us that the central transactions of the world occur when one person talks to another person, one person loves another person, and one person heals another person. This may be trite, but it gives us a focus and beats the alternative of inaction and apathy.

Following our time with Reverend Sharp, the students are sent in groups of four on city excursions. Using public transportation and city maps, they venture to preassigned eateries in Greektown, Bridgeport (Lithuanian), Andersonville (Swedish), and an Indian and Pakistani neighborhood. They are fairly well-seasoned public transit riders at this point, but the opportunities to see the diversity of Chicago's neighborhoods—and have a great lunch—are much appreciated.

As we rendezvous for our trip to Union Station, the sleet that had begun this afternoon is now a blinding blizzard. The chill outside is bracing. One student mutters, "It's the kind of cold that bites at you and makes you tense all over." After this day, the cold has to join a long line of things that are making us tense all over. Buses are delayed and roads are closed as cars careen along and patience runs short. Finally, somehow, we all make it to the station. Pending our first Amtrak experience, I remind the students of some basic train etiquette: stay in the seats assigned to them, keep their voices low, restrict their wanderings from car to car, and, most important, do not get off the train until we hit Memphis.

After some of us lighten the mood by re-creating the "Kevin Costner saving the baby" scene from "The Untouchables" on the great marble staircase of Union Station, we finally board the train. We are looking forward to the pleasures of Memphis—the ducks at the Peabody Hotel, Graceland, red beans and rice, and Beale Street blues. In the back of our minds, though, we also begin to prepare for one of the most sobering experiences on the tour—standing by the balcony where Martin Luther King Jr.'s life ended. In Atlanta, we will see where his life began. In Birmingham, we will see where much of his most important work took place. In some ways, we wish we could miss having to see where he died. If we could avoid that, we might be able to live in the false hope that King and his dream are still alive.

5. MEMPHIS:
A GRIEF OBSERVED

Behold, here cometh the dreamer. . . . Let us slay him and see what becomes of his dreams.

Genesis 37:19–20

Amtrak: Experience the magic. From the very first day I began planning these tours, I saw Amtrak as the way for us to traverse America. On the 1996 tour, we rode Amtrak from coast to coast and only flew for our return from Washington, D.C., to Spokane. However, the rigid calendar limits of the January term, coupled with a desire to add an additional stop, made me revise the 1998 itinerary. I dropped train travel between Los Angeles and San Francisco and, more importantly, the brain-scalding fifty-hour leg between California and Chicago. From Chicago on, though, the 1998 tour rode the rails of Amtrak.

There seemed to be several ways to justify choosing rail over air travel for the tour. Passenger trains save energy, reduce car and air traffic, are more efficient, and promised to be a better financial option. As it turns out, I am not sure any of these publicity brochure promises are actually true. For instance, a study by the Cato Institute for Policy Analysis found that intercity buses are actually more fuel efficient than Amtrak's trains. They also reported that eliminating travel on Amtrak would only add approximately one car every 1.3 minutes on roads that are built to handle a car every 1.5 *seconds*. In the Northeast corridor, which annually accounts for about fifty-six percent of Amtrak's revenues, the study concluded that the disappearance of Amtrak service would result in *no* additional airline flights. As a matter of fact, all of Amtrak's passengers would not fill the unused portion of Northeast-corridor airplanes. What about efficiency? That depends on your schedule. Unless you have three and a half days to go from Memphis to Seattle, you likely will not be drawn to Amtrak's leisurely pace. Even for shorter trips, not many people are drawn to the rails. Amtrak carries only about 0.007 percent of American commuters to work, which is 4 percent of the number that *walk* to work. Finally, for a cross-country trip, Amtrak is only a better financial option if you choose to bring your own food and have a sadistic preference for sleeping in a semireclining seat while in perpetual motion. Otherwise, you will spend hundreds of dollars for sleeper compartments that, although they come with free meals, are only a little less uncomfortable than the reclining seats.

So what is the advantage of traveling on Amtrak? Maybe I am just a romantic, but there is something about riding on trains that seems enlightened. The late John Chancellor once described passenger trains as a sign of a civilized society. They facilitate reflection, contemplation, and leisure. Seeing the landscape, homes, and people between point A and point B is a smoother and more satisfying passage than being airlifted like a sack of potatoes down into your final destination. It helps ease the transition from getting there to being there.

January 15

We arrive at Memphis' Central Station, stagger off the train, reacquaint ourselves with our land legs, and are greeted by amazingly cold drizzle. Memphis was by far our coldest stop on the 1996 tour, and I wonder if this morning is a harbinger of more foul weather. Only two students opted to pay extra for a sleeper compartment on the overnight leg from Chicago to Memphis. As I look at the rest of the bedraggled lot, I suspect a few would sell bone marrow to get enough money to reserve a sleeper for the upcoming Atlanta–Washington, D.C., overnight leg. In a rare flash of insight, I had anticipated their post-Amtrak haze and scheduled no tour activities for today. We will have a short meeting tonight. Until then, there will be a lot of sleeping and washing of clothes.

Some of the more adventurous embark on a trip to Graceland. They seem surprised when I decline their invitation to visit one of the most often-visited residences in the United States—second only to the White House. I have my reasons, though. My mother and sister are convinced that Elvis was a deity. They sustain their delusion with a ready store of comparisons between Elvis and Jesus: Jesus was part of the Trinity; Elvis's first band was a trio. Jesus is the Lord's shepherd; Elvis dated Cybill Shepherd. Jesus was the Lamb of God; Elvis had mutton chop sideburns. You get the picture. As a result of their obsession, I have been dragged to Graceland more times than any human ought to be expected to withstand—despite my rebuttals that the most common mistyping of "Elvis" is "Evils."

In 1998, *American Heritage* magazine proclaimed Memphis their "Great American Place." Located in the southwestern corner of Tennessee, with the Mississippi River and Arkansas to the west and the state of Mississippi to the south, Memphis is a cultural and social crossroads. As characterized by University of Pennsylvania historian Thomas Childers, Memphis—while certainly steeped in the Deep South—looks upriver as well as down, not only to New Orleans, but to St. Louis and Chicago and beyond.

In 1541, Hernando de Soto's expedition passed through the mid-South and claimed the site of present-day Memphis for the Kingdom of Spain, casting a blind eye to the centuries-long residence of the Chickasaw nation. Over the next centuries, claims of the Memphis area would shift to the French, back to the Spanish, and finally to the land-hungry Americans. The Chickasaws signed a formal agreement with the U.S. government in October 1818 ceding all of western Tennessee to the United States. In the following year, three land speculators, one of whom was soon-to-be President Andrew Jackson, founded the settlement of Memphis. Eventually, the city's prominence as a river port midway between St. Louis and New Orleans, coupled with the new Memphis-Charleston railroad line, led to rapid economic expansion and stability. By the mid 1850s, the city of Memphis had grown to be the sixth largest city in the nation. However, it was the Civil War that brought the greatest change to the face and culture of the city.

As Childers describes, Memphis had been overwhelmingly white during its early years. The first immigrants to settle there in large numbers were the Irish, who came to Memphis to escape Ireland's potato famine in the 1840s. In the midst of the Civil War, however, Union authorities established a freedmen's camp for escaping slaves just south of town. The camp population mushroomed with the mounting losses of the Confederate campaign. When the war ended in 1865, most of the freedmen decided to remain in Memphis. Many moved into the south part of town around Beale Street. Soon the black population in Memphis had grown from 4,000 to 15,000. Word spread quickly and Memphis became a favorite destination of blacks from the rural South—not too far north, but far enough north to promise a better life.

Over the next decades, Memphis was besieged with catastrophic yellow fever epidemics (two-thirds of the population was killed or left town because of the disease), bankruptcy, and the loss of its city charter. In 1922, a Prudential Life Insurance Company statistician announced that Memphis—with 67.4 murders per 100,000 population, compared to New York City's meager 5.8—was "the murder capital of America." In its subsequent recovery, Memphis continued to draw a rising tide of black laborers, erstwhile entrepreneurs, teachers, and musicians. Although the city remained strictly segregated, the south side, which was centered around Beale Street, housed a vibrant black community. As Childers notes, this community was "complete with doctors, lawyers, druggists, insurance brokers, schools, churches, retail stores, and theaters, unfettered by the oppressive Jim Crow laws or intrusive white police." At the dawn of the twentieth century, Beale had become "the Negro Main Street of America" and held a magnetic fascination for many in the mid-South region. In the words of blues great Rufus Thomas, "If you were black for one night on Beale Street, never would you want to be white again."

The debriefing part of our meeting is relatively short. The last two days in Chicago were packed and many of our reactions have been processed in informal groups on the train, during the free day in Memphis, over meals, and in 2:00 A.M. bunk-bed conversations. Although I regret not being privy to each of these discussions, it is clear that a cohesive and healthy group dynamic is emerging. Yes, some small cliques are forming, as would be expected, but the sleeping and travel arrangements make it impossible for the cliques to remain secluded. As a result, group conversations are beginning to flow more easily as we become increasingly self-transparent and comfortable with expressing our various opinions and reactions.

The group who went to Graceland relates an interesting encounter with someone they met on the bus. The black woman was an off-duty Memphis police officer who was visiting some friends across town.

When she learned about the purpose of our tour, she spoke openly for nearly forty minutes about the state of racism in Memphis. In her view, Memphis remains a racially divided city. She is aware, as a gainfully employed citizen in a well-respected profession, that she has many more opportunities than were open for her parents and grandparents. She is also aware, though, that when she is not wearing a uniform, she is subject to many of the same slights and harassment that her ancestors suffered through. Just yesterday, she tells the group, she was tailed by a "rent-a-cop" in a music store while browsing for CDs, while other, white patrons went unmolested.

In one simple example, she has articulated the crucial distinction between what psychologists call old-fashioned and modern racism. "Old-fashioned racism" refers to the open flame of racial hatred. It describes the type of blatant racism in which people openly state that they are against social desegregation, they view members of racial minority groups as inferior in various ways (for example, intelligence, ambition, honesty), and they would consider moving away if minority members took up residence in their neighborhoods. Old-fashioned racists still exist and their actions of hate continue to mar the landscape of race relations in America. By and large, however, the beliefs of old-fashioned racism are no longer considered socially acceptable in most circles.

Like most other racial minorities in America, the experiences of this woman likely do not include numerous examples of such overt racism (at least in comparison to the countless examples that could be told by her parents and grandparents). However, we must not take this to mean that racism has disappeared. Like a resistant virus, old-fashioned racism has mutated into more insidious forms of discrimination, persecution, and exclusion.

"Modern racism" is the term given this new face of racism prompted by changes in societal norms and the adoption of antidiscrimination legislation. Inherent in this term is the understanding that racial stereotypes, bias, and resentment still lurk beneath the veneer of a "racism-free" society. This "everyday" racism does not express itself in the blatant, sensationalistic forms of its ancestor. Instead, it manifests itself in more subtle, indirect, and less-objectionable ways than old-fashioned racism. Because of this, modern racism leaves few defining moments for its victims. Instead, it leaves a legacy of "minor" and "forgettable" slights and mistreatments that nonetheless result in debilitating consequences. The tax of modern racism is cumulative, draining, energy consuming, and ultimately life consuming. It is this face of racism that continues to take its toll on this woman and millions of other racial minorities in America. It is this face of racism that whites must come to understand and fight against.

The students also recall that she is especially perplexed about an upcoming assignment where she will be asked to protect a group of Ku Klux Klan members who are planning a downtown protest in Memphis. In her mind, Memphis' inability to stop these people from spewing the message of hate is just another sign of the community's reluctance to actively confront issues of racism—overt or otherwise. She warns the group to look beneath the surface of what the National Civil Rights Museum and Beale Street will suggest and to try to talk with "real" people about the "real" Memphis—the Memphis where some white people would give the group a hard time for talking to her on the bus and some black people would give her a hard time for talking to them. She is exactly right. She's the type of person with whom we should be spending more of our time. As the tours evolve from year to year, I need to continue to make the move from impersonal museums to "real" people, similar to what we did in Chicago.

Several of the students then digress a bit to ask the group about Graceland. After the usual touristy descriptions of excess and bad color schemes, one student makes a statement that illustrates how our perceptions are now being affected by our attempt to see with the other's eyes: "It's funny because I didn't expect Graceland to relate to the course at all and, for the most part, it didn't. However, there was a quote that Elvis always said that captured the essence of our trip. 'Don't criticize that man, you never walked a mile in his shoes.' One of the most important things I've been learning is how many different pairs of shoes there are and how oblivious to them I have been. I know there are things and people out there that I sincerely don't understand. But, I keep thinking of that idea of trying to visualize what it would be like to walk a mile in the shoes of the people we've met and the exhibits we've seen. Although that experience has been different each time, the resonant conclusion has been that I can't do it."

On the heels of that remark, I remind the students that the process of seeing with the other's eyes is a journey and that part of that journey is the frustration of realizing just how gauzy our view always will remain. Despite that, each of us is beginning to see the world in a different way. Things previously unnoticed are now being noticed. Things previously unheard are now being heard. Borrowing Reverend Sharp's analogy, this is the way in which we will each begin to eat our bite of the five-hundred-pound elephant.

For the rest of the meeting, I simply review our Memphis schedule, remind the students to watch their decorum in the hotel, and prepare them a bit for tomorrow's tour at the National Civil Rights Museum. I tell the students that *Time* magazine's Walter Shapiro has called the museum "a classic American jumble of laudable intentions, questionable aesthetic judgment, outside experts, and civic boosterism." Despite the lessons learned at the Museum of Tolerance, they are struck to hear such a negative appraisal of a place each has assumed to be almost beyond reproach. I challenge the students to keep their critical antennae up to rebut or defend Shapiro's perceptions, while allowing themselves to be caught up in the story of the Civil Rights movement and the loss of its greatest dreamer.

Throughout the twentieth century, racial tensions were never far from the surface in Memphis. Like so many other cities across the country, the city's already fragile racial "peace" was challenged by the inexorable march of the Civil Rights movement. The simmering racial tension in Memphis needed only one spark to be ignited into action. That spark was provided by a strike of city sanitation workers, most of whom were black, in February 1968. The workers wanted union recognition and decent wages. As prolonged negotiations groped toward a settlement that always seemed just out of reach, local civil rights leaders used the opportunity to apply nonviolent protest to an economic problem.

In March 1968, Memphis pastor James Lawson persuaded the Reverend Martin Luther King Jr. to pledge his support to the strike. King did so and agreed to lead a protest march. However, the march degenerated into violent turmoil. The "Invaders," a black youth gang who were unswayed by King's appeal for nonviolence, went on a burning and looting rampage. In Reverend Ralph David Abernathy's recollection, "It was the first time that people within our march had actually gone and inflicted violence upon the oppressors." Memphis police retaliated with tear gas, billy clubs, and bullets. King escaped the melee only by jumping into the back seat of a passing car.

King was shaken by the Memphis march. The legitimacy of his movement was already in question. The previous year, King had made opposition to the Vietnam War his top priority. In so doing, he burned his bridges to the Johnson administration, Congress, and many of his allies. The intensification of black violence and white backlash that year also underlined his ineffectuality. All of that had come on top of his disappointing Chicago freedom movement of 1966. Assailed by critics and losing power and status, King was determined to prove the viability of nonviolent protest in the struggle for civil rights. He vowed to return to lead a peaceful and successful march to the Memphis city hall. It was that vow that pulled Martin Luther King Jr. back to Memphis just a week later and, on that fateful day of April 4, 1968, to the balcony of the Lorraine Motel.

January 16

We intentionally arrive several minutes before the National Civil Rights Museum is scheduled to open. I want the group to meet a remarkable person that we met on the 1996 tour. As we approach the museum, Jacqueline Smith, a forty-four-year-old black woman, is just beginning to remove the plastic tarp from a worn sofa and a makeshift cart. As the students look at the layers of clothes Smith wears on this frigid morning, they realize that she spent the night on the sofa. As a matter of fact, Smith has spent the night on that sofa for 3,659 consecutive nights.

Smith is a former desk clerk who lived at the Lorraine Motel from 1977 to 1988. In March 1988, she was evicted to make way for the construction of the National Civil Rights Museum. Since that time, when most of my students were still in grade school, she has lived on the sidewalk facing the museum and fought, in vain, to have the soil where King fell more accurately reflect his vision. Smith claims that all of the former tenants of the motel are now homeless and their treatment is a glaring violation of King's spirit. In her words: "The National Civil Rights Museum is a disgrace to the life and works of Dr. King, a scam, and a land grab that is inflating real estate values and displacing people who have lived in the area for years." She argues that the best monument to King would be a center at the Lorraine offering housing, job training, a free community college, a health clinic, and other services for the poor.

Jacqueline Smith is a flesh-and-bones protest of the museum. Twenty-four hours a day, seven days a week, in the frigid cold and the ceaseless heat, she camps across from the museum and continues her one-woman vigil. She explains—in a monotone way that betrays the thousands of times she has explained this—her protest to our group, gives us pamphlets, and wishes us well. One student asks if the museum can be justified as an important place to learn about King and nonviolent protest. She counters that such things could and should be learned from books, not an impersonal museum. She knows we will end up visiting the museum—the museum authorities say that very rarely are people turned away by her protest. However, she also knows that it is incumbent upon her to stand up and be heard. To do any less would be to deny her self-appointed responsibility.

So, it is with a little heavier step that we walk into the National Civil Rights Museum. The face of the motel, with its distinctive green doors and yellow trim, has been maintained as it was in 1968. However, the interior of the motel has been gutted and expanded into 10,000 square feet of display space and galleries. Although it was first thought morbid to build a civil rights museum on the site where King was assassinated, the museum has drawn more than 700,000 visitors since its opening in 1991.

We begin our tour by sitting through a brief introductory film. It offers a strong, if heavy-handed, admonition for all of us to participate in the political process. We then meet our docent for the day, Mr. Donald Letcher. He leads us to the first display, an incredibly dense time line of pre-1954 black history. It begins in 1619 and, using first-person accounts and copies of original newspaper headlines and documents, overwhelms us with nearly 350 years of black history. The time line is chock-full of information, but leaves us with sensory overload. The students, who are trained to digest every scintilla of information, are a bit frustrated at seeing such a library of material but not being able to immerse themselves in it. However, Letcher does an admirable job of highlighting the key points.

Fortunately, the remainder of the exhibits in the museum veer away from the excessive and overcrowded information of the introductory section and lean to a more interactive style. The first such exhibit, on the *Brown v. Board of Education* case, typifies the switch. In 1954, the U.S. Supreme Court voted unanimously in favor of a black Kansas man named Oliver Brown who believed that his eight-year-old daughter should not have to walk twenty-one blocks to attend grade school when there was a perfectly good one two blocks from his house. One entire wall is covered with a photograph of the triumphant attorneys on the steps of the Supreme Court and an inset picture of black schoolhouses—a visual relief in comparison to what has come before. This is then followed by the Little Rock school-integration story; depictions of the Montgomery bus boycott; a Greensboro Woolworth sit-in panorama; the march on Washington, D.C.; and the Selma-to-Montgomery march.

Each of these exhibits impacts the students in ways that the printed word cannot. As we walk on to a green and yellow Montgomery city bus, for instance, we find the first five rows reserved for whites. A mannequin of Rosa Parks sits defiantly in the second row. As we take our seat in the bus, a driver's voice menacingly barks: "I need that seat now. Please move back. If you don't move from that seat now, I'll have you arrested." Shouts and taunts from other riders barrage us. As we leave the bus, we see photos of real boycott participants and read a brief chronology of the protest.

Something may be lost as we move from documentation to approximation. However, something important is gained. We begin to be inserted into the Civil Rights movement. As we take our place at a lunch counter and watch the television news reports of what the sit-in protestors went through, we begin to see with the other's eyes. No, we are not actually there and, yes, maybe it sanitizes the real experience to a dangerous degree. However, we do begin to have an appreciation for what people went through in their struggle for civil rights. As one student later writes, "I am reminded of the final pages of *To Kill a Mockingbird* when Scout stands on Boo Radley's porch and thinks about Atticus and his lesson about standing in someone else's shoes and walking around for a little while. The National Civil Rights Museum allowed me to stand on the porch of the Civil Rights movement."

As much as the interactive exhibits begin to redeem the museum, I am still struck by a few inconsistencies. The National Voting Rights Act of 1965, for instance, was a pivotal piece of civil rights legislation. Some mark it as the unofficial culmination of the Civil Rights movement. Curiously, it warrants only a single panel on the wall. Similarly, the life of Malcolm X is encapsulated on a single panel. As Amy Wilson of the Smithsonian Institution points out, more prominence is given to the shooting of James Meredith during his march across Mississippi than is given to either of these legacies of the Civil Rights movement.

As our tour winds toward its completion, the educational mission of the museum becomes plain. Above an exhibit on the Memphis sanitation strike, a quotation from Thomas Jefferson reads, "A little rebellion, now and then, is a good thing. . . . It is a medicine necessary for the sound health of government." In this simple quote, the museum effectively places the Civil Rights movement within the mainstream of America's revolutionary tradition. However, even as I read this, I find myself feeling more sympathy for Jacqueline Smith's protest. True, barring the initial introductory exhibit, the museum has been engaging and well done. It is certainly far superior to the Museum of Tolerance in both its conception and execution. However, the museum easily could have been located elsewhere and been just as effective. Maybe this space *should* have been used for something more in line with King's life and work.

We then turn away from the quote and enter the glass-enclosed motel rooms where Martin Luther King Jr. and his colleagues spent his last days in Memphis. An unmade bed. A room service tray with dirty dishes. That day's *Memphis Press-Scimitar.* A butt-filled ashtray. Looking out of the window, we can see the spot where King fell, now marked by red and white carnations. Looking up, we can trace the path of the assassin's bullet from the rooming house across the street. Standing in the presence of history, I now realize why this museum *must* be located on this site. It is the presence of the *place* that ultimately grabs us. It is the presence of the *place* that engages all of our thoughts, emotions, and senses. It is the presence of the *place* that makes the sense of loss unbearably palpable.

The mournful mood is enhanced by a recording of the great gospel singer Mahalia Jackson singing "Precious Lord," just as she did at King's funeral. We also hear the poignant recollection of Reverend Ralph David Abernathy, one of the men at King's side when he died: "Andy Young was the first to get up there by me. And Andy said, 'Oh God.' He said, 'Ralph, it's over.' I became furious. I said, 'Don't say that. Don't you say that, Andy. It will not be over. It will never be over.' "

Within hours after the announcement of King's death, uprisings flared in the ghettos of more than a hundred cities. Twenty blocks of Chicago's West Side went up in flames before Mayor Daley ordered the police to "shoot to wound" any looter and to "shoot to kill" any arsonists. In Washington, D.C., hundreds of fires lit up the night as army units in full combat gear took up battle positions around the Capitol and on the grounds of the White House. By the end of the week, 21,000 federal troops and 34,000 national guardsmen had been called out to quell the unrest that had left 46 dead, more than 3,000 injured, some 27,000 arrested, and an estimated $45 million of property lost.

The greatest loss, of course, was that of the dreamer who had tried to redeem the soul of America. Martin Luther King Jr. was not a perfect man. Part of his legacy, in fact, is a mythology that neglects the reality that he was more human than saint. For many, King's martyrdom has led to a kind of historical revision in which we forget his limits as a man and leader and focus only on his incredible achievements. In truth, like each of us, King did have limits. For instance, he was still learning his way through the art of political strategy and negotiation. It also was unclear if his principles of nonviolence could translate from the familiar soil of the South to the unfamiliar terrain of the North. Regardless, as Harvard Sitkoff argues, King was our last best hope for fundamental change. "Alone among the leaders of his era," Sitkoff writes, "King had been able to inspire African-Americans to struggle against racism *and* to encourage whites to acknowledge their responsibility for the plight of blacks without turning them against the movement. . . . No other African-American leader could keep hope alive, could galvanize the struggle, could inspire dreams."

A week after King's assassination, Memphis authorities recognized the sanitation workers' collective bargaining rights and raised their wages.

After the tour ends, most of us head back toward Beale Street. Following last night's storm, Memphis is not officially "closed for business" today, but it's close. Looking for a lighter—and warmer—mood, I join several students for a steaming bowl of red beans and rice at the Rum Boogie Cafe. I then twist their arm into a brisk walking tour of Beale Street. By the 1960s, the four-block area that is now the revived Beale Street was a dismal wasteland. After several aborted efforts, a redeveloped Beale Street was opened in 1983 and today is a thriving entertainment center. With a dozen or so blues clubs, cafes, record shops, and restaurants, the street jumps with entertainment nightly. In 1997, Beale Street received the stamp of tourist legitimacy—its own Hard Rock Cafe. On most weekends, two blocks of Beale are blocked off to traffic and a tide of people having a good time flow from club to club along the street. As Thomas Childers points out, some disparage the new Beale Street as little more than an artificial and touristy blues theme park. The less cynical, though, see in Beale Street an attempt to embrace the musical and cultural heritage of old Memphis.

Our informal walking tour of Beale Street ends just in time for us to get good spots at the Peabody Hotel for the second of their two daily duck marches. The students think I am a little weird to be so excited about a duck march, but I have yet to have anyone see this ritual and not break out in a wide smile. The Peabody, the "South's Grand Hotel," opened in 1925. Its huge lobby, where ducks swim in the central fountain, has been a gathering place for Memphians for decades. Daily, at 11:00 A.M. and 5:00 P.M., the ducks are regally escorted to and from the fountain on a red carpet leading to a brass elevator. This is one of those southern eccentricities William Faulkner used to write about, when he was not getting lubricated in this very lobby.

We are just in time to get a good spot next to the fifty-foot red carpet as it is unrolled. At 5:00 sharp, in true Skinnerian form, the five ducks flop out of the fountain, line up single file, waddle down the carpet, and huddle into the corner of the elevator for their short ride up to their coop on the roof. Then everyone leaves. Maybe it's difficult to appreciate the ducks unless you are there. Regardless of how hard they try, though, the students cannot hide their smiling faces from my "I told you so" eyes.

Whenever I am in Memphis, I take advantage of another of the great gifts that accompanied the blacks up north during the Great Migration—blues music. Despite the storm, it looks like at least a few blues clubs will be open this evening. So, with only minimal prodding from the students, I quickly agree to an early debriefing to be followed by a night of blues on Beale Street.

Reactions and opinions flow easily in that night's debriefing. The free day in Memphis appears to have allowed many of the experiences to catch up with and wash over the students. We begin with a discussion of Jacqueline Smith's protest. The students are clearly moved by her mission and persistence. However, some are moved in conflicting directions. "The woman on the sidewalk frightened me," one student confesses. "That someone would dedicate their life to a losing cause, one that was arguable on a number of grounds. I respect her dedication, but wonder why anyone would fight so hard for something that seems so trivial, to me. The museum offered her a job, a place to stay. It sounded like the others in the building found other housing and were not left out on the street. She should be praised and yet I can't do it. Something about the whole scene hit me as wrong." Even the students who originally had the greatest sympathy for Smith's protest find themselves swayed by the awesome power of the National Civil Rights Museum. Contrary to

Smith's arguments, most saw the museum as a legacy and call to a *movement*, not just a monument to a man.

There is a deep sense of empowerment left by our visit to the museum. Many of us thought that visiting the place where the dreamer was slain would only reinforce our sense that the dream had died. However, it was just the opposite. Being at the museum and ending the tour on the balcony brought home the point that *we* are part of the dream. As long as there are people with the passion and commitment to carry that dream, the dream will never die. We have become the dream and the hope of racial reconciliation. All of our callings will be different than that of King's. But, if we retain our commitment to the dream and carry that commitment over into actions, we have the capacity to make a difference in our world.

The blues is one of those rare musical expressions that almost defy description. Finding an agreed-upon definition of the blues is more difficult than finding a consensual definition of "sexual activity" in the White House. As Gerald Early, director of African and Afro-American Studies at Washington University, writes: "The blues can be happy or sad, fast or slow, played by jazz musicians, sung with some alterations by pop singers, twanged by country and western stars; the blues can be down-home and rural, with guitar and harmonica, or uptown and urban, with brass and reeds, electrified or acoustic, folkish or hard and loud. Blues can swing, jump, shuffle, or slow-drag. The blues can be about sexual prowess or sexual defeat, about betrayal or commitment, abandonment or return, masculinity or femininity, boasting pride or stoic humility, fortune or debt, aggressive violence against fate or fatalistic resignation to it." Despite its disguises, no other music is so instantly recognizable.

Fortunately, the blues does have some distinctive signatures, at least on a technical level. Chicago bluesmen like Muddy Waters and Willie Dixon, for instance, relied on guitar and harmonica leads, Mississippi Delta styles of singing and playing, a rhythm section, and electronic amplification. Most blues also includes the use of "blue notes" or "bent" pitches and a definite song form (twelve bars, one-four-five). Lyrically, the blues contains some of the most fantastically penetrating autobiographical and revealing statements in the Western musical tradition. The lyrics bemoan our fundamental helplessness even as they glory in our ability to press on. In truth, though, the singer's vocal timbre drives the emotional impact of the song as much as the lyrics.

Getting a handle on where the blues came from is much easier than describing what it is. We know that the blues is a native American musical and verse form, with no direct European and African antecedents (although some argue the style represents a distillate of African music brought by slaves). The blues sprang from spiritual music and field hollers in the Mississippi Delta. It gave voice, like a great collective wail, to a mood of alienation and despair. As Charles E. Cobb Jr. says, the blues was "born as a lamentation for physical hardship, . . . [and] evolved to address the heart's every yearning." Although the blues often is tied to jazz music, bluesologists claim that the blues is neither an era in the chronological development of jazz nor a particular style of playing or singing jazz.

W. C. Handy, a son of freed slaves, first popularized the blues form. In 1905, Handy was a thirty-two-year-old, formally trained musician and band leader who had just moved to Memphis from his home in Florence, Alabama. Four years later, he was commissioned to write a campaign song for E. H. Crump, a young white candidate for mayor. Crump was courting the black vote and wanted a tune that would attract blacks without alienating white voters. The result was "Mister Crump," which is generally acknowledged as the first blues song and which consecrated Memphis as the birthplace of the blues. During the next decade, the blues became a national craze. Records by leading blues singers like Bessie Smith and, in the 1930s, Billie Holiday sold in the millions. During this period, the blues evolved into a musical form widely used by jazz instrumentalists as well as blues singers.

During the late 1930s and 1940s, a new generation of the blues spread northward with the migration of blacks from the South. Moving up Mississippi's Highway 61, the blues found a home on Beale Street. It was there that two sharecroppers from the Mississippi Delta named Chester Burnett and Riley King—better known as Howlin' Wolf and B. B. ("Blues

Boy") King—electrified the blues with the introduction of the amplified guitar. Blues songs soon became mainstays on the national hit charts.

In the early 1950s, the blues began to progress far beyond its original origins. In 1954, a young, white truck driver who had moved to Memphis from Tupelo, Mississippi, made his first recording for Sun Records. Elvis Presley's style drew from diverse sources—black and white gospel, rural and urban blues, and country. In this first racial crossing in popular music, Elvis personified the younger generation's twinge of respect for and envy of blacks. The resulting racial amalgamation, called "rocka-billy," showed the degree to which poor whites and blacks, who worked and socialized side by side in and around Memphis, had come to share cultural legacies. Later, this synthesis would come to be immortalized as "rock-and-roll."

Last night's Beale Street excursion drew mixed reviews. The storm had closed many of the clubs and cafes. The popular wristbands that are pur-chased for one flat price and used for admission to any club were not available, so the few clubs we could enter each demanded a separate cover charge. Some of us sprung for the experience, others did not. Even-tually, several of us found our way to B. B. King's Blues Club and enjoyed some spicy chicken fingers and loud, if not necessarily authentic, blues music. Needless to say, it was not one of the five or six nights a year that B. B. himself drops in to play a set or two.

Several students and I discuss the legacy of the Beale Street blues. In its heyday, Beale Street was a hub of black social life and the blues were the meaningful music of a dispossessed people. However, as we saw last night, there has definitely been a "whitening" of the blues. The only black faces we saw at B. B.'s were behind the bar and on the wall. (As one student says, "It's funny the things that I notice now.") The stage band was white and catered, as do most Beale Street businesses, to an almost exclusively white audience. This is not just limited to Beale Street. There are now about 165 blues festivals and 125 blues societies. All but a few are dominated by whites. White artists have jumped to the top of most blues charts, often by covering the hits of old black bluesmen. As

Rufus Thomas says, "The blues were born black, but they ain't black no more."

No matter how many "No Black. No White. Just the Blues." sweatshirts are sold on Beale Street, the question remains—why the whitening of the blues? There is no easy answer and the controversy surrounding the discussion shows that race remains a divisive issue in blues circles. On one hand, some argue that whites have stolen the blues away in yet another exploitation of a great black legacy. As Michael Grunwald of the *Boston Globe* argues, the white takeover of the blues reminds some of white minstrels who toured the South in blackface in the 1800s singing spirituals they stole from slaves. From this perspective, it is easy to see the new Beale Street as the ultimate metaphor for the white commercialization of a pure and noble black art form.

On the other hand, some argue that blacks have given the blues away as a symbol of the "bad times" and turned to the forward-thinking amalgams of soul, disco, funk, rhythm-and-blues, rap, and hip-hop. In an ironic twist, white bluesmen are "heroes" for saving the blues and bringing the music to the mainstream. Many white artists who have sprung from the fertile ground of blues culture, like Eric Clapton, Bonnie Raitt, the late Stevie Ray Vaughan, George Thoroughgood, and the young Jonny Lang, readily give credit to their lesser-known black influences. Howard Stovall, director of the Memphis-based Blues Foundation, says, "It's too bad that blacks are drifting away from the blues; it's one of their greatest contributions to American culture. . . . But let's face it. If it weren't for whites, this music might be dead right now."

Regardless of whether it was stolen or given away, the reality remains the same. The separation of the blues from the heritage of the black culture in which it was forged is nearly complete. The blues have become a world music, and as it has grown to speak for humanity at large, it speaks less to the particular people who invented it. Even though the Rufus Thomases and Howard Stovalls are committed to keeping the history of the blues alive, it is likely that the next generation of music buyers will no more connect the blues to the black experience in America than they will the setting of the sun to the sharpening of a pencil.

As we leave to catch our early morning train to New Orleans, I reflect on 1990s Memphis. The 1990 census counted its total metropolitan population at 981,747. Of those nearly one million residents, 42.4 percent were minorities—almost all of them (40.6 percent) black. No other city on our itinerary has blacks making up that large a proportion of its total population. Why? As we have seen, part of the answer lies in the past, part lies in the present. Scholars contend that changes in race relations and the effect upon America of homogenization have ushered in an episode of black history that is repeating itself in reverse. The Great Migration has turned around and is returning to the South, telling us at least a little something about the success of the Civil Rights movement. From March 1985 to March 1988, for instance, 586,385 blacks went from the North back to the South. In those same years, only 326,842 blacks followed the original pattern of the Great Migration and went from the South to the North. Memphis, always a home to many blacks, has been one of the recipients of this reverse migration.

The large black population has made itself known in Memphis' business, community, and political arenas. In 1991, for instance, Willie Herenton was elected (by a margin of 142 votes) as the city's first black mayor. His election perhaps speaks most strongly to the strides made by blacks in Memphis. Herenton grew up in a segregated area of Memphis in the 1950s. He remembers the "colored only" water fountains, the segregated public schools, and that he and his family had to enter theaters through the back doors. From this, Herenton grew as Memphis grew. He attended LeMoyne-Owen College, received his master's and doctoral degrees, and became the first black superintendent of the Memphis public-school system. Today, he is in the midst of waging his third mayoral campaign against the latest wrestler-turned-politician, Jerry "The King" Lawler.

Under Herenton's leadership, Memphis, which is now the eighteenth-largest city in the United States, remains a prosperous and thriving community. Over the past decade, it has enjoyed a seventeen percent drop in the crime rate and solidified its standing as the region's preeminent tourist and convention destination. However, this is not to say that Memphis is without its problems. For instance, it has the highest bankruptcy rate in the country, with one in every twenty-three households facing bank-ruptcy during 1997—almost four times the national average. (This explains why it is almost impossible to cash checks, including traveler's checks, in Memphis). Memphis' divorce rate is about ten percent above the national average, which may at least partially explain the high bankruptcy rate. A marked increase in gang activity has left residents wary of alleged gang boundaries and cautious of accidentally making hand motions that could be misinterpreted as gang signs in certain areas of town.

From the standpoint of racial relations, locals seem split on how much Memphis has healed from its troubled racial past. Some see growth, others re-entrenchment. Measures of residential segregation do not clarify the picture too much either. On the measure of dissimilarity (that is, segregation) of blacks, Memphis (0.692) rates right at the national average (0.686) and nowhere near Chicago's highly segregated measure (0.855). Similarly, Memphis' measures of concentration, centralization, and clustering reveal a city relatively free of the racial and ethnic enclaves that make up Chicago. Memphis' clustering score (0.147), for example, is well below the national average of 1.869 and is by far the lowest such score of any of the cities we visit on the tour. The only statistical hint of residential segregation lies in the relatively low measure of interaction (0.250) and corresponding high measure of isolation (0.750), suggesting that the degree of potential for interaction between minority and majority group members in Memphis is scarce.

The fairest analysis is that Memphis remains a community struggling with, but committed to, its goal of finding unity in diversity. There is a code of ceremonial affability in the way blacks and whites talk to one another in Memphis. There is a deep and strained history just below the surface, but years of forced proximity has forged a conversational etiquette. Outsiders find themselves grateful for this veneer, for its civility, grace, and peaceful promise. However, they also find themselves feeling like they have missed the punch line of a tragic inside joke.

Often, Memphis' place in history as the site of King's assassination—the news that stays news—puts it under the critical microscope of the nation's eyes. Just hours after we board today's train, for instance, the Ku Klux Klan will hold a rally on the streets of downtown Memphis. The occasion will be modest in size, if not in passions. The total Klan turnout of members and supporters will only be about fifty-five. They will protest the national holiday in honor of King and point out that January 19, when the nation observes King's birthday this year, is also Robert E. Lee's birthday, which is not a national holiday. A poor loudspeaker system and a blasting wind will conspire to render most of their inane rhetoric unintelligible. A crowd of 1,200 to 1,800 black and white anti-Klan protestors will outnumber them. However, this is Memphis, and the news of the Klan rally will make national headlines and reinforce slow-dying stereotypes of the good old boys in the Deep South.

What will not make headlines are the ironic facts that the founder of the original Ku Klux Klan, Nathan Bedford Forrest, is buried in a Memphis park that is now used mostly by blacks; that the Klan members who planned the rally had to ask a black mayor for permission to assemble and a black chief of police for protection; that most of the Klan members who actually participated in the rally came from Indiana, Illinois, Wisconsin, Ohio, and Maryland; that the Klan only has about five thousand members nationwide and the South no longer stands as its membership stronghold; that the city of Memphis now has more blacks than whites and that, generally, substantial and tangible process has been made in the arena of race relations.

Regardless, Memphis' hard-won measure of racial peace remains brittle, at best. Also, the threats do not come only from whites. Underlying racial divisions among minorities were revealed in a 1996 Memphis school board decision that defined a minority as "black American(s) . . . having origins in any of the black racial groups of Africa." The vote, with the five blacks voting in favor and the four nonminorities voting against, means that only black businesses will be allowed to participate in the school's minority procurement program. As the debate continues, many wonder if blacks can risk alienating other minorities when the battle against affirmative action appears to be spreading east from California.

As Amtrak's *City of New Orleans* begins to roll to its namesake, I leave impressed with a city that is still struggling to live down the impact of one fatal moment on its national image and on the hearts of its residents.

6. NEW ORLEANS: AN INTERLUDE

"Unique" is a word that cannot be qualified. It does not mean rare or uncommon; it means alone in the universe. By the standards of grammar and by the grace of God, New Orleans is the unique American place.

Charles Kuralt, American journalist

January 17

We enjoy bright daylight for the nine-hour trip from Memphis to New Orleans. It is a welcome opportunity to soak in the scenery that gives so much flavor to the South. Some students, who are playing their perpetual game of Pinochle in the snack car, find that the learning experiences on the tour are not limited to our listed itinerary. During the game, a young, white man engages the group in some informal conversation. After a bit, the group tells him about the tour. He gives a sharp whistle and is silent for a few minutes. Then, in a mocking tone, he asks if the group has come up with any answers about fixing racism. Without waiting for anyone in the group to respond, he offers his own solution: "Well, I think we could cure racism if we just gave the blacks a lot more guns. Then they would just kill each other off. Nine times out of ten, when someone is murdered it is black on black." One member of the group mumbles something about an unfair stereotype. The others sit mute. Having lost his audience, the man wanders away.

Stopping down in the snack car for a disgustingly soft apple, I have caught the last few minutes of the conversation. Even I remain silent. I am reminded of a time several years ago when I was riding an elevator to the eighth floor of an office building in Texas. Also on the elevator were two black men, two other white men, and a white woman. For the first four floors, we minded our elevator etiquette and remained silent. After the black men exited on the fourth floor, however, one of the white men turned to the other and said: "Damn niggers. They could have jumped all the way to the fourth floor." The woman and I exchanged a glance of discomfort. It was clear that we both were made uneasy by the comments. It was equally clear, however, that neither of us was going to say anything. In my silence, the two bigots assumed companionship. My silence sent the message that I was in agreement with them. They thought I was one of them. However, I was not one of them, and I should have summoned up the courage to let them know that.

So why am I silent today? Haven't I grown at all in the years since that elevator episode? In some ways, yes; in other ways, no. Today, my silence did not come from cowardice. It came from the weariness of "problem fatigue." Even if you have the energy, how do you counter someone with such an intractable bias? Statistics will mean little to this guy; reason even less. This is one part of the elephant that I choose not to bite off. Later, I will wonder if I made the right decision. Silence is silence regardless of whether cowardice or fatigue motivates it. It is a reminder that short-term enthusiasm will not win the struggle for racial reconciliation. It is a war with a million battles and the worst mistake is to do nothing when you could have done something. I let one battle slip away by not more actively confronting his biased stereotypes.

The next seventy-two hours comprise the whirlwind part of our tour: two cities and more than sixteen hours of Amtrak travel in only three days. Our thirty-six hour stay in New Orleans is an interlude. With its eclectic cultural history, I know there is a wealth of local resources we could mine for this tour. However, the fall of the calendar places us here on a weekend and I have had no success lining up speakers or visits to relevant sites. So, why are we stopping here? Amtrak passes through New Orleans on its way from Memphis to our next major itinerary stop—Birmingham, Alabama. Most of my West Coast students have never experienced the charm and eccentricities of New Orleans. To pass that opportunity by seemed a shame. I have no illusion that a Saturday night on Bourbon Street will offer a deep understanding into issues of race in America. Nor do I deceive myself into thinking that a laid-back Sunday morning of beignets and chickory coffee in the French Quarter will give us any striking insights into what we are studying. New Orleans is a unique American city, though, and I do not think any of us are reluctant to have a few hours of rest and relaxation.

New Orleans has been described as the "inevitable city on an impossible site." As a glance at any map shows, New Orleans is inevitable because it sits at the mouth of the most important waterway system for moving people and goods in North America—the Mississippi River. From this position, New Orleans can easily control the trade between the vast interior of North America and the rest of the world. Although early explorers recognized the strategic value of a city placed at the mouth of the third longest river in the world, they also recognized the apparent impossibility of such a city. From the mouth of the Mississippi to a point about two hundred miles upstream (Baton Rouge), there was no ground high enough to provide a natural site for the "inevitable city." The swampy land was between earth and sea—belonging to neither and alternately claimed by both. In addition, the region was prone to excessive heat, annual floods, heavy rain, hurricanes, mosquitoes, and disease. The "inevitability" of the city, however, drove its citizens to heights of drainage creativity. New Orleans became a city where, in fact, no city should be. Today, thanks to about 180 miles of canals and levees, New Orleans stands (soggily) as the only major American city below sea level.

The cultural legacy of New Orleans is as intricate as the Mississippi Delta. Because it is essentially an island and has been very insulated from the mainland for much of its history, New Orleans has developed a culture very different from any place else in the United States. Originally, Choctaw and Chickasaw settlements prevailed in the area. Eventually, though, New Orleans would pass through French, Spanish, and again French hands before becoming part of the United States as a portion of the Louisiana Purchase in 1803. In the mid 1700s, she was blessed with a group of French exiles from Canada, those charismatic Cajuns (a corruption of the term "Acadians"), who brought with them soul-stirring, foot-stomping music and intoxicating cuisine. In the ensuing decades, slow immigration created labor shortages that encouraged the importation of slaves. As a result, by 1800 more than fifty percent of the colony's population was black (although more than half of them were free persons of color). Also thrown into the cultural gumbo was the compelling influence of the Creoles, who were a product of the merging of French and Spanish settlers born in the colony. American annexation brought even more diversity as Anglo-Saxons flocked to the unique economic opportunities offered in New Orleans. Finally, as an oasis of civilization in a hostile swamp, New Orleans' standing as an international port led to unique worldwide connections, and the cultural gumbo was made that much spicier. It is little wonder that Walker Percy has called New Orleans the only "foreign city in the United States."

After arriving at the Amtrak station, we ride the "city's movable museum," the oldest continuously operating street railway system in existence, to our hostel, the Marquette House. Most of us are famished, so we quickly unpack, have a very brief orientation meeting, and head back to the streetcar and a Saturday night in the *Vieux Carre,* the French Quarter.

As a seaport and major point of entry for the country, New Orleans has always had a transient population of seamen, immigrants, and tourists. As a result, it also has always had a "hospitality" industry—restaurants, theaters, operas, bars, gambling houses, and red-light establishments. This industry is obviously much larger than what the resident population alone would support. Although only one facet of New Orleans, the seventy-block area of the French Quarter is the city's great drawing card. Visitors throng to its superlative restaurants and luxurious hotels. But on a Saturday night in January, it's Bourbon Street that draws the crowds.

Bourbon Street is the carnival that students always imagined it would be and more—or less. It's not just that the street is more commercial than the students expected, it's the type of commerciality that throws them off. As are many first-time tourists, they are surprised by the degree to which the adult entertainment sleaze merchants have bought off Bourbon Street. I don't know if the merchants' presence is a *consequence* of the hedonistic ethos on the street or the *cause* of it. Regardless, most of the students are less than impressed with their night on Bourbon Street. Rather than losing their inhibitions, most of them had their inhibitions raised to full mast. One student's tongue-in-cheek comment is revealing: "I usually like to hang out with rude, drunk, belligerent, and pornographic people that I have never seen before. I don't know what my problem was."

At first, I chalk their lack of enthusiasm up to yet another manifestation of that priggish streak running through Presbyterianism. Later, though, I wonder if their lack of enthusiasm is not simply a consequence of how they are being impacted by the tour. We have spent so much of our time with deep issues of exclusion and the future of America, that maybe trivialities—and Bourbon Street is the height of trivialities—just don't catch our attention the way they used to. Maybe we have become too aware of the important issues underlying American life to allow ourselves to be swept away by the inane and meaningless. Or maybe there is an underlying recognition that the pornographic exploitation of something like Bourbon Street is anything *but* trivial in the myriad ways it influences our culture and interpersonal relationships. At any rate, I find myself defending the French Quarter. I promise the students that—if they look hard enough—they can still find that magic and romance in the French Quarter that runs deeper than the lethargic striptease acts, walk-up daiquiri stands, and two-drink-minimum bars on Bourbon Street.

January 18

We begin Sunday morning with a leisurely breakfast of beignets and café au lait at Café du Monde in Jackson Square. The air-light French doughnuts and steaming coffee hit the spot. Café du Monde is open around the clock and, from the look on the students' powdered-sugar-coated faces, I suspect more than a few will return to stock up before tomorrow's early morning train ride to Birmingham.

While we eat, we are "entertained" by a small boy shuffling his legs in a pantomime dance. He has tacked bottle caps to the bottom of his sneakers, and an older boy looks on, waiting to pocket the money dropped by passers-by. On most weekends, there are at least a dozen such dancers here in the French Quarter. All are children (most younger than eight or nine). All perform beside a crumpled cardboard box. All of them are black. All are from poor neighborhoods that lie just out of sight and mind of the city's tourism epicenter. Some of them will make $20 or $30 a day, the only income their family will receive outside of a government check. "These are kids who are holding down jobs," says Joel Devine, a professor and chairman of the Department of Sociology at nearby Tulane

University, "and making a very appreciable difference in a household income that is close to nonexistent. The sad thing is that it's not just a hobby. These are kids with very few alternatives. They go out and do put food on the table. That's the sadness. That there is a need for them to do it."

In addition to the sadness of children working for a living, there is the question of whether these boys and girls perpetuate an offensive "Bojangles" racial stereotype. Barbara Guillory Thompson, an expert on the dynamics of black families and professor of sociology and chair of the Division of Social Sciences at neighboring Dillard University, finds nothing offensive about it. "For me, it's just part of a New Orleans tradition, and I did not find it personally offensive," she says. "For me, it's perfectly good and honorable and honest." In the harsh realities in which these children live, Thompson sees their street performing as "better than stealing."

In the context of this city, maybe there is something honorable and culturally enriching about such street performers. Still, we are pulled back to the South Side of Chicago and forced to ask if this is how a child's life is meant to be lived. Today, each of us will enjoy the material riches of the French Quarter. As one student describes her experience, she will be "cursed by the Visa today, the devil of the French Quarter will grasp me by my wallet and pull me in." In the midst of such affluence, how can we sleep at night knowing that grade school children are hoofing for tourists simply to put food on their family's table? What switch do we flip in our conscience that allows us to steep ourselves in excess, while so many around us live in abysmal poverty? How do a democracy's priorities become so warped that the plight of the poor is not even on our radar screen? These are not questions with easy answers, but they are questions that must be asked. As I leave Café du Monde, the beignets and café au lait do not sit as well as I thought they would.

We spend the next several hours browsing the French Quarter. The quaintness of the open-air flea market, fruit stands, and upscale shops begins to redeem the area for most of the students. After noon, we reconvene for a gospel brunch at the House of Blues. It is a pricey chunk of the course fee, but I suspect we all are due for a good meal. "All you can eat" takes on a special meaning for a group of college students traveling across country with their backpacks. We consume vast amounts of jalapeño cornbread, cheese grits, fried nuggets of alligator and chicken, shrimp, smoked turkey, bread pudding, croissants, jambalaya, fresh fruit, and the requisite champagne mimosas. On a trip where good food has been scarce and budgets tight, it is nice to engage in a brief respite of unrestrained gluttony. While we eat, we are entertained by the soulful four-part harmony of the Mount Zion Harmonizers (who are celebrating their fifty-ninth year together). Although the show is brief, the gospel music is moving. We finish by waving our napkins in the air and joining in on a rousing rendition of "When the Saints Go Marching In."

I am not as thrilled with our gospel brunch as most of the students seem to be. The all-black musical group performing for the all-white audience that had shelled out a ridiculous amount of money for the brunch does not sit any better with me than the poverty-stricken street dancers performing for the beignet-eaters and café au lait–drinkers at Café du Monde. There is something about it that is too voyeuristic and imper-sonal. I am reminded of a quote by Dr. bell hooks, distinguished professor of English at City College of New York: "American culture is obsessed with blackness, but primarily in a commodified form that can then be possessed, owned, controlled, and shaped."

Given our lack of a substantive itinerary for the past two days, I decide to focus Sunday night's debriefing around a "minilecture" on public housing. I suspect the students will not have a lot to discuss, and a dinner conversation I had with a friend from Tulane University seemed a perfect follow-up to our discussions on public housing in Chicago. Besides, I had not lectured for a while and, frankly, I was tired of facilitating discus-sion—reflecting the not-so-admirable trait that most college professors have of wanting to talk rather than to listen.

The New Orleans region, with a population of 1.3 million, is a two-tiered society. A quarter of all households have annual incomes over $50,000 and another quarter have incomes of under $15,000. The poorest of the poor are overwhelmingly black and Hispanic (some twenty-eight percent of whom have not completed high school, compared with four-teen percent of whites). In the city's poorest neighborhoods, the average annual household income is only slightly more than $5,000. These neighborhoods rely on ten government-subsidized, public-housing proj-ects that house about 55,000 people—ten percent of the city's popula-tion. These projects are governed by the Housing Authority of New Orleans (HANO).

In 1996, the U.S. General Accounting Office labeled HANO as one of the worst housing authorities in the United States. They claimed that HANO had failed to carry out routine maintenance (such as repairs to plumbing, heating, and electrical systems) and modernization work (such as replacing roofs and razing unsafe buildings). Tenants would often wait *years* for simple services. As a result, more than twenty-five percent of the apartments sat vacant because of neglect and deteriora-tion. Oddly enough, the problems were not due to a lack of federal fund-ing. HANO had nearly $200 million in unspent modernization grants and other funding (representing eighty-two percent of the total funding to the housing authority during the last decade). Neither were the problems due to an unresponsive local government—New Orleans has had a black mayor since 1978 and the proportion of black registered voters has risen from forty-nine to sixty-one percent. Rather, the problems stemmed from bureaucratic bungling and chronic mismanagement.

The U.S. Department of Housing and Urban Development found itself with two choices: place HANO under jurisdiction of a federal judge or find an outside institution free of HANO's own dubious fifty-eight-year history to run it. Federal officials decided to hand over the housing authority to the most unlikely of candidates—Tulane University. Tulane is a highly selective, overwhelmingly white, old-line southern school in a postcard neighborhood in uptown New Orleans. Ronald Mason, a senior vice pres-ident and general counsel for Tulane, was appointed de facto head of HANO. What could he know about public housing, let alone about fixing it? As it turns out, he knew a lot.

According to the federal government's rating system, Tulane has pulled off one of the most dramatic turnarounds in the history of public housing. How? First, they evicted criminals and drug users, reduced the backlog of work orders by nine thousand and improved response times for such things as plumbing repairs from months to day or hours. Just as important, they enlisted the support of citywide tenant groups who had once fought HANO bitterly. In addition, a cooperative-agreement program recruits residents to do maintenance and help with security and job placement.

However, Tulane's plan went far beyond simple management of real estate. Under the Campus Affiliates Program, some 150 faculty and 500 students from Tulane and nearby Xavier University now go to the projects and do everything from private tutoring to teaching courses on health, parenting, job training, teen pregnancy, high school equivalency, and college readiness. They also help residents find jobs and even provide seed capital to help them start small businesses.

Similar to the long-range plans in Chicago, Tulane's fifteen-year vision is to reshape neighborhoods by razing many of the existing public-housing projects and replacing them with single-family units. Mason even dares to believe that more than a third of the city's public-housing units could one day be privately owned. It may be too soon to call Tulane's program a "miracle," but it offers an innovative urban experiment that compels us to rethink issues of public housing in America. It also reminds us that the mission of higher education has three branches— teaching, research, *and* service. Too many colleges and universities across the country pride themselves only on the first two. By taking service to new heights, Tulane and Xavier remind us that higher education's greatest calling is to make the world a better place for everyone.

After the lecture/debriefing last night, I talked for a few moments with a student who was lingering on the veranda. He is a thoughtful young man who has clearly been wrestling with the material we have encountered on the tour. I do not always agree with his perspectives, but I appreciate the effort he is putting into processing his experiences. Over the past few days, though, he has begun to pull away from the group discussions.

As we talk, it becomes clear why he has pulled away. In general, this is a group that *feels* very deeply. Tears are common and emotions, especially as the trip wears on, are at the surface. However, this is a young man who is somewhat suspicious of feelings. To his credit, rather than criticize others, he is turning a light on his own soul and wondering if he is not feeling what he is supposed to feel. "I don't know how I should respond to all of this that I'm seeing," he begins. "I'm not a very emotional person. I usually objectify things and think rationally about them without letting my emotions affect my thoughts. I've always been wary of people who are really emotional. I think that the problem that we're studying has its roots partially in the fact that people make decisions based on emotion. A white teenager ends up in a situation where he is outnumbered and intimidated by blacks. His emotions of fear and uncertainty lead him to decide to see blacks as a threat to him that he begins to hate. Maybe he joins in hate crimes and other racist activities. Instead, he should separate himself from his emotions and objectively realize that he's become a domino in the cycle of hate that has been going on for centuries."

Even as he describes his rational prescription for ending hate, he recognizes that perhaps he's not giving enough credit to the power of emotions. "But I feel like I'm not allowing my emotions to play enough of a part. Should I allow my emotions to affect me more? Have I conditioned myself to deny emotions rather than channel them? Things don't affect me as much as they seem to affect other people. And, if that's a weakness, I don't know what to do about it."

I empathize with all of his questions. I work in a field where reason and the intellect are prized and emotion and the heart are suspect. I even cut off students in my courses who begin a statement with "I feel" and urge them to rephrase it as "I believe" or "I think." I am not apologetic about that practice. To some degree, higher education serves as a necessary corrective to a society where reason and intellect are viewed with suspicion. I think of recent movies like "Forrest Gump," "I.Q.," "Nell," "Dumb and Dumber," and "Jungle Book" in which there is a head-heart split that makes intelligence the villain or, at the very least, leads to a suspicion of the mind. In those movies, simple is good. Simple virtue, often linked with a lack of intelligence, is equated with inner goodness and leads to earthly rewards. Following the heart always leads to the right answer. In that context, higher education *should* be about reclaiming the promise of rationality and the value of intellectual pursuit.

As I listen to this student, though, I wonder if we have done *too* good a job of that. Have we committed the opposite mistake of deifying the head and disparaging the heart? Are we raising a generation of students with the capacity to think but not to feel? If so, what are the implications for their social awareness and involvement? If they only intellectualize the suffering of others without feeling that pain, will they be moved to action? As the student closes, he articulates the dilemma: "Am I failing to act on my responsibility to the world because I am able to separate myself from the emotions of sadness? And if I let my emotions take control somehow, will it cause me to be depressed rather than helpful?"

I think American society does need to reclaim the value of reason. We have become too suspect of it and base too many of our decisions and actions on shallow pools of emotion. But we cannot make the opposite mistake of denying the importance of the heart in human affairs. We must retain the capacity to feel and to somehow strike a balance between head and heart that lets each inform, and be informed by, the other. I want my students to intellectualize much of the material they encounter on the tour. I want them to learn names, dates, places, and events. However, I also want them to feel the sufferings and passions of those who have struggled for civil rights in America. Those feelings will animate the substance of what they have learned. They will give depth to the breadth of knowledge. To lose either would be a shame.

January 19

We leave the hostel at 5:00 A.M. on Monday morning and make our way to the New Orleans Amtrak Station. I feel a little dissatisfied with our time in New Orleans. There is so much more here that we could have learned and so many other people with whom we could have talked. Weekends happen, though, and I suspect there are not many more interesting places to spend one than in the "City that Care Forgot."

Birmingham was a relatively late addition to our itinerary. Because of that, I have had little success in setting up much other than our Tuesday trip to the Birmingham Civil Rights Institute. Unfortunately, Amtrak's schedules did not give us the option of leaving New Orleans yesterday to arrive in Birmingham in plenty of time to scope out the area for events commemorating Martin Luther King Jr.'s birthday on Monday. We will arrive in Birmingham about 2:00 P.M. and simply catch whatever we can of the day's festivities. Surely there will be a lot going on in the city where Bull Connor's dogs helped galvanize the Civil Rights movement and lead to the passage of the Civil Rights Act of 1964.

7. BIRMINGHAM: "BOMBINGHAM" REVISITED

We will accept the violence and hate, absorbing it without returning it.

James Lawson, Civil Rights activist

January 19

After an uneventful seven-hour trip, the owner of Point A–Point B Transportation Services meets us at the Birmingham Amtrak station. Dorothea, a black woman born and raised in the area, is immediately captured by the purpose of our study tour. She enthusiastically tells us about the many human rights activities in which she is engaged. Just this morning, she attended the Martin Luther King Unity Breakfast at the Civic Center. That was followed by a Freedom March through the six-block area of the Birmingham Civil Rights District.

"Unfortunately," she goes on to say, "those were the only major civic events planned to celebrate Martin Luther King Jr.'s holiday." At the sound of the word "were," both the students and I let out an audible groan. I assumed, incorrectly it now turns out, that speeches, marches, and activities would be going on all day. But Dorothea is a woman not easily deflated. "On a beautiful afternoon when most everyone else in town will be enjoying the day off," she says, "you all should walk down to Kelly Ingram Park and dip your toes in history. You've come too far to just sit in your hotel rooms!"

With a population of nearly 350,000 in 1960, Birmingham was Alabama's largest city. As a steel town, it was one of the region's major business centers. The city's industrialization was based primarily on abundant local deposits of coal, limestone, dolomite, and iron ore—all essential for making steel. However, as a company town of the U.S. Steel Corporation, Birmingham's industry was actually controlled from corporate boardrooms in New York City and Pittsburgh. Northern industrialists derived part of their profits from the low price of labor, and the "Pittsburgh of the South" proved to be a profitable outpost of cheap, unskilled workers. In addition, the use of a discriminatory race wage kept the working class divided along racial lines, with white workers earning more than black workers, although both were below the national average.

Discriminatory training and hiring practices compounded the economic impact of the race wage. For instance, only one of every six black employees was a skilled or trained worker, as compared to three of every four whites. It was common practice for industries to openly reserve the better-paying jobs for white workers. As a result of these disparities, the median annual income for blacks in Birmingham was $3,000, which was less than half of that for white workers. In addition, blacks were three times less likely than whites to hold a high school diploma. Only ten percent of the county's black population was registered to vote.

The problems ran deeper than economics, education, and voting rights. Martin Luther King Jr. called Birmingham, where blacks accounted for forty percent of the population, "the most thoroughly segregated city in the United States." In a wire to President Kennedy, he further described it as "by far the worst big city in race relations in the United States." Advantaged by the discriminatory race wage, the white lower middle class had mobilized to dominate the electorate and keep in office candidates pledged to segregation. They wanted to defend "whites only" jobs from black competition and viewed desegregation as a threat to their schools, neighborhoods, and communities. Their voice was so strong that, in 1962, the city closed sixty-eight parks, thirty-eight playgrounds, six swimming pools, and four golf courses to avoid complying with a federal court order to desegregate public facilities. Birmingham abandoned its professional baseball team rather than let it play desegregated clubs in the International League. Birmingham segregationists even banned a textbook because it had black and white rabbits in it!

Often, segregationists were violent in their demands for the status quo. For instance, Birmingham was the infamous site of the 1961 Mother's Day vigilante attack on the Freedom Riders, when police failed to intervene. Other white mob attacks on integrationists such as the Reverend Fred Shuttlesworth (head of the Alabama Christian Movement for Human Rights) buttressed the official use of police brutality to defend racial norms. Between 1957 and 1963, eighteen unsolved bombings in black neighborhoods (which brought the total of unsolved racial bombings in Birmingham in the postwar period to more than fifty) earned the city its well-known moniker of "Bombingham."

As the city's national reputation became increasingly tarnished, its economic development began to lag. A group of white moderates, headed by chamber of commerce president and local realtor Sidney Smyer, recognized that racism was bad business for Birmingham. Smyer's group proposed a change in the structure of the city government. They wanted to switch from the existing system of three city commissioners to a mayor-council form of government. Underlying their proposal was a desire to rid Birmingham of their most embarrassingly strident segregationist—Theophilus Eugene "Bull" Connor, the commissioner of public safety.

In his book *Why We Can't Wait,* Martin Luther King Jr. included a chapter entitled "Bull Connor's Birmingham." In that chapter, King described a city ruled by the fear, hatred, and bigotry of the ironically named "commissioner of public safety." What was life in Birmingham like for blacks living under the reign of Connor? "You would be living in a city where brutality directed against Negroes was an unquestioned and unchallenged reality," King wrote. "One of the city commissioners, a member of the body that ruled municipal affairs, would be Eugene 'Bull' Connor, a racist who prided himself on knowing how to handle the Negro and keep him in his 'place.' As commissioner of public safety, Bull Connor, entrenched for many years in a key position in the Birmingham power structure, displayed as much contempt for the rights of the Negro as he did defiance for the authority of the federal government. . . . In Connor's Birmingham, the silent password was fear."

How did Bull Connor come to such a position of power? In 1937, Connor entered the race for the Birmingham city commission and won one of the three slots. After that, he remained a longtime recipient of the electoral support of the white lower middle class that dominated Birmingham politics. For nearly twenty-five years, Connor had consistently won reelection as a union-busting, segregating defender of public virtue. As a matter of fact, before earning a reputation for racial brutality, he was known for violently preventing the unionization of Birmingham's heavy industries.

As commissioner of public safety, Connor saw himself as entrusted with the protection of the morals of Birmingham society. He carried out this trust by enforcing city ordinances that concerned everything from liquor licenses to segregated seating. He often acted as the sole arbiter of public taste, banning movies that he deemed deviant and even yanking "offensive" comic books from newsstands. However, his specialty was advocating segregation. It was in that area that his individual racism became institutionalized in the Birmingham police department and judicial system. As Glenn Eskew writes in his compelling book *But for Birmingham*, "In the eyes of local law enforcement, black people were inferior beings, singular manifestations of a monolithic mass. . . . Police brutality like vigilante bombings represented manifestations of community-sanctioned violence in defense of racial norms." Connor made Birmingham into his private realm of segregation, while most locals turned a blind eye to his bare-knuckled tactics.

On November 9, 1962, Birmingham voters unexpectedly approved the new form of government—a mayor and nine council members. The next step was a mayoral election. Undaunted by the vote, Connor declared his candidacy. After losing to Albert Boutwell (a "moderate" segregationist) by eight thousand votes in a special mayoral runoff election in April 1963, Connor resorted to another strategy. He went to court asking that he and the two other commissioners be allowed to complete the terms of office they had earlier been elected to serve, before the voters had decided to do away with the commission form of government. While waiting for the dispute to be settled, the citizens of Birmingham found themselves with two city governments. It would not be until May 21, 1963 that the Alabama Supreme Court would rule in favor of Boutwell and the new form of government and order the three commissioners to vacate city hall. In that brief period of governmental turmoil, however, the eyes of the nation would focus on Birmingham's showdown with the Civil Rights movement.

Birmingham was to be a pivotal point in the civil rights drama. In 1963, the Civil Rights movement was still reeling from a devastating setback in the southwestern Georgia town of Albany less than two years before. King believed that the failures in Albany had stemmed from a complete lack of strategy and purpose. There were no planning sessions, little cash, and no provisions to get protestors out of jail or provide legal services. There were deep and substantial divisions among the black leadership. In hindsight, King realized the painful mistake he made by getting involved in a movement for which he was unprepared.

King's biggest mistake in Albany, though, came following his arrest for leading a march on city hall. Arrested on December 16, 1961, King vowed to refuse bond and stay in jail until the city agreed to desegregate. In addition, he publicly stated that he expected to spend Christmas in jail and told reporters he wanted thousands to come to Albany and join him in jail. King was bailed out of jail after only two days (most believe as a result of a scheme by Albany's white city fathers to undermine King's leverage). The negative response to King's "evasion" of his vow to stay in jail was immediate and vociferous. The national media, having already given King more than his fifteen minutes of fame, roundly denounced him as a failure and the Albany movement as a defeat. New York's *Herald Tribune* called Albany "one of the most stunning defeats of King's career" and "a devastating loss of face" for King. *Time* magazine openly questioned King's commitment to the moral struggle of civil rights—a far cry from the image of the man who had triumphed in Montgomery and been featured on the cover of the magazine five years before.

Many alleged King's Albany "sellout" as the real telling point on his leadership. Other leaders of the Albany movement privately blamed him for the meager settlement and questioned both his abilities and commitment. In his 1962 study entitled *The Negro Revolt,* journalist Louis E. Lomax foresaw the implications of Albany: "The next town he [King] visits to inspire those who are ready to suffer for their rights he will find people saying, 'Remember Albany' . . . 'We got to watch our nigger leaders. They'll lead you into trouble with the white folks and then run off and leave you like he did them people in Albany.' " Clearly, King's "crusader" image was on the wane.

Two subsequent stints in Albany's jails would do little to quell the emerging questions about King's leadership ability and the efficacy of the movement. The *New York Times* published a profile suggesting that King was out of his league in politics and "woefully inadequate in organizational ability." Movement critics compiled a catalog of his tactical mistakes. As journalism professor Richard Lentz wrote, "King was The Loser—a failure at nonviolence, rejected by his own people, swallowed up by success, unable even (the final indignity) to remain in jail as a martyr." By Labor Day weekend of 1962, King had retreated to Atlanta and the Albany movement was over for good—a devastating defeat, for both the movement and King, by any measure.

The reputations of both the movement and King were seriously damaged. Malcolm X, representing an increasingly popular alternative solution to the racial conflict, remarked that "the civil rights struggle in America reached its lowest point" in Albany. Exaggerated or not, it was clear that another Albany could destroy the entire movement. King needed a success to restore his reputation and that of the movement. Reverend Shuttlesworth convinced King and the Southern Christian Leadership Conference that Birmingham offered them their best opportunity. Shuttlesworth said, "I assure you, if you come to Birmingham, this movement can not only gain prestige, it can really shake the country."

As Taylor Branch argues, King always had entered popular movements more or less haphazardly. After Albany, though, he "needed control of a concentrated effort, maximizing both his risk and his chances for spectacular success." In other words, there had to be no more spontaneous rescue missions. If Birmingham was *the* place, a plan had to be developed. A plan that would be aggressive and resist an easy truce. A plan that would mobilize on a precise target area and specific issues. Wyatt Walker, a colleague at the Southern Christian Leadership Conference, dramatically christened their Birmingham plan "Project C"—for "confrontation." It would be launched in March 1963 (the year of the one-hundredth anniversary of the Emancipation Proclamation) and—although Branch contends it was actually more of a cold plunge than a rational exercise of any kind—would become a masterpiece in the use of media to explain a cause to the general public.

Project C called for King to subject himself to arrest in Birmingham on April 12, Good Friday. In a meeting earlier that same morning, some of King's colleagues—including his father—had urged him to remain free and raise new money for the movement rather than risk a prolonged imprisonment. Most said they would support whatever King decided. After stepping out of the room for a moment, King returned and said: "I don't know what will happen. I don't know where the money will come from. But I have to make a faith act."

Later that day, a half-mile into a march toward downtown Birmingham, King was arrested along with more than fifty other demonstrators. Media cameras captured the event. For many, this was the beginning of King's true leadership. King was placed in solitary confinement in Birmingham's jail. His requests to make phone calls or talk with his lawyers were refused. He had no mattress or linen and was sleeping on metal slats.

On April 13, a thirteen-paragraph statement by eight members of the local white clergy appeared in the *Birmingham News.* The ad, entitled "White Clergymen Urge Local Negroes to Withdraw from Demonstrations," called King's activities "unwise and untimely" and branded him a troublemaker. King's twenty-page response, first written in the margins of newspaper and on scraps of toilet paper, would be immortalized as a classic of protest literature. Ironically, initial reception to the now-famous "Letter from Birmingham Jail" was cool. Not a single mention of it reached white or black news media for a month. It was only *after* the success of the Birmingham campaign that several national periodicals published it in its entirety and reprints were distributed across the nation. Eventually, the letter would prove to be one of the most potent weapons in the propaganda battle to legitimize the Civil Rights movement and the strategy of nonviolent civil disobedience.

On April 20, 1963, fearing a loss of momentum in the Birmingham campaign, King accepted release on bond. In contrast to the indecision following his release from Albany's jail, King used the occasion of his release from Birmingham's jail to decisively implement the next phase of Project C. James Bevel, a member of the Southern Christian Leadership Conference, suggested using Birmingham's black children as demonstrators. He argued that children would be less fearful than would adults, who were reluctant to march due to concern of losing their jobs and income. From a media standpoint, the sight of young children being hauled off to jail would dramatically stir the nation's conscience and would more than offset any potential criticisms of unjustly using the children as battle fodder. With more than a little trepidation, King agreed to commit his cause to the witness of school children.

On Thursday, May 2, the children—ranging in age from six to eighteen—began their demonstrations in Birmingham. By the end of the day, the "children's crusade" saw 959 children taken to Birmingham jails. The next day, more than a thousand children stayed out of school and gathered at the Sixteenth Street Baptist Church to march. With the jails already near capacity, Connor hoped to keep the demonstrators out of the downtown business section without making arrests. He brought out the city's police dogs and, acting with less and less restraint, he also ordered fire fighters to turn their high-pressure hoses on the children. At one hundred pounds of pressure per square inch, the water was capable of knocking bricks loose from mortar or stripping bark from trees at a distance of one hundred feet. The water rolled the children weightlessly like pea gravel on a sidewalk. Three teenagers were bitten severely enough by the German shepherds to require hospital treatment. The police, swinging nightsticks indiscriminately, beat protestors and onlookers. Those jailed that Friday night brought the number of children arrested in two days to nearly 1,300.

Birmingham's blacks were now galvanized. The next day, the confrontation moved into the downtown area and Bull Connor again summoned his dogs and the water cannons. Using an armored police tank, he penned nearly four thousand protestors in Kelly Ingram Park. Across the nation, people could not pull their eyes from television pictures of children being blasted with water cannons and chased by snarling police dogs. Newspapers and magazines around the world were filled with stories and photographs. The conflict and coverage continued to escalate uncontrollably. The marches grew in size and intensity. By May 6, more than two thousand demonstrators had been jailed.

I heed Dorothea's advice and follow up a brief introductory meeting with a walk down to the Birmingham Civil Rights District. Among other sites, the district includes the Birmingham Civil Rights Institute, Sixteenth Street Baptist Church, and A. G. Gaston Gardens. It is designated as the city's tribute to the monumental fight for human rights in this country. On this late afternoon, the area is napping from the morning's events.

As dusk approaches, we enter the historic Kelly Ingram Park. This four-acre park was the focal point of the Birmingham struggle. Again, it was here that Bull Connor's helmeted troops, snarling dogs, water cannons, and armored police tank cornered thousands of protestors. Images from this park pricked the national conscience and proved to be instrumental in overturning legal segregation in our nation. As we approach the park, we are not sure what to expect. How a community memorializes events and people from its past reflects how it has processed the meaning of those events and people. None of us know Birmingham well enough to predict what the park will have become.

As we enter the park, which is adjacent to the Birmingham Civil Rights Institute, we stand by an elevated statue of Martin Luther King Jr. He is clutching a Bible in his left hand and facing the Sixteenth Street Baptist Church. The statue is still festooned with brightly colored wreaths from the morning's activities. Other statues of prominent blacks in Birmingham's history are situated throughout the park.

Most noticeable, though, are the several metallic sculptures on the perimeter of the park. These sculptures, we will later discover, were commissioned specifically for the park, which was subtitled "A Place of Revolution and Reconciliation" by Mayor Richard Arrington. Three of the sculptures, created in 1992 by James Drake, depict the children's march, police dog attacks on demonstrators, and the hosing of marchers. Another sculpture by Raymond Kaskey is a tribute to the clergy's contributions to the movement. For many of the students, this sculpture of the three ministers kneeling in prayer surrounded by the four broken pillars representing the four little girls killed in the bombing of the Sixteenth Street Baptist Church was particularly moving.

A Freedom Walk that meanders throughout the park connects all the sculptures. Some of the pathways, which refuse to let us be passive by-standers, even take us *through* a particular sculpture. In sharp contrast to the realities of the 1960s, the pathways all converge on the center of the park, where a fountain and pool represent a peaceful and meditative life spring of hope. As we sit at the pool, the sound of the cascading water—suggesting continuation, purity, and baptism—drowns out all else around us.

I am impressed with the brutal honesty running throughout Kelly Ingram Park. Attempts to memorialize are often simply facades for sanitizing parts of our history we want to repress. However, the planners of this park have been as faithful to the cowardice and bigotry of some of Birmingham's citizens as they are to the hope and promise of a brighter tomorrow. The park conveys a sense of regret and repentance, while pointing to a future that we cannot yet see. As one student notes, the fact that the flowers are still in bloom in the dead of January fits nicely with the contrasting themes of the park.

Later that evening, several of the students get their first glimpse of the racist undercurrent still swirling in Birmingham. On their way back from dinner, they hail a cab. The driver is a white woman in her fifties who was born and raised in Birmingham. When she found out where our group was staying, she said: "Be careful—there are a lot of blacks, drugs, crime, and other problems in that area." One of the students asked why she so easily spoke of blacks as if they were some kind of disease, social ill, or problem. Her terse reply: "They're the cause of all of it." Another student, trying to spin the conversation in a slightly different direction, asked the woman if she had seen any of that day's Martin Luther King Jr. festivities. "No, I don't agree with that stuff," she replied. "After all, we should celebrate Robert E. Lee's birthday. He was here first." Having at least a modicum of social awareness, she went on to try and establish herself as open-minded: "Everyone has been discriminated against one time or another. It's those Indians I feel sorry for. They're the ones who are still getting screwed, still having to live on reservations."

Ironically, when she dropped the students off, she encouraged them to keep learning because one can never know too much. This was probably not the introduction to the city that the chamber of commerce would have arranged. Nonetheless, it was yet another graphic reminder of how deeply ingrained racial hostility is in America.

On May 10, 1963, a settlement between Birmingham's leading business owners and the Southern Christian Leadership Conference was announced. For the retail merchants, who were stung by the boycott of local businesses, it was less an accord with their conscience than it was an accord with their pocketbooks. The merchants agreed to desegregate lunch counters, rest rooms, fitting rooms, and drinking fountains. In addition, they pledged to hire black workers in clerical and sales positions. Labor unions created a bail fund to secure the release of the eight hundred blacks still in jail. The Southern Christian Leadership Conference acquiesced on a timetable of planned stages, relenting on its insistence that these changes take effect immediately.

Connor and his fellow commissioners condemned the deal as "capitulation by certain weak-kneed white people under threat of violence by the rabble-rousing Negro, King." That night, more than one thousand Ku Klux Klansmen rallied outside the city and bombs exploded at the home of King's younger brother and at the Gaston Motel, where King had been staying. Rioting erupted. The violence in Birmingham finally aroused a national consensus that demanded a federal response. Only after President Kennedy dispatched federal troops to nearby Fort McClellan was the eruption quelled. The conflict ended altogether when the Alabama Supreme Court recognized Mayor Albert Boutwell and the new council as the legitimate government of Birmingham. Boutwell had initially suggested that he would not be bound by the merchants' settlement. Later, however, sensing a change in the direction of the political winds, he agreed to honor the negotiated accord.

January 20

The morning begins with our tour of the Birmingham Civil Rights Institute. Dedicated in November 1992, the institute is the centerpiece of the Civil Rights District. It stands as the community's commitment to telling the story of the Civil Rights movement through the prism of the Birmingham experience. On a broader level, the institute also is committed to telling the story of the national struggle for civil rights as well as human rights worldwide. It is a "living institution" that views the lessons of the past as a positive way to chart new directions to the future. In addition to a museum, the institute accomplishes many of its purposes through promoting research via a well-respected archives department and oral history project; disseminating information through changing exhibits and an active education department; and encouraging discussion on human rights issues locally, nationally, and internationally.

It is clearly a slow day at the institute. There are only a handful of other visitors—a small group of military personnel from Washington, D.C., and a family from Germany. After the traffic jam of visitors at the Museum of Tolerance in Los Angeles, each of us sigh with silent appreciation at the opportunity to have a museum almost all to ourselves. In contrast to the National Civil Rights Museum in Memphis, our tour here does not include a docent. It is completely self-guided and promises the opportunity for self-paced, contemplative reflection.

The tour begins with a twelve-minute film about the history of Birmingham from its founding in 1871 through the 1920s. Then the screen lifts to reveal the entrance to the rest of the permanent exhibits, beginning with a display of water fountains designated for either whites or blacks. In the first galleries, the museum effectively demonstrates the racial inequities that had become so accepted in Birmingham from about 1920 to 1954. Included are replicas of an iron ore mine entrance, segregated streetcar, "shotgun" house, church, and two classrooms, one for whites and the other for blacks, juxtaposed side by side. The replicas are complemented with compelling information that gives a texture to the inequities. In 1944, for instance, the average class in a black school in Birmingham had forty-three students, compared to twenty-four at white schools. A series of heart-rending pictures depict the climate of violence and intimidation that reinforced segregation in Birmingham.

We then move into the main gallery, which chronicles the history of the Civil Rights movement from 1955 to 1963. Several small theaters depict various episodes in the movement. The most captivating video is "Birmingham: The World Is Watching." The video plays on television sets in a replica of an appliance store from that time period. Although we have seen the searing visual images of Kelly Ingram Park often enough to become nearly desensitized, the inclusion of recent interviews with the same people gives their suffering a fresh meaning. A "water wall" with water cascading in front of images from the demonstrations reinforces our understanding of what thousands went through in their struggle for civil rights. Similar to the adjacent Kelly Ingram Park, the framers of this exhibit in the museum spared no honesty in depicting the injustice and brutality of their hometown. They bared their souls while facing their past and giving the most accurate depiction possible of the depths of segregation and exclusion in Birmingham.

Also in this area, we stand next to the bars of the actual jail cell that confined King in 1963 when he wrote "Letter from Birmingham Jail." The experience is made all the more salient as we hear King's voice reading the letter that we have read time and time again. We also see copies of his police fingerprint sheet and, for a brief moment, glimpse the fear that a black man, famous or not, must have felt in standing on the threshold of a jail where any pretense of civility would soon be disregarded.

Although it is a self-guided tour, we have pretty much stayed in step with the small group of military personnel, most of whom are black. It is interesting to watch our reaction to them and their reaction to us. Over the course of the tour, we have become increasingly sensitized to both the legacy of hatred that our ancestors perpetrated and the myriad ways in which we, as whites, continue to benefit in a country dominated by whites. Now we stand shoulder to shoulder with an anonymous black person and view the horrors of Kelly Ingram Park. Scores of questions run through our minds. What were their parents doing in 1963? What were our parents doing? It is unlikely that any were involved in these specific events. But how were they reacting as they read the newspaper and saw the graphic evidence? What *were* they involved in? It is a moment of historical imagination that is very unsettling. One student later says: "I wondered today what the black group with us on the tour of the museum thought as we watched the film and walked through and read the material. I know that I felt ashamed as I sat there in front of them and I wondered what, if anything, they were thinking of me. Do they look at me and feel anger? Do they wonder what I think or wonder why I am here? I also wonder if I was to step forward and be active in this fight for equality like I want to, what will blacks think? Will they be in support of me participating or think that I am doing it for some other motive? Will they think I think they can't do it alone? Or will they think it doesn't have to do with my people so I can't relate and shouldn't be a part of the fight?"

At least one member of the military group senses the discomfort. She strikes up a brief conversation with one of the students. As I pass by, I hear the student say, "I'm sorry that I didn't learn more about this before college. I can't change the past, but I need to understand more about how it shapes the present." The young black woman responds, "You know what? It's okay. I didn't know about a lot of this either."

In the last gallery, I find myself standing at a large window that overlooks the Sixteenth Street Baptist Church. Photos and copy describing the events of September 15, 1963 flank the window. The entire exhibit area is understated. That subtlety is fitting because the events of that day stand, in Howell Raines's words, as "the most terrible incident of racial violence during the peak years of the Southern civil rights movement."

It was about two weeks after the march on Washington, D.C. On that September Sunday morning, a bomb constructed from twenty pounds of dynamite shattered the peace of the Sixteenth Street Baptist Church. It was Youth Day at the church and dozens of children attending a Bible class were injured. Four black girls—three of them fourteen and one eleven—who had been changing into choir robes in the basement, lay dead and buried under the debris. They died in a struggle they were only just beginning to understand. Years later, Walter Cronkite echoed the enormity of the bombing: "At that moment that bomb went off and those four little girls were blasted and buried in the debris of the church, America understood the real nature of the hate that was preventing integration, particularly in the South, but also throughout America. This was the awakening."

Six years later, Alabama's new attorney general, William Baxley, began an eight-year crusade that finally culminated in the accusation and trial of Ku Klux Klan member Robert Edward Chambliss. Chambliss was convicted, after two trials, in 1977. He died in prison in 1985 at the age of eighty-one, while still maintaining that the FBI was behind the bombing.

The day after the Sixteenth Street Baptist Church bombing, a white attorney, Chuck Morgan, addressed the all-white Young Men's Business Club of Birmingham. Responding to the question of *who* bombed the church, Morgan cried out: "The 'who' is every little individual who talks about the 'niggers' and spreads the seeds of his hate to his neighbor and his son. . . . The 'who' is every governor who ever shouted for lawlessness and became a law violator. . . . Who is really guilty? Each of us. Each citizen who has not consciously attempted to bring about peaceful compliance . . . each citizen who has ever said, 'They ought to kill that nigger.' Every person in this community who has in any way contributed to the popularity of hatred is at least as guilty, or more so, as the demented fool who threw that bomb." After Morgan finished, another member moved that the Young Men's Business Club of Birmingham admit a black to membership. The motion died for lack of a second.

The Young Men's Business Club of Birmingham notwithstanding, the tragedy of that Sunday produced outpourings of sympathy, concern, and financial contributions from all parts of the world. More than $300,000 was contributed for the restoration of the bombed church. It was reopened for services on June 7, 1964. The people of Wales, England, gave a special memorial gift, a large stained glass window with the image of a black crucified Christ. That window still sits in the rear center of the church at the balcony level.

In July 1997, Spike Lee's feature-length documentary "Four Little Girls" opened for a two-week run at the Film Forum in New York. In February 1998, during Black History Month, the Oscar-nominated documentary would be broadcast nationwide on HBO. The film is a tribute to the lives, family, and friends of the four victims of the 1963 bombing—Carole Denise McNair, Cynthia Wesley, Addie Mae Collins, and Carol Rosamond Robertson. Although his film will not reach the large audience he did with some of his early works, Lee is telling a story that should be remembered. In Lee's words, "African Americans are far too quick to want to forget. We don't want to remember. It's always: 'Let's forget about slavery, Emmett Till, Rosa Parks, Medgar Evers. Why you wanna go back and bring that up—dredge up that stuff?' Consequently, we have a generation of black kids who think this is the way it always was—that we could always live where we wanted, eat where we wanted, have church where we wanted. We need to remember." The importance of remembering was brought home when Lee noted that his brother, David, went to the premiere with a date who "had lived in Birmingham all her life and hadn't even heard of the bombing."

In the same month as the opening of Lee's documentary (purely coincidental, according to authorities), the federal government reopened the church bombing case after the finding of "new information." The case was also reopened in 1980 and 1988, but with little effect. Despite that erratic investigative history, this most recent reopening seems to hold more promise. More than a year before, the FBI and the Birmingham police had responded to a tip with an extensive review of investigative files. That tip, combined with a subsequent analytical review, led them to conclude "there existed sufficient basis to reopen this investigation so that all persons responsible for this heinous crime would finally be brought to justice."

Long ago, investigators had publicly identified three other men as suspects: Herman Cash, who died in 1994; Tommy Blanton of Birmingham; and Bobby Frank Cherry of Mabank, Texas. However, J. Edgar Hoover ordered his agents to shut down the federal inquiry in 1965, even after the agents cabled him that they had evidence so strong that even a white Alabama jury would convict. Why did Hoover overrule his agents? Two reasons are commonly mentioned. First, he did not want to expose FBI spies within the Ku Klux Klan. Second, Hoover may have thought a conviction would help the Civil Rights movement and, thus, his enemy, Martin Luther King Jr., who had conducted funerals for three of the bombing victims.

The newly reopened case focuses on Blanton and Cherry, both of whom have denied involvement. Some are elated at the new investigation, hoping to finally bring to justice the perpetrators of a particularly brutal bombing. Others are skeptical of the new probe. Ahmed Obgfemi, director of the Malcolm X Center for Self-Determination in Birmingham, remarked: "The FBI has new information? Who are you kidding? Any accomplices he [Chambliss] had are probably eighty-five or ninety years old by now. They have lived their lives and gotten away with it." In October 1998, federal grand jurors in Birmingham began hearing testimony in the case.

As we file out of the museum, the group seems a little flat. This has been a difficult stretch of the trip. The hours on Amtrak, coupled with the whistle stops in Memphis, New Orleans, and Birmingham, have taken their toll. Information overload, fatigue, and complacency are beginning to overwhelm even the hardiest among us. In addition, there is a definite sense of being "museumed-out." One student remarks on our way back to the hotel: "Walking through the museum today, I was amazed at how much information was there. I could've stayed there for two days and still not read everything and explored every display. But I didn't have as much interest as I did earlier on the trip. Most of it was what I'd seen, heard, or read before, often multiple times. I would most prefer spending my time talking with people who have been impacted by prejudice. A man that I met at the Sixteenth Street Baptist Church told us that racism is still alive and well, it's just done in the form of 'mind games' now. I would have rather sat down over coffee and talked with him for a couple of hours about his experiences and opinions than go to another museum. I can't decide exactly what I think is true and what I should do about it and how I should feel about it until I know people who have been and are being impacted by racism."

Those comments are helpful reminders to me that the heart of this trip should be in face-to-face communication with others. Future tours must continually add those opportunities wherever they can be added. Passively absorbing museum reader boards will take us a step toward seeing with the other's eyes. However, the biggest step will be taken when we commit to a conversation with someone different from us—a conversation in which we refrain from trying to persuade or impress and simply listen. Listen to the pride, the pain, the hope, and the frustration. Only through that commitment will we begin to see with the other's eyes and make progress toward racial reconciliation.

At the 1963 march on Washington, D.C., Reverend Fred Shuttlesworth said, "But for Birmingham, we would not be here today." Indeed, were it not for Birmingham, the eventual accomplishments of the Civil Rights movement would have been jeopardized. Following Birmingham, the hearts and minds of millions of white Americans were altered. In Taylor Branch's words, events in Birmingham set off "the greatest firestorm of domestic liberty in a hundred years." The sound of the explosions in Birmingham reverberated across America. Government statisticians counted 758 racial demonstrations and 14,733 arrests in 186 American municipalities over the ten weeks following the Birmingham accord. The aftermath of national protest, urban rioting, and international pressure forced the Kennedy administration to propose the most comprehensive civil rights legislation since Reconstruction. Eventually, this legislation was passed as the Civil Rights Act of 1964. It prohibited discrimination in most places of public accommodation, authorized the government to withhold federal funds to public programs practicing discrimination, banned discrimination by employers and unions, created an Equal Employment Opportunity Commission, established a Community Relations Service, and provided technical and financial aid to communities desegregating their schools.

It is easy to contend that the climax of the civil rights struggle occurred in Birmingham. Despite its apparent success, however, many scholars maintain that the true legacy of Birmingham is the narrow focus of civil rights reform that has left the perpetual promise of the movement unfulfilled. For instance, Glenn Eskew, assistant professor of history at Georgia State University, argues that the moderate approach to reform inherent in the Civil Rights movement never challenged the structure of the white power system. Yes, blacks gained access to public accommodations and equal employment opportunities. Yes, the integrationists received the inclusion for which they fought. In his opinion, however, this "token desegregation" was a poor substitute for the radical reform that was necessary to challenge the white power structure. As a result, the dominant and unassailable structure of exclusion remained in place even while giving the appearance of inclusion.

It is easy to let Birmingham be defined by its history. However, the story of Birmingham continues after Kelly Ingram Park and the Sixteenth Street Baptist Church bombing. Birmingham desegregated with the Civil Rights Act of 1964. Through court cases, blacks began to receive "whites only" jobs and freedom as consumers. The Voting Rights Act of 1965 succeeded in registering Birmingham's black population as voters. Black political empowerment continued with the appointment of Arthur Shores to the city council in 1968 and the election of Dr. Richard Arrington as mayor in 1979. Arrington remained in office for nineteen years before being replaced by Dr. Bernard Kincaid, the black son of a Birmingham coal miner and housewife. Chris McNair, the father of the youngest victim of the 1963 Sixteenth Street Baptist Church bombing, is one of two blacks on the five-member board of commissioners for Birmingham's Jefferson County. Economically, a growing black middle class has joined many white people in the march of upward mobility.

Even though we had only been in Birmingham less than twenty-four hours, we had heard enough to know that not all blacks in 1990s Birmingham have benefited from political empowerment, equal access as consumers, and equal employment opportunities. As Eskew summarizes it, "In 1990 skyrocketing homicide rates among African Americans in Birmingham set new records for violent deaths in a city known for brutality. Outside the system and abandoned by black and white, inner-city residents faced insurmountable problems: unemployment, drug addiction, teen pregnancy, gang warfare, AIDS, and grinding poverty. After two decades of work by the Jefferson County Committee for Economic Opportunity, scandals revealed that it had done little more than line the pockets of its minority directors. The corruption spilled over to the Birmingham Housing Authority, which was so poorly managed that the U.S. Department of Housing and Urban Development—itself a troubled agency—had to intervene. Meanwhile, public-housing projects resembled war zones as drug lords and gang members fought over the units of the Collegeville and North Birmingham Homes. With drugs and gangs came an increase in violence and black-on-black homicides. Although the white power structure joined the black city government in efforts to reclaim the downtown area by containing the violence, both largely ignored the inner-city poor. Extremism characterized the desperation of the decade as nihilistic black youths shot each other over tennis shoes while elderly civil rights heroes concerned themselves with gaining access to private country clubs. No wonder, then, that almost all African Americans believed their leadership had lost touch with reality and the problems average black people faced."

This is not to say that hope has disappeared beneath the horizon. When it comes to racial disparities and how to correct them, Alabama has made significant strides from the stereotypes reinforced with every replay of Governor George Wallace's "Segregation now! Segregation tomorrow! Segregation forever!" speech. Segments of the Birmingham community are especially active in the search for racial reconciliation. At Monday morning's Martin Luther King Unity Breakfast, for instance, the Community Affairs Committee unveiled its "Birmingham Pledge." Established in 1969, the committee is a biracial organization dedicated to achieving racial justice and harmony in the Birmingham community. The Community Affairs Committee—comprising business, civic, and religious leaders—meets every Monday morning at the Birmingham Civil Rights Institute to discuss community concerns and to develop concrete ways of bringing the races together. The "Birmingham Pledge," now a national campaign whose signers include President and Mrs. Clinton, reads: "I believe that every person has worth as an individual. I believe that every person is entitled to dignity and respect, regardless of race or color. I believe that every thought and every act of racial prejudice is harmful. I believe if it is my own thought or act, then it is harmful to me as well as to others. Therefore, from this day forward I will strive daily to eliminate racial prejudice from my thoughts and actions. I will discourage racial prejudice by others at every opportunity. I will treat all people with dignity and respect; and I will strive daily to honor this pledge, knowing that the world will be a better place because of my effort." Signed pledges returned to the Community Affairs Committee appear in a registry at the Birmingham Civil Rights Institute. To date, several thousand signatures from around the world have been returned.

The church, a moving force behind so many civil rights leaders and activities, has also joined the struggle to reclaim the soul of Birmingham. Gerald and Gwen Austin, for instance, founded the Center for Urban Missions in 1986. This nonprofit corporation was "founded on the hope of bringing the power of God" to inner-city Birmingham. Just seven years ago, the Austins began the New City Church, which ministers to a nondenominational, multiracial, and inner-city congregation. Through the center and the church, the Austins are specifically targeting Metropolitan Gardens, Birmingham's largest housing project and home of the poorest area in the nation. Working with the ardent belief that the church can be part of the solution and not just part of the problem, the Austins can point to several success stories and even claim that the crime rate in Metropolitan Gardens has been reduced by forty-two percent since their ministry began its work.

These are just two examples of people who have chosen to take their bite of the elephant. However, they remind us that no attempt at change is too small. One student, spiraling in a deep period of self-introspection, later writes about this very issue: "The thing I see missing from this generation is emotion—passion for doing what is right and what is good. The willingness to be bold, to sacrifice, and even to die. The frustrating part of all this is wondering how I can use my passion to contribute to change. The blatant racism of the past made blatant revolution the necessary response. Today, the need is there all the same, but I just don't sense the passion for revolution. I see individuals with their politically correct opinions living their lives unaware and unexposed to the urgent reality of the racism that still exists."

Refusing to only focus on the speck in the others' eye, she reflects on the beam in her own. "And what does it mean for me, someone who is seeing it firsthand? And yet I have dreams to go back to my isolated, comfortable world of education and family. My dreams are to minister and counsel families and individuals that struggle with relationships, trauma, and the stress of life. I hope to be married, live in the suburbs, have children, travel, and see the world. Can I still make a change in the world while filling these dreams and hopes? If I'm so passionate about the necessity for change, wouldn't I be willing to sacrifice my 'comfortable' dream and live life in the inner city, seeking out an unknown and unstable career devoted to a cause? . . . I just don't feel that is my call. How do I reconcile this? I may not be a revolutionary leading marches and motivating the masses, but I *will* make a change in my little corner of the world. This trip has not informed me as to the end of my search for knowledge, but has taught me to have an ever-increasing awareness—a presence that screams out 'This is what I stand for!' and at the same time seeks to know more. Regardless of what I do or where I go, this is who I am."

Interestingly enough, fellow Spokanites are the harshest critics of these study tours. In their mind, I should be keeping the students in Spokane and exposing them to the issues of race and exclusion in our own community. Among my many replies to this particular criticism is the fact that there is something about being on the road that encourages a deeper level of self-introspection than does the comfortable confines of a Pacific Northwest classroom. This student's journal entry is exhibit A.

On our ride back to the Amtrak station, I ask Dorothea about the reputation of the National Association for the Advancement of Colored People (NAACP) in Birmingham. During the civil rights era, segregationist authorities throughout Alabama had declared the NAACP a "foreign corporation," thus rendering its activities illegal, to prevent its interference in their local machinations. Although she is a member, Dorothea believes that there are several other organizations in Birmingham, and throughout Alabama, that are more active in addressing issues of racial equity and reconciliation. Unfortunately, she is not alone in this opinion. In one

1992 poll, more than ninety-four percent of black respondents suggested that the NAACP (as well as the Southern Christian Leadership Conference) had "lost touch with problems blacks face." For some, particularly the young and the poor for whom the organization purports to speak, the lack of familiarity with the NAACP is striking.

It is easy for detractors to blame the present problems of the NAACP on leadership that left the organization rocked by scandal and mired in debt. As a matter of fact, disclosures in 1994 revealed that then executive director Benjamin F. Chavis Jr. had committed more than $330,000 of the organization's money to forestall a sexual harassment and sexual discrimination suit by a former employee. Hoping to restore the organization to prominence, in 1995 Myrlie Evers-Williams (widow of the slain civil rights worker Medgar Evers) was elected as the new chair and Representative Kweisi Mfume, a Maryland Democrat, was appointed as the new president and chief executive officer. Julian Bond, a former Georgia state senator and activist who marched with King, was elected as chairperson of the NAACP board in February 1998. Each of these appointments drew praise among many blacks active in business and politics. Today, hopes run high for a rebirth of the NAACP and a return to the prominence it has enjoyed since 1909.

However the problems of the NAACP run deeper than their internal struggles and will not be easily fixed by new bodies in administrative seats. Many blacks simply do not identify with the organization's purpose in today's world and its relation to their daily lives. Rather than having a specific focus, the NAACP has taken on a wide range of issues and handled most of them ineffectively. Doubts about the organization's purpose are especially acute given the large number of blacks who have been elected to public office—particularly in the South—since the 1970s. In a 1996 interview, New Orleans's Mayor Marc H. Morial said: "I think that, in the past, the NAACP was so important in the South, particularly in the pre-black electoral area. But to a great extent in the electoral era . . . the advent of African-Americans serving in elected positions, plus our increasing ability to influence elected leaders, has probably created a necessity to question the relevance of the organization."

In August 1999, the NAACP, hoping to show the nation its relevance, announced plans for an economic boycott of South Carolina. The boycott's aim is to force the state to lower the Confederate battle flag that flies over its Capitol dome. "The NAACP," Mfume explained, "has the moral authority to speak out vehemently against going back . . . to a symbol that represents so much that was wrong with the nation." At stake for South Carolina is the more than $280 million that black travelers are estimated to spend each year in the state. Other civil rights leaders, including Jesse Jackson, are backing the boycott and the NAACP. The boycott was unanimously approved by the NAACP board in October 1999 and was slated to begin January 1, 2000.

As we wait to board the Amtrak bus (the rail line is under repair) to Atlanta, the group fatigue has given way to general silliness. Somehow, everyone in the group now knows Joy's most carefully guarded secret (she cannot stand for anyone to touch her face). I am the only one who originally knew about it, so I can't imagine how it got out. . . . Regardless, most of us are now taking turns slyly conniving ways to get close enough to her to touch her face and then streak away. In the midst of our reindeer games, though, I am brought back to the sobering plaque bearing the smiling faces of the four young girls killed in the 1963 bombing. Its simple inscription is a hopeful plea of forgiveness and possibility: "May men learn to replace bitterness and violence with love and understanding."

8. ATLANTA: ''DON'T TELL ME IT'S ON PEACHTREE, AGAIN. . . .''

If Atlanta could suck as hard as she blows, it could be a seaport, too.

Popular nineteenth-century joke, particularly in Savannah

Hotlanta. A City Worth Seeing. The City Too Busy to Hate. The Next Great International City. The City without Limits. The Brave and Beautiful City. The Black Mecca. Capital of the New South. Atlanta: Come Share Our Dream. Star on the Rise. From its earliest days, Atlanta has used sloganeering, self-promotion, and boosterism to create the image it wished to present to itself and the rest of the world. From your first entry into the city limits or your initial step onto the airport concourse, you are assaulted by the city's pride in itself. This pride is both gratingly annoying and candidly refreshing.

After the jovial bus ride from Birmingham (we got free lunches!), most of us are ready to swallow whatever image the civic leaders wish to give us. We collect our bags and hop on the Metropolitan Atlanta Rapid Transit Authority (MARTA) subway—the city's clean and efficient, if limited, public transit system. Just out of the station, though, we soberly notice a billboard that slaps us back to the reality of the tour. On a sign advertising MARTA, someone has scrawled "Moving Africans Rapidly Through Atlanta."

January 21

After a sound night's sleep and a quick-fix breakfast of Krispy Kreme doughnuts, we head north to the upscale district of Buckhead. The students take excessive delight in repeating the name "Buckhead" to each other and speculating on its origin. Much less interesting than their speculations, in fact, the name is painfully literal. It derives from the mounting of a buck's head on a post near a settler's crossing in 1838. Today, this twenty-eight-square-mile area of north Atlanta is thick with pubs, music venues, luxury goods, high-powered business centers, glitzy malls, and grand living. Buckhead does not sound like it fits the tour's itinerary. However, the Atlanta History Center is housed here. Although not specifically devoted to issues of race, the center is a great introduction to the history of the South's greatest city—its birth, destruction, rebirth, struggles, achievements, and legacy. The center tells Atlanta's story with award-winning museum exhibitions, two historic houses of different periods, and a range of beautiful gardens that detail the horticultural history of the area. For students who have not spent a lot time in this part of the country, much of the material in the center will provide a larger introduction to the South.

The Atlanta History Museum opened in 1993 and is the entry point for the entire Atlanta History Center. In addition to its changing exhibits, the museum houses three permanent exhibitions. One describes folk art traditions in the South; another, the largest in the museum, chronicles the Civil War. However, our major interest is in the permanent exhibit entitled "Metropolitan Frontiers: Atlanta, 1835–2000." The exhibit puts a positive spin on Atlanta's inexhaustible supply of self-promotion and revolves around one theme: "the creative, regenerative abilities of Atlantans that serve them so well in times of crisis and that direct them in times of growth and change." To be sure, Atlanta has had its fair share of crisis, growth, and change.

Originally, Cherokee and Creek Indian tribes populated what is now the Atlanta area. The Cherokee settled north and west of the Chattahoochee River, with the Creek populating the area south and east. Even as late as 1788, when the U.S. Constitution was ratified, eighty percent of Georgia remained Indian territory. Between 1790 and 1830, however, the western push of settlers increased the population of Georgia sixfold. In 1821, the land that is now Atlanta was opened for white settlement.

Increasingly, Indian tribes were forced into the frontier. By 1827, the Creek were gone. The following year, gold was discovered in the northern Georgia mountains, which gave additional impetus to Indian removal efforts. In a sham council meeting attended by fewer than 500 Cherokee (most of whom were part of a tiny pro-removal faction) of a population of more than 17,000, a treaty was negotiated for Cherokee removal. Most of the Cherokee refused to migrate. In the brutal winter of 1838–1839, the Cherokee were forcibly moved westward to reservations in Oklahoma. The route they traversed and the journey itself became known as the "Trail of Tears" or, as a direct translation from Cherokee, "The Trail Where They Cried" *(Nunna daul Tsuny)*. More than four thousand Cherokee, nearly one-fourth of this exiled Indian nation, died as a result of the removal.

Legend has it that Cherokee mothers grieved so much that the chiefs prayed for a sign to lift the mothers' spirits and give them strength to care for their children. From that day forward, a beautiful new rose grew wherever a mother's tear fell to the ground. The rose is white, for the mother's tear, and has a gold center, for the gold taken from the Cherokee lands. The seven leaves on each stem represent the seven Cherokee clans that made the journey. To this day, the Cherokee rose—now the official flower of the state of Georgia—prospers along the route of the "Trail of Tears."

Following the removal of the Cherokee, there was an immediate land rush for the former Indian territories in the Southeast. In 1837, a spot in the center of present-day Atlanta was selected as the southern terminus of a railroad to be built northward to Chattanooga, Tennessee. The spot was first known as Terminus, then as Marthasville, and finally as Atlanta in 1845. Lying at the junction of three granite ridges connecting the Southeast's coastal, piedmont, and mountain areas, it became the gateway through which most overland traffic had to pass between the southern seaboard and the region to the west.

During the Civil War, Atlanta became a supply hub, relief center, a safe site for southern war industries, and the keystone of Confederate rail transportation east of the Mississippi River. Richmond, Virginia, may have been the political capital, but the strategic heart of the Confederacy was in Atlanta. That was the good news. The bad news was that Atlanta therefore became the prime military objective of General William Tecumseh Sherman's invasion of Georgia. After a bloody four-month siege, the city fell to his Union troops on September 2, 1864. On November 15 of that year, Sherman departed on his famous march to the sea, but not before all of the railroad facilities, almost every factory, warehouse and military target, and more than two-thirds of the homes in Atlanta had been burned to the ground. (Sherman had ordered that private homes and churches not be harmed. However, fires at other sites often spread to residential neighborhoods. This prompted the classic line from Henry Grady, the young editor of the *Atlanta Constitution*, upon meeting Sherman—"some people think you are kind of careless about fire.")

During Reconstruction, Atlanta was faced with the challenge of rebuilding from an infrastructure of ashes and a civic treasury of $1.64. The city adopted as its symbol the Phoenix rising from the ashes and the motto "Resurgens." More pressing, Atlanta had to create an identity that was compatible with national norms, while not wholly separate from southern culture. Over time, Atlanta came to epitomize the spirit of the "New South," having risen from the ashes of the Civil War (literally) and become an advocate of reconciliation with the North to further the South's economic agenda. Local leaders began to push for economic diversification and industrialization of the region. By 1890, Atlanta was a southeastern leader in commercial development. By 1910, forty railroad lines had returned to Atlanta, united the local economy, shaped the city's layout, established the focus for financial activities, located the labor centers, and connected the Southeast to the nation.

Atlanta's population quadrupled in the decades following the Civil War. Blacks now made up at least half the city's work force and were employed in jobs to reconstruct the city and carry out its commerce. The museum exhibit puts a delicate frame around race relations during this time: "Two parallel societies emerged, one for blacks and one for whites, each with distinctive characteristics and completely segregated from one another." However, as the turn of the twentieth century approached, these parallel societies began to intersect with increasing tension and volatility.

On opening day of the 1895 Atlanta Cotton States and International Exposition, black leader and educator Booker T. Washington gave a rousing speech signaling an unprecedented acceptance of social and political racial segregation in exchange for allowing blacks to make economic progress within a well-defined sphere. In this address, known as the "Atlanta Compromise," Washington declared that the agitation for "social equality" was the "extremist folly." "In all things that are purely social," he continued, "we can be as separate as the fingers, yet one as the hand in all things essential to mutual progress." For the white community, Washington's words were exactly what they wanted to hear. The governor of Georgia rushed across the stage to shake the hand of the man who would accommodate the status quo and give Atlanta its much-needed facade of racial harmony.

Although Ronald Takaki argues that Washington was actually not a conservative accommodationist, it was clear that his approach to racial reform differed greatly from one being advocated by a professor at Atlanta University. W. E. B. DuBois's radical protest urged the creation of an educated black leadership, the "Talented Tenth," that would be committed to racial advancement. Under the direction of this intellectual "yeast," blacks would be empowered to rise collectively. DuBois's strategy was based on a deep conviction that superior intelligence, scientific investigation, and collegial effort would solve the race problem. He was convinced that Washington's compromise represented capitulation and had failed as a vehicle for racial progress. DuBois was zealous in his bitter opposition toward the suffocating effects of accommodationism and racial subservience.

Both of these men's platforms would be challenged by the events of September 1906. On a Saturday evening, precipitated by four extra editions of the *Evening News* trumpeting successive cases of alleged black rape and the supposed discovery of white pornography in black brothels, a mob of 10,000 frenzied whites beat or shot at every black in sight. During the five-hour massacre, the mob committed unspeakable atrocities—using a small black child for target practice and beating to death two barbers. Rioters crucified several bodies on utility poles and threw three corpses on the monument to Grady, Atlanta's leading architect of racial reform. They attacked juke joints, pool halls, and stores and overturned streetcars. The massacre finally ended in the face of sheer exhaustion and a fortuitous downpour. Violence erupted again on the following Monday evening. By the end of the riots, 25 black Atlantans (and 1 white) were dead, 150 were wounded, and more than 1,000 people, mostly blacks, would leave the Atlanta area in fear of their lives.

As Dominic Capeci and Jack Knight have outlined, the Atlanta race riots of 1906 were a litmus test for the contrasting philosophies of Washington and DuBois. Both leaders were rocked by the unimaginable outbreak of violence. Washington held fast to his belief that his compromise had survived the bloodshed by viewing the violence as simply a tragic aberration in race relations. He blamed the riots on the riffraff of both races and, primarily, on black radicals who wrought much more than the "extremist folly" he had described in 1895. Washington reiterated his public offer of black cooperation to the southern elite and promised a tightened, self-imposed segregation by the black community. Washington actively relished the role of peacemaker and his compromise policy, although itself compromised, dominated the aftermath of the riots.

In contrast, the viability of DuBois's protest was dashed in the fallout of the riots. His reliance on rationality to lead to racial reform could not answer the extreme irrationality of the Atlanta riots. DuBois had attributed racism to ignorance and meanness and had looked for its remedy in rationality and moral argument. In the bloody face of the Atlanta riots, he seemed paralyzed by the long-range ramifications of urban disorder on his philosophical beliefs and protest strategies. It was this paralysis and DuBois's corresponding silence that gave unintentional credence to Washington's accommodationist policies. Washington's compromise strategy did not have all of the answers, but at least it offered *something*.

During the early decades of the twentieth century, racial relations in the South would reflect much of Washington's accommodationist policies. Underpinning the racial subservience was the 1896 U.S. Supreme Court *Plessy v. Ferguson* ruling. That decision, which emphasized the doctrine of "separate but equal," had made segregation the law of the land. In addition, poll taxes and literacy requirements for voting rights were effectively disenfranchising blacks. Worst of all, hundreds of blacks were being lynched annually. By the early 1940s, the South had lost a significant portion of its black population to the Great Migration. It was clear that the possibility of progress for blacks in the South was distressingly remote and that the decades of the 1950s and 1960s would demand an alternative strategy for racial reform.

The museum exhibit shamelessly displays the Atlantan trait of self-promotion. This is perhaps partially excusable, given the fact that the exhibit was developed as the cornerstone presentation of Atlanta's history during the Olympics. Not as well chronicled, however, are some of the numerous problems facing Atlanta at the turn of the millennium. Atlanta, with a metropolitan population of nearly 3.5 million, continues to grow like kudzu. Since 1990, the region has drawn 415,000 out-of-state residents—the most in the nation. All told, the ten-county metropolitan Atlanta area has grown by roughly a quarter just since 1990. Studies show that a one percent increase in population growth results in a ten to twenty percent growth in land consumption. Indeed, without topographic obstacles, Atlanta has grown far beyond its own borders, bumping up against its rural neighbors. The Atlanta countryside has gone from rural to suburban in character without ever passing through an urban phase. By combining all of that data, it becomes clear that Atlanta has grown faster than any human settlement in history—from 65 miles north to south to 110 miles since 1990. According to one estimate, the northern Georgia mountains could become part of metropolitan Atlanta by 2002!

With this growth have come the triple evils of suburban sprawl—pollution, traffic congestion, and visual blight. Pollution from cars and power plants have caused air quality to deteriorate so quickly that, in 1997, the Environmental Protection Agency curtailed further road building in the area. Until the region complies with the Clean Air Act, it cannot draw on federal highway funds, which account for eighty percent of new-road financing. Los Angeles is the only other major city with similar restrictions. In addition, metropolitan Atlanta suffers from a disruption of wildlife habitats and the noxious alteration of rivers, streams, and landscapes. Atlantans have the longest average round-trip commute to work in the nation—36.5 miles daily, more than Dallas' 29.5 and Los Angeles' 20.5. As any commuter will tell you, this takes valuable time away from family and work. Atlanta is a city even more dependent on the automobile than Los Angeles and notoriously lacking in public transportation. An expansion of the city subway system, which promises to decrease pollution and commuting time, is resisted by the major suburban counties for fear that its trains would bring in urban crime. Finally, every day more than fifty acres of green space in the metropolitan area is plowed under for more houses, strip malls, Wal-Marts, and convenience stores.

The suburban sprawl also has implications for the urban center of Atlanta. It is the smallest central city of the nation's ten largest metropolitan regions—the hole in the doughnut. According to the 1990 census, the population of Atlanta proper *dropped* to 394,017 from 425,022 in 1980. From 1986 to 1996, Atlanta's population declined by five percent as increasing numbers of people moved to the outlying suburban neighborhoods. Atlanta's Mayor Bill Campbell now represents fewer constituents than the chief executives of four of the five counties that constitute the metropolitan area.

This movement is not just "white flight." It is more accurately "blight flight" because the city has a significant black middle class that has fled from downtown as well. Downtown commerce has been hurt as shoppers are pulled from locally owned stores and restaurants to large, regional, cookie-cutter malls. This flight further leads to a concentration of poverty and other social ills in the urban core of Atlanta. For instance, Atlanta has led the nation in homicide rates for several years and consistently has some of the highest crime rates in the country. Thirty-two percent of the city residents live in poverty, thus ranking Atlanta fifth among American cities. In 1990, the average black family's income was an astounding twenty-six percent of the average white family's, down from fifty-two percent in 1970. The 1990 census found that forty-three percent of Atlanta's children lived in poverty and 14,000 homes did not even have a telephone.

Although an early leader in desegregation, the city remains geographically segregated with only a handful of neighborhoods being truly integrated. Ronald Bayor, a historian at Georgia Tech, even argues that much of the continuing geographical segregation is a vestige from the time when the city's highways and roads were designed to enforce rigid segregation. Three interstates converge on Atlanta and cut off its black and white sides. Some roads literally change names to separate black from white. Monroe Drive, for instance, becomes Monroe Boulevard as it enters the urban center of Atlanta.

Racial segregation also has returned to Atlanta's public schools. Atlanta's city schools are now virtually all black. This return of racial segregation to the public schools is not limited to Atlanta. A 1999 study by the Civil Rights Project, a research and advocacy organization run by the Harvard Graduate School of Education and Harvard Law School, found that seventy-five percent of Hispanic students and sixty-nine percent of black students attend schools in which most of their classmates are also members of racial minority groups. The continuing trend toward resegregation, the largest backward movement since the 1954 Supreme Court decision declaring school segregation laws unconstitutional, is proceeding fastest in the South. The study also found that segregated minority schools almost always have high concentrations of poverty, which adversely impacts student achievement.

However, good news may be on the horizon for Atlanta. In 1997, the population of the city proper grew for the first time in thirty years as traffic-weary suburbanites moved back. With the construction of more than a thousand lofts, new retail stores, and an explosion of public art and pedestrian corridors, downtown Atlanta is experiencing a dramatic revitalization. Mayor Campbell's office takes credit for various efforts that, during the past three years, have reduced violent crime in Atlanta by 16.5 percent. Islands of old neighborhoods in town are being gentrified as nearly every unit of public housing undergoes renovation. New, affordable homes are being built in neighborhoods long ignored by developers. To become a sterling example of urban revitalization, Atlanta still has a long way to go. It seems clear, though, that a commitment is in place and resources are being sought.

After our time at the Atlanta History Center, we disperse for a free afternoon and evening. Some students head to the Jimmy Carter Center and Presidential Library, others opt for shopping at Lenox Square, some try to catch a tour of Turner field, others stay at the Atlanta History Center, and a few romantics find their way to an Buckhead theater for a showing of "Titanic."

Later that evening, we reconvene for a short debriefing in the basement of the hostel. The students loved the Atlanta History Center, but
it's difficult to separate their positive reactions to the center from their
even more positive reactions to a free afternoon. Regardless, the center
definitely left its impression. Several of the students had spent the rest of
the day touring the center's other exhibits, historic homes, and gardens.
Afterwards, one was reminded of a comment made by Reverend Sharp in
Chicago. He had said, "To understand race in America today, you have
to go back to slavery." That comment really resonated with this student,
our only Southerner. Making Sharp's general comment even more specific, she said: "I think to understand the South today, you have to go
back to the plantations. The South grew up around cotton and a way of
life that was not that ethical or just to all that lived in it. It is that heritage, though, that still surrounds the South today."

Another student was struck by the center's permanent exhibit on the
Civil War. "The artifacts were incredible and the story has always capti-
vated me," she later wrote. "However, there was an exhibit that offered
a perspective on war that I had not honestly pictured before. We are the
children of Vietnam vets. We are the generation raised by adults who
were children when wars were fought for unknown purposes. We did not
learn about fighting for a cause. We learned about the horrors of fighting,
period. Because of this, I grew up thinking that wars simply reflected the
fallen nature, mostly of men, in inflicting suffering on another group of
people. I seldom thought of it as conflict resolution, and I never considered the strategic side of battle. But this exhibit portrayed that strategic
side in a way that made me look at war as a problem-solving measure."

A couple of students spent their afternoon at the Carter Center and
Presidential Library. In what has been called the most beautiful of our
nation's presidential libraries, they saw photos, memorabilia, state gifts,
a re-creation of the Oval Office, and audiovisual presentations. One of
the students, who I expect to run for president someday, also spoke with
a staff member about the Atlanta Project—the center's ambitious program of urban renewal. This effort, which is led by Carter himself, was
created in October 1991 to help Atlanta's neediest communities gain
access to vital resources. It is yet another example of Carter's genius

for creating public-private partnership ventures. The Carter Center also brings a similar approach to countries all over the world. It is active in bringing warring parties to the negotiating table, monitoring elections, safeguarding human rights, fighting disease, increasing group production, and promoting preventive health care.

My future-president is impressed. "His [Carter's] focus on sociopolitical justice and his realistic personality really are atypical of American presidents. Furthermore, his international emphasis has really set some important foundations for much of the growth of the global community. It is as though he was completely ahead of his time in addressing the growing interconnectedness of the global community as well as the natural environment." This student is not the only one impressed. On August 9, 1999, President Bill Clinton came to the Carter Center to present Jimmy and Rosalynn Carter the Presidential Medal of Freedom—the nation's highest civilian honor.

Following the race riots of 1906, most black Atlantans followed Booker T. Washington's strategy of tightened, self-imposed segregation. They withdrew their businesses and homes from downtown and established themselves along Auburn Avenue—"Sweet Auburn," as it came to be called. In this relatively affluent neighborhood was an economic cross-section of people—railroad porters, preachers, doctors, servants, lawyers, college professors, and business executives. Here, black institutions grew strong, even though they lacked the resources of their white counterparts. In the commercial district of Sweet Auburn, more than one hundred businesses and public services thrived—banks, insurance companies, builders, jewelers, tailors, doctors, lawyers, funeral parlors, a newspaper, a library, and a business college. All were black owned or black operated. In Sweet Auburn, blacks could spend their whole lives in a black environment, while seldom glimpsing a white face. Consistent with Washington's compromise, they accommodated segregation by secluding themselves in a well-defined enclave that promised independence and relative freedom from persecution and discrimination.

In 1929, Martin Luther King Jr. was born at 501 Auburn Avenue. Today, this is still a black neighborhood, but a less prosperous one than it was when King was alive. Middle-class blacks have other shopping and residential options now. The area, which has been preserved as a national historic site, has several dozen houses nicely restored to the way they looked in the 1930s when King was a boy. In particular, the block of Auburn Avenue where King was born reflects the neighborhood's former status as the wealthiest black community in the nation. Along the length of Auburn Avenue, the city is upgrading the street with paving stones and lighting reminiscent of the community's heyday during the 1930s. However, houses outside the historic district remain dilapidated and many once-thriving storefronts are shuttered.

Annually, more than three million people visit the Martin Luther King Jr. National Historic Site. Despite its popularity, many have long held that this site is not what it should be. Instead, it reflects years of distrust between the King family and the National Park Service. This distrust culminated in the early 1990s when the service went ahead with plans to build a visitor's center on land the Kings had wanted for a multi-media museum and theme park. Coretta Scott King and her family withdrew support, denouncing the National Park Service in the media. Mrs. King even accused the National Park Service of harboring "dark ambitions." The conflict came to a head in December 1994, when the King family halted service tours of the King birth home. In the face of mounting criticism and accusations of greed, however, the King family struck an uneasy truce with the National Park Service. Tours of the home could resume in return for the National Park Service's support of the future development of the King's museum and theme park, which the family still wants to build.

January 22

We arrive a few moments before the Martin Luther King Jr. Center for Nonviolent Social Change opens. The center was founded in 1968 by Coretta Scott King and others. Today, the King's younger son, Dexter Scott King, heads the center. More than simply a memorial to the slain leader, the King Center is a living, action-oriented monument to nonviolent social change through educational and community action programs.

While we wait, we walk the length of the long reflecting pool in which the marble tomb containing King's body stands. On this cold, early morning, the eternal flame has an unusual luminescence. There is a somber silence to the place. I get the sense that the silence would be there regardless of how many visitors were milling about. However, this silence is broken by the words etched on the side of his crypt: "Free at Last. Free at Last. Thank God Almighty I'm Free at Last." The inscription is perfect in its simplicity.

While Joy leads one group to the tour of King's birth home, I join the others in the small museum adjacent to the pool. Here, in Freedom Hall, photographs and signs form a brief chronology of King's life in the Civil Rights movement. Four small cases display a few things he left behind— some clothing and a small travel kit; his Nobel Peace Prize; the tape recorder Coretta Scott King used to take down his speeches in Montgomery, Alabama; and the key to the Memphis hotel room where he was assassinated. After all we have seen in Memphis and Birmingham, it is easy to be unimpressed by the scarcity of items displayed in this quasi-museum. However, as journalist Henry Wiencek writes, the scarcity of items "is [part of] the power of the place—the sense of a great invisible legacy that can't be displayed or contained but that is all around us."

We then cross the street to the new 21,000-square-foot visitor center operated by the National Park Service. The visitor's center is connected by a recreational "green belt" to the nearby Carter Center and Presidential Library. The center features two films, one about King and the other about the Sweet Auburn business district. It also includes a modest exhibit of videotapes and text about the movement, with King's biography used as a contextual framework. At one point, a young black child—no older than five—hears King's voice on a video screen, turns, becomes incredibly excited, and screams: "There, there, there he is! I heard his voice, there he is, I see him!" One student standing beside me says, "I am amazed that this child knows more about King than I did when I came to college. It shows why we need to teach multicultural history to our young. Why teach eight years of European history when there is so much more to our country and culture than just European ancestry?"

As the students meander through the exhibits, I ask one of the National Park Service personnel about the status of the relationship with the King family. Speaking circumspectly, he tells me that the National Park Service is presently negotiating with the King Center about the possibility of taking control of the center. It sounds like the uneasy truce has not gotten any easier. Regardless, I think the visitor's center is a welcome addition to the national historic site. Before its completion, the historic site had no comprehensive interpretive displays. As a memorial to one of the world's most important civil rights leaders, it really was lacking. The new visitor's center at least partially corrects that. As Don Barger, the National Parks and Conservation Association's Southeast regional director, said in a 1996 interview: "We had preserved the place, but we had not preserved the meaning, and now we have."

Finally, Joy's group has returned from the tour of the birth home and it is our turn to go. We cross the street again, head east for a block, and find ourselves on the doorstep of the upper-middle-class home where King was born and three generations of his family lived. It is a nine-room, two-story Queen Anne–style home that was built in 1895. In a clipped, monotone manner, the park service ranger reels off plenty of King family lore. As always, the crowd's favorite is the story of how young Martin would unscrew the piano stool just to the point where it was unstable enough to collapse when the music teacher sat on it. Hoping to shirk a music lesson, he usually just ended up with a longer lesson and the wrath of Daddy King when he got home. As one student says: "There is something about the mischievous little Martin that makes him more human and, in a strange way, even more admirable." We also see the dinner table, set with the original china, where Daddy King used to hold court and talk politics. We walk by the bathroom young Martin would hide in so he would not have to do the dishes, the small bed he slept in with his brother, and the high ceiling his father jumped to touch in joy when King was born. Sets of Chinese checkers and a Monopoly board round out the sense of familial closeness in the home.

After our tour of the birth home, we reunite with the other group and walk west to 407 Auburn Avenue. Here is the Ebenezer Baptist Church where King, his father, the Reverend Martin Luther King Sr., and his maternal grandfather, the Reverend A. D. King, all preached. An incredibly welcoming church receptionist takes us through the sanctuary and gives us a brief history of the church. She reminds us that the young King preached his first sermon here at age seventeen and joined his father as copastor from 1960 to 1968. She also notes that Ebenezer was the scene of tragic episodes. In April 1968, crowds gathered here to view Martin Luther King Jr.'s body as it lay in state. In 1974, an assassin fatally shot King's mother as she was playing the church organ.

We had hoped to attend a weekly Bible study at the church, but the hoopla and preparations surrounding a recent visit to the church by Vice President Al Gore on Martin Luther King Day has cancelled this week's study. As we leave the sanctuary, the receptionist goes on to say that, in a deal with the National Park Service, Ebenezer is about to complete construction of a larger glass and steel sanctuary and church building next to the visitor's center. The original Ebenezer Baptist Church will then be leased to the National Park Service, which should offer a wonderful opportunity to interpret the vital role played by the black church in the Civil Rights movement. In response to my parting question, she says that, yes, the proposal was publicly endorsed by Mrs. King and other family members involved with the King Center.

Leaving Ebenezer Baptist Church, we see a line of children from a local Head Start program winding their way from the National Park Service visitor's center to the King Center. Although they are all bundled up against the bracing cold, most appear to be black. As they walk, they are singing "We Shall Overcome." It is mesmerizing. I wish the National Park Service and King Center officials could hear these children. It makes me think that maybe their uneasy truce might become a bit easier.

In the 1950s and 1960s, Atlanta took the lead in the Southeast in strengthening minority rights. The decision to do so was based less on an altruistic view of relations between blacks and whites in the region than it was on a pragmatic realization that disruptions like those seen in other major cities during the Civil Rights movement would be devastating to the image of a "New South" being created for Atlanta. The business leaders themselves described their actions as "enlightened self-interest." Regardless of motivation, Atlanta found itself taking the right fork in the road.

Boasting itself as the "City Too Busy to Hate," Atlanta's strongest identification with the movement for racial reform was through its native son, Martin Luther King Jr. He was only the tip of the reforming iceberg in Atlanta, however. Prominent black universities and a wealthy black bourgeoisie produced a black leadership—including Julian Bond and John Lewis—with which to be reckoned. Many whites played key roles as well. *Atlanta Constitution* editor Ralph McGill, for instance, was a freethinking, liberal-leaning advocate for civil rights who served to annoyingly prick Atlanta's conscience. "They used to say there are two types of people in the South," said the journalist George Goodwin, "those that couldn't eat breakfast until they'd read Ralph McGill, and those that couldn't eat breakfast *after* they'd read Ralph McGill." Mayor Ivan Allen Jr. was the only southern mayor to endorse Kennedy's civil rights bill, the forerunner of the Civil Rights Act.

Under the leadership of Chief Justice Elbert Tuttle, the desegregation process in Atlanta and throughout the region was relatively swift and peaceful. As early as 1961, President Kennedy urged Americans to "look closely at what Atlanta has done" in desegregating its schools. By 1964, Atlanta had integrated its parks, golf courses, buses, swimming pools, theaters, schools, public libraries, and most of its hotels and restaurants. The transition was not without incident, particularly in surrounding counties in the region. In comparison with the violence in other parts of the Deep South, however, it was almost exemplary. It can be rightly said that Atlanta epitomized the southern transition in positive race relations and provided an enviable role model, even for its rival Birmingham, for progressive leadership in the region.

Desegregation was followed by political empowerment. In 1973, Atlanta became the first major city in the South to elect a black mayor, Maynard Jackson. He was re-elected twice by overwhelming margins. Andrew Young, one of Martin Luther King Jr.'s top lieutenants, became Georgia's first black Congressman since Reconstruction, represented the United States at the United Nations, and then followed Mayor Jackson to city hall. In 1993, Bill Campbell became the city's third black mayor in a landslide victory, garnering seventy-three percent of the vote. Beverly J. Harvard, a black woman, was appointed chief of police in 1994 and is responsible for the overall operation of the largest municipal law enforcement agency in the state of Georgia.

In 1970, Atlanta's population was predominately black (51.3 percent) for the first time in its history. At that time, it was one of the nation's three majority black cities. More than 200,000 blacks migrated to Atlanta between 1980 and 1990. In 1990, the estimated racial distribution in the city was 67 percent black; 31 percent white; and less than 1 percent each for American Indian, Asian, and Hispanic. In 1996, blacks made up nearly half of the newcomers to the city, where they now represent more than 70 percent of the population. Those figures give the city of Atlanta, sometimes called a "Black Mecca," the highest ratio of blacks to total population of any U.S. city except Detroit.

How do we explain Atlanta's overwhelming appeal for blacks? Mayor Campbell offers one perspective: "Atlanta is justifiably known as the Mecca for African-Americans because of our incredible history as the birthplace of the Civil Rights Movement, our unyielding commitment to African-American businesses, and our unprecedented array of African-American colleges and universities." Lest this appear as yet another example of Atlanta's "boosterism," a 1997 *Ebony* survey asked the one hundred most influential black Americans to select the dream city they would live in if they could live anywhere they want. By a three-to-one margin, they considered Atlanta to be the best city for blacks, the city with the most employment opportunities for blacks, the city with the most diversity, and the city with the best schools and the most affordable housing for blacks.

For many, Atlanta has long been seen as the land of milk and honey for blacks. Indeed, its great selling point to the world is as a model of black middle-class achievement. Atlanta's establishment has long been (relatively speaking) a bastion of black power and affirmative action. In 1973, one-tenth of one percent of the city's contract dollars went to companies with minority and female owners. Upon taking office in 1974, Mayor Jackson sent a strong message to the white business community by holding up the construction of Hartsfield Atlanta International Airport until contractors took on minority partners. Over time, black politicians developed programs that, by city statute, require thirty-six percent minority participation in public projects. The result was an increase in the number of minority-owned and minority-run (primarily black) construction and service companies. These companies tend to have far more minority employees than do white-owned companies. In 1995, forty percent of the city's contract dollars went to companies owned primarily by minorities and women. Sixty percent of the revenue generated by concession businesses at Hartsfield Atlanta International Airport, the world's second busiest, is now earned by minorities. Such numbers are unheard of in the private sector.

Even as national trends retreat in the opposite direction, Atlanta's political establishment still embraces affirmative action with enthusiasm. Mayor Campbell articulates that enthusiasm: "Everybody who is a person of color in this country has benefited from affirmative action. . . . The sad truth in this country, the sad truth even in the city of Atlanta, is that without our affirmative action programs, our minority businesses would wither."

Nowhere was the enthusiasm for affirmative action more evident than in the commitment to minority participation in preparing for the Olympic Games. The Atlanta Committee for the Olympic Games, the private corporation established by city officials to run the event, doled out fully one-third of $387 million in Olympic construction money to companies owned by minorities and women. As a result of encouraging joint ventures between white-owned companies and those with minority or female owners, virtually every new site for the Summer Olympic Games was built with significant minority participation. Mayor Campbell is especially proud of the way in which the policies of the Atlanta Committee for the Olympic Games have left a legacy of biracial business relationships.

Not everyone is thrilled with the legacy of affirmative action, however. Atlanta's program has been criticized for adding costs to some public works projects, temporarily supporting minority businesses that later failed, and disproportionately helping a few minority companies with big contracts. In addition, black-owned companies continue to get far more business than do companies owned by women or other minorities. Some argue that placing all minority groups in competition for a limited number of set-aside programs maintains the old power structure by preventing permanent coalitions between such groups. Finally, the system in Atlanta can be particularly difficult for small, white-owned businesses squeezed out when minority companies are linked with large white-owned companies that have plenty of capital. Many whites rarely bid on public works projects now because of the difficulty in finding minority partners and the increased paperwork required of joint ventures.

Nowhere has governmental policy on race relations been more incendiary than in the practice of affirmative action. Some people view it as a milestone; others as a millstone; and still others regard it as a necessary, but imperfect, remedy for an intractable social disease. However, most do not even know what the term "affirmative action" means. For the general public, affirmative action can mean anything from the demeaning use of quota programs for supposed incompetents to the meritorious practice of extending a hand to eminently qualified people previously held back by racial, ethnic, or gender bias. A wide range of government documents even acknowledges that the term has come to have different meanings in different contexts. Is it any wonder the public debate is so confused?

In its classical definition, affirmative action occurs whenever people go out of their way (take affirmative or positive action) to increase the likelihood of true equality for individuals of differing categories. Affirmative action policies and programs rest on the assumption that nondiscrimination alone is not sufficient to overcome the effects of past discrimination. Active policies and programs must be implemented to ensure fair representation. In practice, affirmative action policies and programs focus on recruiting, hiring, retaining, and promoting more of certain *underrepresented* groups of people into an organization. By consciously taking race, ethnicity, and gender into account, affirmative action promotes the inclusion of a group that has had a history of exclusion.

In addition to a growing number of judges who believe the Constitution does not allow government to categorize people by race, even to benefit those who have long been disadvantaged, there is an increasingly vocal public resistance to affirmative action programs. It is a gross misstatement, however, to categorically assert that the public does not support affirmative action anymore. The myth that the public opposes affirmative action is based largely on public opinion polls that offer an "all-or-none" choice between affirmative action as it currently exists and no affirmative action whatsoever. In truth, most members of the public oppose extreme forms of affirmative action (such as quotas, set-asides, and reverse discrimination) that violate norms of procedural justice. However, they do not oppose the concept of affirmative action itself. When intermediate choices are added, surveys show that most people want to maintain some form of affirmative action.

Much of white America's negative reaction to affirmative action is based on three "sincere," although misguided, objections. First is the objection that affirmative action promotes reverse discrimination. This misguided objection ignores the fact that discrimination against whites is *illegal*. Whites who believe they have been the victims of reverse discrimination can go to court like anyone else and make their case. Despite this legal avenue, actual claims of reverse discrimination are remarkably rare. A 1995 Labor Department draft report reviewing opinions by U.S. District Courts and Courts of Appeal found that between 1990 and 1994, of the three thousand discrimination cases filed, only one hundred (less than four percent) were charges of reverse discrimination. Of the one hundred, only six were found to have merit. If reverse discrimination is so prevalent and unbearable, then why—in a society enamored with legal redress—are its legal manifestations so incredibly scarce?

A second misguided objection is that affirmative action violates the great American ideal of advancement by pure merit. The fallacy in the "pure merit" objection is whites' convenient amnesia of the arrangements that have always gone beyond considerations of "pure merit" in the American job market. Some of the best jobs are not advertised. Rather, they are circulated by word of mouth and filled through networks of friends and associates. Many of us have benefited from such informal "buddy" or "good-old-boy" networks or assistance. We have recruiting and hiring preferences for veterans, special economic incentives for purchase of U.S.-made products, import quotas against foreign goods, and agricultural and textile subsidies.

Third is the misguided objection that discrimination is dead and affirmative action is simply no longer necessary. Some critics of affirmative action argue that the time has come to revise, scale back, or abandon the temporary imposition of affirmative action goals and timetables because the procedures that require fairness have, in large measure, been institutionalized. In other words, today's playing field is fairly level and affirmative action is no longer necessary.

Affirmative action has indeed helped women and racial minorities achieve more equitable representation in the past thirty years. Despite these gains, a wide variety of evidence suggests that the ultimate goals of affirmative action—eliminating the consequences of past discrimination and likelihood of future discrimination—have yet to be reached. The effects of affirmative action across education, employment, and business are fragile. Women continue to earn 72¢ for every male dollar. White males make up only twenty-nine percent of the workforce, but hold ninety-five percent of senior management positions. Black men with professional degrees earn twenty-one percent less than whites with similar jobs and credentials. Although Hispanics comprise 8 percent of our country's workforce, they make up only 0.4 percent of our managers. Most racial minorities continue to suffer from twice the unemployment rate of whites, earn half the median family income, and are half as likely to attend four years or more of college.

How much more dire might the pictures become if affirmative action programs were removed? Unfortunately, we have a clear answer to a question that is no longer hypothetical. In 1995, the state Board of Regents in California banned consideration of race or gender in higher education admissions. In November of the following year, Proposition 209 was confirmed by a statewide referendum. State and local governments were immediately prohibited from discriminating against or granting preferential treatment to any individual or group based on race, sex, color, ethnicity, or national origin in public employment, public education, and public contracting. With the passing of Proposition 209, California became the first state to effectively repeal affirmative action programs. Today, more than two dozen states have pending legislation or voter initiatives aimed at weakening or eliminating racial preferences in education and other areas. Similar legislation already has impacted a wide range of programs in Texas, Louisiana, Mississippi, and Washington.

The intentionally vague wording of California's original proposition enabled Governor Pete Wilson to move against a wide variety of "offending" programs. Although its sponsors claimed that it would not affect educational outreach programs, it most certainly has. Among the many programs decimated or destroyed was the California Summer Science and Technology Academy that identified public high school pupils, with an emphasis on female and minority students, to participate on university-based research projects. The California School Paraprofessional Teacher Training Program, which assists minority school district employees in applying for admission and financial aid for teaching training programs, also fell victim to Wilson's interpretation of Proposition 209. Finally, the American Indian Early Childhood Education Program, which allows school districts with more than ten percent American Indian students to establish an advisory committee on their early education, also was impacted.

The sponsors' claim that educational admissions would be relatively unaffected was just as much of a fable. The elimination of affirmative action in the University of California systems took effect with graduate students entering in 1997. For the 1997 entering class at the University of California's Boalt Hall Law School, twenty-seven percent fewer blacks and twenty-four percent fewer Hispanics applied. Of those, only fourteen blacks were admitted, down eighty-one percent from 1996. Only thirty-nine Hispanics were admitted, down fifty percent from the previous year. Amazingly, only *one* black student and fourteen Hispanic students were expected in the incoming class of 270 at Boalt Hall Law School. The elimination of affirmative action did not apply to undergraduates until 1998. Black admissions for freshmen enrollment in the fall of 1998 at the University of California at Berkeley dropped sixty-six percent from the previous year.

This is not to say that schools have given up on their quest to keep the increased access minorities have gained to quality higher education. Some schools in the California system, for instance, have tried to reclaim room for considering race, ethnicity, and gender in admissions. At the University of California at Berkeley, applicants are invited to write an essay describing how they have "overcome" any limitation or obstacle (race, ethnicity, gender, age, physical handicap, poverty) in reaching their present standing. The University of Texas at Austin Law School also recently added one-on-one interviews and personal essays about overcoming adversity to its admission process.

Affirmative action is not a cure-all. However, it does recognize that racism is self-perpetuating, not self-correcting. It makes us "do the right thing" when we are not naturally disposed to do such a thing. Affirmative action reminds us of some ugly things about human nature. It is, however, the lesser evil. The options of merit-based selection and equal opportunity policies are limited in redressing the continuing existence of racism. The present concept of affirmative action needs to be stabilized and, perhaps, reformed. However, it must not be eliminated.

After our morning in Sweet Auburn, we catch a quick lunch at Underground Atlanta. This is a six-block area in the heart of Atlanta that, in 1989, was transformed into an urban marketplace. On its three levels, Underground Atlanta now has one hundred specialty retail shops, nearly two dozen food-court vendors, and just as many restaurants and nightclubs. The prices are high, but the food is warm, and, being underground, we are spared from the gathering storm that threatens to hit any moment. Of course, the storm hits at the exact moment that we are leaving for our afternoon appointment at the Center for Democratic Renewal (CDR). In this pelting rain, we will be soaked to the bone in a matter of seconds. Most of my students realize that we will start walking anyway. The skies show no immediate sign of letting up and I would rather be wet and on time than be dry and late. Especially for this appointment.

The privately funded CDR was founded in 1979 as the National Anti-Klan Network. It was the first multiracial organization that was established specifically to monitor, expose, and counter hate groups and hate-

group activity. Through its evolution and 1982 name change, the organization has stayed committed to its mission—promoting a democratic
and just society free of racism and bigotry. Several months ago, I saw the
deputy director of the CDR, Dexter Wimbish, interviewed by Tavis
Smiley of Black Entertainment Network. I was impressed both with
Wimbish and the mission of the CDR and thought a visit with them
would be a great addition to our 1998 itinerary.

Unfortunately, the CDR is so frequently the target of hate-group
threats and violence that they are very hesitant to give out their exact
address. So, we are to meet Wimbish at the corner of two pre-assigned
streets promptly at 2:30 P.M. From there, he will take our group to the
offices of the CDR. The cloak-and-dagger feeling of it all has me a little
bit more anxious than usual. I'm afraid that if we are a minute late to
the meeting point that we will blow the whole opportunity. So, it's off
in the driving rainstorm to meet Wimbish.

We arrive at the meeting point, bedraggled and wet to the bone, only
to find that Wimbish is not there. We wait for a few more soggy minutes
and then, hoping to at least wait in a dry lobby, I begin knocking on doors
and asking local merchants if they have any idea where the CDR is located. However, every person I ask says that they have never heard of the
CDR and suggests that my directions are screwed up. After all, there are
forty-three roads named Peachtree in Atlanta and it's not uncommon for
visitors to become disoriented. Discouraged, I return to the group to find
Wimbish waiting patiently under a large umbrella, having just returned
from a march on the Capitol in support of affirmative action. "Didn't
expect you guys to be here on time in this rain," he says. I can't tell if
he is impressed by our fortitude or amazed at our lack of intelligence.
Regardless, he takes us just a few steps away to the offices of the CDR.
The moisture on me turns to steam as I realize that this *very* lobby is
one of the places where I stopped to ask where the CDR was. The receptionist, who just moments before had told me that she had never heard
of the CDR, smiles sheepishly at me and says, "We can never be too careful about who we let in here."

Wimbish then escorts our group to the main offices of the CDR. The
whole place has an eerie "X-Files" feel to it. It's more than the secrecy

that accompanies the place. It's also the sense that they spend their days, like Fox Mulder and Dana Scully, tracking an almost unimaginable evil. An evil that, in some circles, even has a conspiratorial slant. I get the strong feeling that, if need be, this place could be packed and moved at a moment's notice. The CDR staff members, who are obviously unaccustomed to visitors, flock to the briefing room to get a glance at this sodden group.

After a short introductory video, Wimbish begins the briefing with an overview of the CDR's activities. He briefly describes their strategies for organizing the community on a grassroots level, taking the Klan to task in the courtrooms and in congressional offices, researching the opposition, informing the public, educating the activists, assisting victims, and building networks. Because the effects of the far right are more subtle today than a generation ago, the CDR believes that the most effective strategy is to build and support strong human rights organizations that are in touch with the needs of each community and have the tools and resources to bring about positive change.

As a recent example, Wimbish relates some of the center's activities in response to the black church burnings throughout the nation. To respond to the immediate crisis, the center has fielded media questions; assessed actions that need to be taken and monies that need to be distributed; offered services to churches, pastors, and church members; and collaborated with a national network of church, community, and law enforcement agencies to provide accurate information to the public. With their minds continually on their mission, though, the CDR's chief aim has been to move the rebuilding efforts into community empowerment.

In these offices, however, it is clear that the emphasis is on maintaining the CDR's standing as experts on white supremacy and the far right. The offices are filled with dozens of file cabinets that reflect the center's efforts to monitor the activities and movement of these groups. Staff members collect this information from community activists or, in some cases, by surreptitiously subscribing to newsletters and e-mail distribution lists of hate groups. One large room contains all of the "bad guy" files. Some students are disturbed to see that files on James Dobson, founder of Focus on the Family, and the Promise Keepers movement are both included in this room. One student asks why Dobson is included here. The staff member replies that it is Dobson's push to return to traditional values (code language for restricted roles for women and minorities) coupled with his "medieval" views on abortion that merit him this dishonor. Glad to support anything that may diminish Dobson's influence, I smile and make a mental note to send a contribution to the CDR when I get home. Another student asks where the "good guy" files are. Tellingly, a staff member points to one file cabinet in a small closet down the hallway.

The students are surprised, as am I, to find that the CDR's monitoring activities run broader than the Klan and other white supremacist groups. They also include segments of the far right (such as the Christian Coalition, the John Birch Society, and Pat Buchanan's 1992 presidential campaign), Christian Identity Ideology, Christian Patriot–type organizations, Holocaust denial and revisionists, and even the broad ideology of biological determinists. In short, any ideology, group, or person who promotes hatred, exclusion, or the inferiority of others comes under the watchful eye of the CDR.

My writing, and much of this tour, focuses on the everyday racism that continues to plague minorities across this country. I have been less interested in the sensational discussions surrounding hate crimes and hate groups. I think such discussion distracts us from the more important issues. In reality, it is mostly nice, nonhating people who perpetrate racism in America. I have emphasized the ubiquitous nature of everyday racism rather than the sporadic, but violent, outbreaks of hate crimes. I have focussed on the exclusionary tendencies within each of us rather than scrutinize the breadth of hate groups across our country. However, today's time at the CDR challenges me to rethink my views of both hate crimes and hate groups. As Wimbish reminded us, denial and passivity are the major obstacles to successfully confronting these issues.

A 1997 report published by the Leadership Conference Education Fund and the Leadership Conference on Civil Rights offers the first major comprehensive assessment of the hate crime problem in America. The report, "Cause for Concern: Hate Crimes in America," chronicles the persistence of violent crimes against virtually every racial, ethnic, religious, and sexual orientation minority as well as against women. From killings and beatings to acts of arson and vandalism, these hate crimes injure or even kill thousands of people, terrify countless others, divide Americans against each other, and distort our entire society.

The Hate Crime Statistics Act was passed in 1990 and reauthorized in 1996. This act requires the Department of Justice to compile data on crimes that "manifest prejudice based on race, religion, sexual orientation, or ethnicity" and to publish an annual summary of the findings. Between 1992 and 1995, more than 25,000 hate crimes were reported.

However, these numbers paint only a partial portrait of the scope of the problem. For instance, the total number of law enforcement agencies that reported hate crimes to the FBI covered less than three-quarters of the population of the United States. As a matter of fact, only six of every ten police agencies voluntarily report bias crimes to the FBI. Four-fifths of those say they do not have *any*. Imagine, there were no hate crimes in Alabama, Arkansas, and Mississippi in 1997! How can this be? For one thing, many police departments are put off by the extra FBI paperwork and the prospect of determining a motive as elusive as bias or hate. For another, there is tremendous between-state variation in exactly what constitutes a hate crime. Twenty-one states exclude sexual orientation from their laws. Others add age or gender, whereas some stick to race, creed, and color. Eight states have no hate crime laws at all. Nor do the statistics include hate crimes against women simply because they are women.

In a similar way, proud pronouncements that Ku Klux Klan membership is near a historical low of about five thousand mask the continued growth of hate-group movements across our country. In part, the decline in organized hate groups is a result of debilitating lawsuits brought against them by human rights organizations such as the Southern Poverty Law Center and the Anti-Defamation League. With the success of these lawsuits, however, hate groups have begun to adopt new avenues of recruitment—literature distribution, the Internet, public access television, and local grassroots organizations. These groups complement their recruitment of young people who are alienated from society with more mainstream adults who are angry with the federal government. All in all, the CDR estimates that there are about 150,000 to 200,000 hate-group sympathizers across America. Thus, rather than the decline of organized hate groups, we are witnessing their evolution. As a result, the internal existence of hate groups still poses a far greater danger to the peace of America than any foreign enemies.

I return to the hostel that evening to find an urgent message from the public relations director at Whitworth. I check with him every day or so for any recent publicity contacts I need to follow up on. I suspect he is just a little anxious because I have not called in a few days. "Urgent" has a very subjective meaning in the academic world.

Having a few minutes before the debriefing, I decide to try to reach him before he leaves the office. I catch him and he excitedly says, "The White House called and has been trying to reach you for three days!" "What do they want?" is the only reaction I can immediately muster. "I don't know," he replies, "they just want to talk with you ASAP." He gives me the number and name of the person to contact. I swear my firstborn to him that I will call first thing in the morning. As I hang up the phone, I'm really puzzled. A call from the IRS, or even the FBI, I might understand. But the White House? What could they want? As one student later says, "It's like you got a message from Cindy Crawford just saying she wanted to chat."

I head down to our basement debriefing. It has been a long, packed day, but I want to make sure we take this evening to discuss our reactions to Sweet Auburn and the CDR. As usual, much discussion already has taken place during subway rides and over dinners. But, we will see what more we can learn from each other.

The initial part of our discussion focuses on the general theme of urban parks and preservation. To some degree, the experiences of the tour have given the students a starting point from which to understand memorialization and remembrance. They have seen it done well and they have seen it done not so well. In general, they are very impressed with the National Park Service's treatment of the King birth home.

"While it would have been powerful to see in any setting the piano Martin and his brother attempted to avoid," one student says, "it was even more poignant in his actual house. I am impressed that our government and our nation would work to preserve history in this way." One student, though, questions the inclusion of the birth home in the historic site: "I have a hard time thinking that he [King] would want people touring through his home. I don't know that that is something he would see as necessary. Perhaps study and celebration are a better way of commemorating all that he did for our country. I just don't know about touring someone's home. That just seems like a stretch."

The memorialization at the King Center draws mixed reviews. One student says, "I was in awe to be standing at the site of his grave and yet, when I took a second to look around, the setting seemed odd. Surrounded by concrete, brick and a museum. It just didn't seem like the proper burial ground, it seemed very lonely and 'on display.' The personal belongings [in Freedom Hall], I once again felt were out of place. To see the clothes he wore near the time of his death, his jewelry box with a collection of tie tacks and cuff links, his wallet—all seemed a little too tabloidish for me." Another student disagrees: "I really like how his grave was in the middle of the water. I thought a lot about the concept of water and how it relates to peace. It just seemed so cleansing for his grave to be in the middle of a pool. The water was clear and I liked how it rippled down and settled at the bottom near his grave. It was so calm and beautiful. I felt at rest when I was there."

As the discussion continues, it becomes clear that the greatest challenge posed for the students that morning came from several King quotes on display in the visitor's center. As one student says, "His quotes are so clear. They're also very convincing. It makes me think that if we put them up on billboards, the world's problems would end." One particular quote captures the students: "Every man must decide whether he will walk in the light of creative altruism or the darkness of selfishness. This is the judgment, life's most urgent question is—What are you doing for others?" For my students, all of whom will be facing real-world career choices within the next year or so, this challenge really hits home. One student says: "On this trip, we are between two worlds. We come to observe from our positions of comfort and convenience, but the things we see challenge us to constantly ask ourselves where we are going to stand. What are we going to do now that we can no longer live in ignorance of the world's needs?"

For some of the students, a potential answer to the question of "what can I do" was suggested by our time at the CDR. In one student's excited words, "This place [CDR] is doing *it*. I felt like any far-out, idealistic idea I would come up with that would contribute to change would be supported here. They made it clear that they would help make it happen, with concrete steps, funds, and information. They aren't just sitting there, collecting information, lamenting the overwhelming problems we face. They are *doing* things—all over the country." "I really admired the dedication and determination of the people working, in seclusion and secrecy, at the CDR," another student continues. "I guess they feel that they are eating the elephant one bite at a time, they're just eating their bites with plastic utensils because they can't afford real silverware. I hope I can find something I have as much passion about as they do about stopping Klan activity in the United States." Another student sums up many of our reactions: "I'm thankful that those people at the CDR are there."

As expected, however, the inclusion of certain figures in the "bad guys" files strikes some sensitive chords. For some of the students, the shock of seeing James Dobson and the Promise Keepers on the same "wanted" poster as David Duke is just too much. Others, though, use the occasion to more objectively examine the validity of their preconceptions. One student later writes, "I think the reason it was so difficult for me was not because of my disappointment in James Dobson, but in myself. As I became more informed about the things he [Dobson] stands for and specific things he has said, I found myself remembering certain things I had struggled through with his writing, but had brushed aside wanting to support what I thought was a good cause." Other students question how the CDR defines what they defend. "They [CDR] say that others try to remove freedom," one says, "but they dictate what and how freedom is defined. In the case of abortion, maybe freedom *doesn't* include my right to end a life that is not even mine." Another student continues, "It's great that there are groups like the CDR to watch the hate groups, but, at the same time, I feel that I have to do all I can to educate myself because, like any group, the CDR brings their own biases into what they present."

January 23

Given today's overnight leg on Amtrak, I have left the day completely unscheduled. Some students tour the Margaret Mitchell House, visit the CNN Center (everything in Atlanta seems to have a "center" designation), drop by the graduate admissions office at Emory University, see the Picasso exhibit at the High Museum, or go to the World of Coca-Cola. Others just hang out and wash clothes. It is late in the afternoon before I have a chance to return the call to the White House. My contact is Chandler Spaulding. It turns out that Spaulding is an outreach associate for the President's Initiative on Race. Someone with the initiative heard about our tour, and Spaulding asks if a panel of initiative members could possibly meet with our group while we are in Washington, D.C. We arrange a date and time and Spaulding asks me to forward the names and social security numbers of everyone in the group for security clearance. As I hang up, I simultaneously realize what a great opportunity this is and try to develop a way to give meaning to the opportunity that will not leave the students, and me, in a state of panicked anxiety. For now, though, it is time to make our way to the Amtrak station.

As we pull out of the station, I see a sign heralding Atlanta's most recent self-appointed image as the "Next Great International City." Such an image was unthinkable as recently as the early 1970s, when there were fewer than a hundred major multinational corporations in Atlanta, only four consulate general offices, and only one nonstop flight to Mexico City. Since that time, however, there has been a 425 percent increase in foreign-born residents in Atlanta. Atlanta's "fourth-wave" immigrants (those arriving since 1965) now number more than 266,000 (more than nine percent) of the region's residents. There are now increasing numbers of foreign corporations, more than forty honorary and general consulate offices in the metropolitan area, and more than twenty daily international flights out of Atlanta. Mosques and *taquerias* are springing up, a recent Miss Atlanta was Korean American, and even the head of Coca-Cola is Cuban born.

But exactly how diverse is contemporary Atlanta? To answer this question, Georgia State University's Center for Applied Research in Anthropology developed an "ethnic diversity index" to measure diversity in Atlanta and compare the city to other major metropolitan regions. The goal of the index is to provide a comparative measure of how multicultural or diverse a region "looks" or "feels" to the average person on the street. Thus, numbers of newspapers, radio stations, and television programs devoted to particular ethnic and cultural groups are weighed more heavily than numbers of multinational corporations with regional offices. The index ranges from plus one to negative one. A score of plus one represents a world where no particular group has a majority and diversity characterizes the demographic mix. A score of negative one indicates no diversity whatsoever.

As scored on this index, Atlanta is surprisingly monocultural. In other words, there is not an observable "critical mass" of diversity to the average person on the street. In fact, of the ten cities tested, only two (Birmingham and St. Louis, both with negative scores) were lower than Atlanta's score of +0.21. Atlanta's score falls well below such cities as Dallas, Chicago, and Miami and very far below the two most diverse regions—Los Angeles and San Francisco (each around +0.70).

How can a city with such an explosion of growth in its international population "feel" so nondiverse to the average person on the street? Part of the answer lies in the fact that the newcomers are not necessarily those for which the city had planned or wished. The majority of the fourth-wave immigrants are working-class or peasant peoples from Latin America (primarily Mexico) or Asia (primarily Southeast Asia). These are not the middle-class professionals Atlanta had hoped to attract. In addition, these new immigrants do not fit into the dichotomous social categories to which the city historically is accustomed—black or white.

As a result, there has been a predictable backlash against these "newcomers." Today, issues of race in Atlanta are no longer restricted to black and white. Some of the more egregious incidents are described by urban anthropologists Rebecca J. Dameron and Arthur D. Murphy of Georgia State University: "In one famous incident a homeowner suggested that bear traps be placed in people's yards to keep out the undesirables. Neighbors of convenience stores complained about young men who stood out front waiting for work. Police began to harass individuals who 'looked illegal,' asking for immigration documents they had no right to request. An English-only ordinance was introduced and eventually passed in the state legislature. The most popular talk show host in the city responded to white and black resentment against these enclaves by labeling Chamblee [an industrial community on the northeastern edge of Atlanta] 'Chambodia,' a term that was repeated to one of the authors by a state legislator when discussing the question of the role of immigrants in Georgia's economy."

Clearly, the dominant power structures in Atlanta, which still reflect the traditional and hard-won black-white configuration, must accommodate the demands for social change coming from the fourth-wave immigrants. In addition, the newer minorities—taking a page from black history in Atlanta—must develop an active electoral bloc as well as an understanding and willingness to play the insider game of Atlanta politics. The analysis of Alejandro Portes and Alex Stepick in their review of the transformation of Miami applies equally well to these new Atlantans: "Immigrants do not first learn to be 'Americans,' and only then are freely admitted into the mainstream. Rather they become Americans by elbowing their way into centers of local power through the political mobilization of ethnic solidarity." How well Atlanta learns to share the power will greatly affect its viability as the "Next Great International City."

9. WASHINGTON, D.C.: THE BEGINNING OF A COUNTRY AND THE END OF OUR LINE

It is a city of temporaries, a city of just-arrived and only-visitings,
built on the shifting sands of politics, filled with people just passing
through.

Allen Drury, *Advise and Consent*

January 24

We arrive at beautiful Union Station in the heart of Washington, D.C.
We have just a few hours before our afternoon tour with Capitol Entertainment Services. They are a privately owned, black business that offers
guided tours of the national monuments and memorials and—what
brings us to them—a black heritage tour. It is a four-hour whirlwind tour
that comes too close on the heels of an overnight leg on Amtrak. Regardless, for those who stay awake, it does give some redeeming insights into
the story of the black community in the nation's capital.

Our first stop is the National Museum of American History at the
Smithsonian Institution. Here, we take a brisk stroll through the exhibit
"Field to Factory: Afro-American Migration, 1915–1940." We have seen
firsthand the impact of the Great Migration on the demographics of Chicago. However, that mass movement remains one of our century's least
studied and most poorly understood (at least in its ramifications) historical events. This special exhibit is an attempt to rectify that. It interprets
the complexities and effects of the Great Migration by focusing on the
migrants themselves. Here we vividly see the lives of blacks in the
South, the hopes and expectations that prompted the decision to move
north, and the difficulties faced in a new environment—both in the migrants' adjustment and the adjustment of others to them. Included here
are displays of a tenant farmhouse from southern Maryland, a re-creation
of a row house from Philadelphia, and more than four hundred artifacts
and documents. Through it all, one begins to appreciate the significance
and difficulty of the migrants' decision to leave family, home, and
friends.

As we hustle out of the exhibit, we pass by a simple, unobtrusive
display that catches someone's eye and then spreads like wildfire to each
of us: a lunch counter from the downtown Woolworth's store in Greens-

boro, North Carolina. It was at this very counter and on these very stools that four freshmen from a local black college, North Carolina A&T, had sat on February 1, 1960. They were refused service at the sacrosanct whites-only lunch counter, but sat there unperturbed all afternoon and vowed to return at 10:00 the next morning to continue what they called a "sit-down protest." Later that week, sympathetic sit-ins began in Durham, Raleigh, and other North Carolina cities. Within days, the movement leaped across state lines into South Carolina and Tennessee. By the end of February, sit-in campaigns were under way in thirty-one southern cities across eight states. The "sit-down protest" would galvanize the Civil Rights movement among college students and become one of the most effective activist strategies. And it all started on these very stools. Unfortunately, this is not an "official" site on our tour itinerary and we are quickly hustled past the exhibit before we can really take it in.

After some more blurred drive-bys, we arrive at our next stop—the Frederick Douglass home at Cedar Hill. We had read about Douglass's background in our fall preparation course. We knew that he was born a slave in Maryland in 1818 (his mother was a slave and his father white, perhaps her owner). In 1838, Douglass fled to New York and then to Massachusetts, where he joined the abolitionist movement. Entirely self-educated, he became an eloquent speaker, author, and journalist for the abolitionist cause. During the Civil War, Douglass counseled President Lincoln and urged blacks, including his sons, to join the Union Army. After the war, he supported the constitutional amendments that granted blacks citizenship and the right to vote. Douglass also was well-known as a women's rights advocate, bank president, essayist, newspaper publisher, fluent speaker of many languages, Minister to Haiti, and the most respected black orator of the nineteenth century.

Frederick Douglass was nearly sixty years old when he purchased this 1850s brick hilltop house (thus breaking a "whites-only" covenant), which he named Cedar Hill. In his later years, this beautifully situated house proved to be a welcome respite for reading, exercise, and lively discussions about politics. Throughout the house are scattered mementos of his incredible life—Lincoln's cane given to him by Mrs. Lincoln after the assassination, a leather rocking chair from the people of Haiti, and a handcarved German clock. Most fascinating, though, is the desk given to him by Harriet Beecher Stowe. It was on this desk that Stowe penned the history-changing *Uncle Tom's Cabin* in 1851 and 1852. Douglass died at Cedar Hill in 1895. Today, the home is part of the Frederick Douglass National Historic Site administered by the National Park Service.

From the Douglass home, we make a very quick stop at the Anacostia Museum. This museum is devoted to the identification, documentation, and preservation of the black experience in the Upper South. Through a series of special exhibitions, the museum examines contemporary social issues and their impact upon black communities in the region. Although it is a Smithsonian National Museum, the Anacostia is in the southeast corner of the city, distant from its more visited cousins on the mall. However, as the guide explains to us, the thought behind its location was to place it in an area where residents of the district less likely to visit the museums on the mall, predominately lower-income blacks, would have a readily accessible exhibit about their heritage.

On the day we visit, one of the two exhibits is a collection representing decades of work by Muhammad Ali's personal photographer. The collection includes stills from Ali's fights, informal portraits with other famous celebrities, and candid pictures of Ali's private life. The second exhibit is "Man Made: African-American Men and Quilting Traditions." This unique exhibition features quilts made by black men ranging from the 9-year-old Herbert Munn to the 105-year-old Benjamin Jackson. I know it would be enlightened of me to learn more about the "conspiracy of silence" surrounding black men and quilting traditions. In the brief time we have, though, it just does not catch me and I find myself spending most of my time in the Ali exhibit. I console myself by thinking that even the men who made these quilts might have made the same choice.

We are quickly off to a drive-by of Lincoln Park on East Capitol Street between Eleventh and Thirteenth Streets. In 1876, a statue of Lincoln was unveiled in this park named in honor of the Great Emancipator. (This was the city's primary tribute to Lincoln until the Lincoln Memorial was dedicated in 1922.) Called the Emancipation Memorial, the statue was paid for solely with funds donated by freed slaves, many of them soldiers in the Union Army during the war. The life-sized Lincoln, which was sculpted by Thomas Ball, stands with the Emancipation Proclamation in one hand and the other hand extended toward a black man breaking out of shackles. The liberated slave is made in the likeness of Archer Alexander, the last man captured under the Fugitive Slave Law.

Almost a century later, in 1974, a statue of black educator Mary McLeod Bethune was erected in Lincoln Park by the National Council of Negro Women, the organization she had founded in 1935. In an evocative depiction, the energetic teacher is reaching out to two children as if to hand on her legacy of self-respect, pride, and a love of learning. This was the first monument in a District of Columbia park to honor a black woman. The Lincoln statue, which originally faced the Capitol, was turned to face the Bethune memorial.

As our fourth hour winds down, we ride through the historic U Street corridor in the Shaw neighborhood. This mostly black neighborhood is named for Colonel Robert Gould Shaw, the white commanding officer of the Massachusetts 54th Volunteer Infantry, the band of black soldiers depicted in the 1989 film "Glory." In its heyday, the U Street corridor was referred to as "Black Broadway." It was the home of Duke Ellington and the place where Billie Holiday and Ethel Waters performed in velvet-chaired theaters. The corridor is also the home of one of the most prestigious historically black universities in the nation—Howard University. Until the end of legalized segregation in the 1950s, the Shaw neighborhood was the business and retail hub of the city's black community. Following Martin Luther King Jr.'s assassination in 1968, however, the area was decimated by riots. Rebuilding efforts followed, only to be derailed by the extensive construction of a Metro subway stop in the heart of the area in the 1980s. "What the riots didn't do to tear up U Street, the Metro finished," says one longtime resident. Today, the area continues to struggle to rebound from the construction.

Even good news is tainted in the Shaw neighborhood. After two postponements for lack of money, in July 1998 the Shaw neighborhood finally enjoyed the long-anticipated unveiling of the nearly completed African American Civil War Memorial. Designed to honor the more than 180,000 blacks who served with the Union forces during the Civil War, the memorial is a $1.6 million piece of an ongoing effort by black Americans to publicize history often excluded from textbooks, movies, and popular culture. Now, the only question that remains is whether funds will be found to complete the memorial.

Some local activists are doubtful. They argue that when the recipients of the honor are black, funding and accountability are tough to come by—even in a city enamored with memorials. Others even suggest that there continue to be a curse on the black men who took up arms to defend a country that never did much to defend them. Still others blame inept city leadership and political in-fighting for the delays. Regardless of where the blame falls, most agree that the initial enthusiasm for the memorial has waned almost to the point of apathetic neglect. As journalist Laura Lang writes, "What's sad is a city that waits until the 1990s to start building a national memorial to 1860s black Americans, then spends eight years tinkering away without finishing it." Even if the memorial *is* finished, some still will see it only as a salt-in-the-wound reminder that there is no memorial to blacks on the mall. This is just another illustration of an eternal rule—there is no such thing as a controversy-free monument in the nation's capital.

The subtext of the black heritage tour lies in the story of how Washington, D.C., came to exist. Located along the Potomac River, it was chosen as the permanent site of the United States capital by Congress in 1790. It was President George Washington, however, who was given power by Congress to choose the exact site for a federal city where lawmakers could conduct the business of government. The chosen site, from land given by Virginia and Maryland, was a ten-square-mile area. President Washington negotiated with Pierre-Charles L'Enfant to lay out a plan for the new city, making it the first large city in modern times to be planned before its actual construction. Congress mandated a ten-year construction period, with the federal government taking official residence on the first Monday in December 1800. It was more than symbolic that one of the surveyors who assisted in mapping the boundaries of the federal city was a free black, Benjamin Banneker.

The 1800 census listed 3,210 residents of Washington, including 623 slaves (about twenty percent of the population) and 123 free blacks. By 1850, the number of slaves had declined to just five percent of the city's population. By 1860, blacks made up a full one-third of Washington's total population. During and after the Civil War, the district's population more than doubled within a few years to suddenly include 40,000 freed slaves. These former slaves set a pattern of racial diversity that was to have a major impact on the city's life. They exercised their own national ambitions for freedom and established a thriving community in the nation's capital. Looking to northern cities like Philadelphia for models, blacks developed important institutions, including schools, churches and fraternal organizations, which existed apart from whites.

After the Emancipation Proclamation and the passage of the Thirteenth Amendment, new freed blacks from the South continued to find a strong and welcoming black community in Washington, D.C. By the turn of the century, the District of Columbia had the largest urban population of blacks in the United States. However, the Great Migration of the early twentieth century guided hundreds of thousands of blacks directly to northern industrial cities, and by 1930 New York, Chicago, Philadelphia, and Baltimore all had larger black populations.

In the 1960s, the city was home to several pivotal events in the Civil Rights movement—most notably the 1963 march on Washington and King's dramatic "I Have a Dream" speech on the steps of the Lincoln Memorial. More than simply being a stage, however, the city itself was uniquely transformed by the movement. Since its earliest years, the city government of Washington, D.C.—regardless of which of the several forms of government prevailed—had been under the direct or indirect control of Congress. Until 1961, residents of the district were even denied the right to vote. After that year, qualified people could vote in presidential elections, but still had no voice in elections of local officials, all of whom continued to be appointed by Congress.

In the district, the Civil Rights movement translated into a movement for home rule. Residents believed that the responsiveness of Congress to district issues was slow or entirely lacking. Some also noted that the congressional committees charged with district responsibilities tended to be dominated by Southerners who resisted efforts to give home rule to a district with an increasing black majority. In the face of sustained pressure, Congress finally reorganized the district's government in 1967 and, three years later, created the position of a nonvoting delegate to the House of Representatives who was elected by residents of the district. Finally, in 1973, limited home rule was granted to the district—the first measure of self-government in almost one hundred years. With home rule came provisions for the popular election every four years of the mayor and city council members. The city council was empowered to establish and set tax rates and fees, make changes in the budget, and organize or abolish any government agency of the district.

It bears noting, however, that Congress did reserve the right to veto any actions of the district government that threatened the "federal interest." That range of power even extended to cases where Congress believed the district was a threat to its *own* interest. In 1995, after the city's debt had climbed to $722 million and showed no signs of a turnaround, Congress flexed its territorial muscle and created the District of Columbia Financial Responsibility and Management Assistance Authority (more commonly known as the Financial Control Board). The five board members are appointed by the president and approved by Congress. They have the authority to hire and fire personnel, approve budgets and contracts, hold hearings, solicit public input, and restructure the city government. In 1997, a legislative amendment transferred operational control of most of the city's government from the mayor to the board. In many minds, the creation of this "rescue package" board has stripped the district of any vestige of its hard-won right to self-rule.

The Financial Control Board is supposed to retain power until the district eases its debt and operates under a balanced budget for several consecutive fiscal years. Under current law, the board would remain in place through 2001. However, Washington, D.C. Delegate Eleanor Holmes Norton introduced a bill in January 1999 to jump-start the restoration of self-government by returning power to the mayor and the council after the city balances its budget this year. Norton's bill argues that Congress should strip the control board of power one year ahead of schedule because the city's financial recovery has been more rapid than anticipated. Her bill also states that Congress can aid the city's recovery by granting "clear and unambiguous authority" to the mayor to run the city. The bill, known as the D.C. Democracy 2000 Act, became the first bill of the 106th Congress signed into law.

Today, Washington, D.C., is a metropolis with two faces. One face is the 2,809-square-mile metropolitan area (including two counties in Maryland and the cities of Fairfax, Falls Church, and Alexandria and four counties in Virginia). The 1990 census counted nearly four million people in this area. Of that figure, 37.8 percent were minorities, with the greatest portion of those (26.6 percent) being black. Two-thirds of Washington's employed live outside the District of Columbia and represent a work force that is highly specialized, professionally skilled, and well above the national averages in educational level and per capita income. More than one-fourth of the people over twenty-six years of age in the metropolitan area hold college degrees, the highest percentage among the ten largest metropolitan areas in the country. The area's population also has one of the highest annual per capita incomes in the nation.

The other face of Washington, D.C., is the central city core. Here, the complexity of social, economic, and political problems contrasts sharply with the surrounding suburbs and counties. For instance, when one analyzes the racial demographics of the area, sharp disparities arise. A close examination of the distribution of the black population in the metropolitan area makes it apparent that the vast majority is clustered in the central city core of the district. On the relative clustering index of the U.S. Census Bureau, only Chicago (3.039) and Los Angeles (2.853) have a higher degree of racial enclaves (Washington, D.C.'s score is 2.055).

Like the central city core of other metropolitan areas, the district's population is in flux. The population, which was nearly 800,000 in 1965, was counted at 606,900 in the 1990 census. Estimates from the 1998 census indicate that the district was down to fewer than 554,000 residents, a decline of more than eight percent from its 1990 population. The downsizing of the district stems from afflictions familiar to other big cities—private-sector jobs are moving to the suburbs, city services and the tax base are deteriorating, real estate values are dropping, and people do not feel safe from crime. In fact, the major acceleration of population loss occurred in 1989 in tandem with the crack epidemic and a record homicide rate. However, another factor that is unique to the district impacts the exodus—the problem of shrinking government employment.

Both blacks and whites have moved out of the district in substantial numbers. Slightly more than half of the households who left the city for nearby suburbs from 1990 to 1995 were black. In an odd way, this pattern of migration has accentuated even more starkly the racial and economic imbalance in the district. Washington, D.C., has become a place only the rich can afford to live in and the poor cannot afford to leave. Thus, the relatively few people moving *into* the district tend to be single and white. Although that "gentrification" process has resulted in the upgrading of a number of residential areas in the district, it has only aggravated the problems of household displacement among the poor. Those who have no choice but to remain tend to be black families.

When it all plays out, one is left with a city whose majority population (about two-thirds) is black and where the unemployment rate, especially among youth, ranges well above the national average. Educational level and per capita income are considerably below the averages found in the surrounding suburbs. In fact, as of 1996, 24.1 percent of the city's residents lived below the poverty level (compared to a nationwide figure of 13.7 percent). Outside of the major tourist avenues, large areas of the city are in advanced stages of physical and spiritual decay. Add to this an incredibly high rate of crime, and it is easy to see why a 1999 study by the Children's Rights Council listed the District of Columbia as the worst place in the nation to raise kids.

Further exacerbating the differences between the city and the metropolitan area is the reality that the living and working populations of Washington, D.C., are among the most transient in the nation. Thus, there is neither the social stability nor the continuity that provides the lifeblood of most other large cities. A high proportion of government and service workers commutes into the city from suburban homes. These more affluent workers typically spend most of their income and pay most of their taxes in adjacent counties and states. City residents, who are mostly black, also depend on the opportunities offered for federal employment, but generally lack the educational qualifications for jobs at higher incomes.

Differences between the city and the metropolitan area also can be seen in life-span statistics. Men in the district have nearly the shortest life span of any population group in the United States. Their counterparts across the Potomac River in Fairfax County, however, are nearly the longest-lived men. An average man's life span in the two places differs by 14.5 years. The picture is even more bleak for black male Washingtonians. Their 1990 life expectancy of 57.9 years was the second shortest in the country. Only Oglala Sioux men of the Pine Ridge Reservation, who live an average of 56.6 years, are likely to die younger. These life expectancies are similar to ones seen in many countries of sub-Saharan Africa and are lower than those of any nation in this hemisphere, except Haiti.

Unfortunately, the future for both the district and its residents is not much brighter. The city has minimal local control of its revenue system, it lacks a significant taxable industry, and the great majority of its real estate is tax exempt. As a result, Washington, D.C., is forced to depend heavily on intergovernmental revenue and monies that, in effect, constitute payment by the federal government in lieu of the taxes it would pay if it were a private industry.

At that night's debriefing, it is clear that a shower, change of clothes, and relaxing dinner has done wonders for all of our spirits. In retrospect, it is also clear that the black heritage tour *did* give us some important insights into the black presence in the development of our nation's capital. Students were especially struck by the authenticity of the Douglass home and the experience of standing on the floorboards where so many luminaries—Harriet Beecher Stowe, Elizabeth Cady Stanton, John Brown, and Harriet Tubman—had stood. Had we been better rested, chances are we would have taken away even more from the tour. Regardless, it connected our reading with some actual historic sites and reminded us of why we are here—to see with the other's eyes.

I close the debriefing by reminding the students to be diligent about their personal safety. I emphasized this in the fall preparation course and

I have occasionally reiterated it in discussions throughout the tour. However, this city scares me. It is up to its monuments in crime. As much as I love it here, the high crime rate raises my *in loco parentis* antennae to the nth degree. The city has at least 6,100 armed federal law enforcement officers—more than twice as many as most *states* have. And that figure does not even including the district's 3,600 municipal police officers. In a city with a population of about 540,000, that is 18 law enforcement officers for every 1,000 residents—more than seven times the national average.

Despite that presence, there is an average of about 60,000 serious crimes committed annually in the city. That rate dwarfs those of such similarly sized cities as El Paso, Seattle, and Boston. In 1996, the violent crime rate per 100,000 residents was nearly four times higher than the rest of the nation. The number of federal and state prisoners per 10,000 residents was also nearly four times higher than the rest of the nation.

How can this be? Part of the reason can be attributed to mismanagement. A 1996 study, for instance, found that only between 350 and 700 officers in the 3,600-member municipal force were assigned patrol cars last year. The study also found that the officers on this force did not see crime reduction as their responsibility, their leadership lacked vision, and morale was low. Complicating the matter further is the fact that most federal officers are assigned to fixed posts in secure federal facilities with narrowly defined jurisdictions that barely extend to the city's sidewalks. In many cases, a federal officer who witnesses a crime on a city street must call 9-1-1 to notify the local police. All told, a surprisingly small number of the city's law enforcement officers actually patrol the streets.

Another part of the reason can be attributed to ignorant denial. On a July 5, 1996, CNN program, then mayor Marion Barry announced that Washington, D.C., was as "safe or safer than Topeka [Kansas]." During that same holiday weekend, however, there were six murders in the city—as many as Topeka had all year to that point. Whatever the reason, I zealously remind the students that Washington, D.C., isn't Kansas and that we must not let the fortunate fact that we have gone relatively unscathed through the tour cloud our judgment in these last days.

Political controversy in Washington, D.C., has never been limited to the federal government. Locals have had their fair share of fodder from sexual escapades, mismanagement, and drug use among their politicians. In a city where the majority of residents are black, race has often played a role as well. In the most recent example, the city is still buzzing over the December 1997 Financial Control Board appointment of Camille C. Barnett, a white woman, as the city's new chief management officer. The fact that this new chief management officer's annual salary of $155,000 was about $65,000 more than that paid to the mayor did not sit well with Barry. The fact that Barnett was white did not sit well with most of the city's residents, the majority of whom are black.

"The appointment of the new city manager reminds me of a story they tell in black churches," one e-mail to a local columnist began. "The preacher said to the congregation 'Let us pray for Sister Mary who is sick.' 'How sick is she?' shouted one of the congregants. 'She's sick enough for a white doctor.' I guess that's the way the control board feels about D.C., also." "It's not about talent, Sir," the e-mail continued, "it's about us being able to seem like we are fixing our own problems. Some of the sting would've been taken out of this had she been a local woman with local ties [Barnett was then working with a consulting firm based in Raleigh, North Carolina]. She said she's going to live in a 'funky' neighborhood. Great start! This is the new version of *Out of Africa*."

Other people agreed that the city had been handed the crowning racial insult—the appointment of a white woman to oversee a majority black work force. Another e-mail to the same columnist said, "There is no way that a thinking person could conclude other then [sic] that the appointment of a white woman to fix the problems of D.C. was a calculated act to further embarrass the citizens of color in the District." One local talk show host said that the move had rekindled discussion of "The Plan" among his listeners, many of whom believe that the white power structure is moving to retake control of the district. Mark Thompson, cochair of the Stand Up for Democracy Coalition, warned: "The appointment of Camille Cates Barnett could right now be the city's greatest potential for racial division. To have a white person come in and effectively be made mayor *de facto*, and appoint her to that position, is an insult."

Others countered that the Financial Control Board, with four out of five black members, selected Barnett *in spite of* her being a white woman and simply because she was the best person for the job. As columnist Colbert I. King of the *Washington Post* argued, "I believe it is logical, morally consistent and well within the range of normal intelligence to conclude that a majority black financial control board had something in mind other than the humiliation of black people when it chose Barnett to be chief management officer." At times, the dialogue reached scathingly sarcastic depths. "The very idea, a white person having a job of significance in the District," one letter to King began. "Don't we all know only black people can have jobs running the District? Of course, the fact that only black people have been running this town over the past 20 years—and running it into the ground—seems to escape attention."

Just over one year later, on January 7, 1999, Barnett resigned as Washington's chief management officer. She said her resignation was best for the new administration of Mayor Anthony A. Williams because the city is speeding toward the restoration of home rule. However, locals said she had underestimated the racial divisions in the district and was never able to overcome the animosity engendered by her initial hiring.

January 25

Psychologist James Jones of the University of Delaware has developed a model reflecting the basic ways in which individuals and cultures orient themselves to life. His approach, the TRIOS model, contends that there are five dimensions of human experience relative to this orientation: time, rhythm, improvisation, oral expression, and spirituality. These dimensions refer to how we experience and organize life, make decisions, arrive at beliefs, and derive meaning. Individually, we vary along these dimensions. Culturally and ethnically, we vary as well. As such, the dimensions can serve as tools in helping us appreciate the richness of America's racial diversity.

On this Sunday morning, the students and I will get a chance to experience one of the five dimensions of the black experience—spirituality. It is especially germane because poll respondents routinely credit black churches with having the greatest influence on improved conditions for black Americans. We will be attending the Sunday morning worship service at Metropolitan Baptist Church in the Shaw neighborhood. Founded in 1864, Metropolitan Baptist has nearly five thousand members and stands as one of the most active and respected black churches in the district. Under the leadership of Dr. H. Beecher Hicks Jr., this middle-class church has expanded its social activism in the Shaw neighborhood.

Following the church secretary's suggestion, we arrive about twenty minutes before the morning service is scheduled to begin. At my suggestion, the group disperses in small groups of two or three to sit throughout the sanctuary. Metropolitan Baptist is a predominately black congregation and the thought of twenty-two white faces sitting in a clump seems too forced. It could only be worse if we hung placards around our necks. I want the students to melt into the setting as much as possible and have a host of individual experiences rather than one big group experience.

We have been on the road now for nearly three weeks. Everywhere we have gone, we have been a visitor. There is something deep inside each of us that yearns to be "home" again, to feel the comfort of a heartfelt welcome, to know the ease engendered by a friendly smile and warm hug, to feel the consolation that only similarity brings. I did not necessarily put Metropolitan Baptist on the itinerary to fill any of these yearnings. Over the next three hours, though, the "academic" goal of passively experiencing spirituality in a predominately black church will be swept away as the congregants of Metropolitan Baptist take us to their hearts and welcome us like long-lost children.

To most of us, our time at Metropolitan Baptist is one of the highlights of the trip—even for the several among us who would not identify themselves as having a strong religious conviction. At a point where we have begun to wonder if simple peaceful, parallel coexistence is the most realistic hope for race relations in America, the parishioners at Metropolitan rekindle the hope that our similarities can unite us more than our differences divide us. Perhaps actual friendship—deep, abiding, significant relationships—between people of different races is possible, if only we can keep our eyes on the things that join rather than those that split. Over the next three hours, religion redeems itself as we glimpse its promise of reconciliation.

At its best, religion can unite its followers in a way that few other experiences can. In pursuit of a common ideal, religion can mask—or at least render secondary—many of the differences that we use to draw lines of demarcation between "us" and "them." From the beginning of the service, the students and I feel part of "them." "Even when we all stood up as visitors," one student later wrote, "I never felt 'white' or something 'other' than these people." Another wrote, "When we first got there, I thought that everyone was looking at me because I was white. I thought people would be thinking, 'What's she doing here?' As soon as we sat down, a woman to my left greeted me with "Good morning!" She reached for my hand and held it tight. She lingered there and smiled. I felt welcomed and relieved. . . . In church, she felt like my sister. . . . It was strange. I felt like I knew them. I felt also that we were so much alike."

For most of the students, this was their first experience with the spiritual diversity of a predominately black church. "What do you say about your first time?" one wrote. "I was a virgin at attending black worship services and the only word I can think of is beautiful. This described the service to me in every way. The music was such, the people were such, and the words were even such. . . . They were open to reconciliation and were happy to see that we were there. . . . After seeing so much hopelessness in the area of race relations, it was refreshing to be welcomed and to see a community so alive." Another student thoughtfully considered the implications of religion for the larger issue of reconciliation: "I am left to wonder if racial reconciliation is possible only through spiritual healing. I ultimately believe it is, but how this is to function in a secular state really frustrates me at times. I do not believe in constructing a religious state, but I do not see the vibrancy in political thought that I see in this church."

After the service, we are greeted by dozens of people who want to express their thanks for our attending their church. I don't think I have shaken so many hands since the birth of our first baby. Finally, we make our way out and several growling stomachs head with me to Ben's Chili Bowl, a U Street institution. The sense of renewal we feel stands in marked contrast to the isolation and tiredness we felt just hours before.

If someone had told us earlier this morning that we were about to be subjected to a nearly three-hour church service, I think "renewal" would have been the last word to come to mind.

At the posted recommendation of Bill Cosby, I order a bowl of chili and a side of fries. As I listen to the students excitedly process their reactions to our time at Metropolitan Baptist, the cynic in me returns and hopes we do not forget that—despite what we experienced today—religion divides more often than it unites. It is at least partially instructive to recognize that Sunday morning remains the most segregated time of the week in America. Even in its pursuit of a common ideal, religion can institutionalize a bland "sameness" that neglects the diversity of heritage, history, and gifts in its members. I also hope we remember that the road to racial reconciliation is long and difficult. If there were an easy answer (such as, "Let's all go to church together"), we would have solved the problem by now. I think it is time for me to get some fresh air.

For the rest of the day, students are off to tour various sites, rest, or do a final load of laundry. Most will be jockeying for prime seats at a local bar or restaurant to watch John Elway finally get his coveted ring as the Denver Broncos beat the Green Bay Packers in Super Bowl XXXII. I have the final galley proofs of my book to review and rush back to the publisher. As the students head off, I remind them of our 10:30 A.M. appointment tomorrow at the U.S. Holocaust Memorial Museum.

January 26

The Dalai Lama of Tibet became the U.S. Holocaust Memorial Museum's first visitor when it opened its doors on April 22, 1993. In addition to being our national institution for the documentation, study, and interpretation of Holocaust history, the museum also serves as our country's memorial to the millions of people murdered during the Holocaust. Like any memorial, though, the museum became quickly steeled in the hot fires of controversy.

Edward Linenthal's *Preserving Memory: The Struggle to Create America's Holocaust Museum* chronicles the obstacle course of political, logistical, ideological, and spiritual dilemmas in the fifteen-year struggle surrounding the birth of the museum. When the Carter administration decided to create a commission to recommend an appropriate national Holocaust memorial, it was often derided as simply a move to appease domestic Jewish interests—especially after Carter's decision to sell a fleet of F-15 fighter planes to Saudi Arabia in 1978. On a larger political scale, the memorial was seen as a gratuity in the administration's support for the State of Israel. More significantly, many wondered about the impact of the museum on the ongoing Israeli-Arab conflict. Would the museum foster the use of the Holocaust as a weapon by which Jews claimed innocence and righteousness and, thereby, become blinded to the injustices they inflict on Palestinians?

Logistical questions regarding the appropriate location of the memorial and the appropriate building were equally contentious. For survivors, a museum within the monumental core of the mall was especially important. It was viewed as an eternal insurance policy, proof that the Holocaust actually happened. However, when the government donated the land for the museum just adjacent to the mall and only a few hundred yards from the Washington Monument, controversy arose regarding the appropriateness of that placement. Many argued that the museum was misplaced because the Holocaust was not an American event. Both Jews and non-Jews worried that resentment about Jews "pushing their way onto the mall" would spark a new wave of antisemitism. One survivor, Dr. Laszlo Tauber, was so concerned about this possibility that he personally offered to provide funding and land in Virginia.

Ideological debates also raged over exactly what and how the museum would depict the Holocaust. Survivors often expressed their fear of again being victimized through the murder of memory. Who would be included as victims of the Holocaust? What about representatives of non-Jewish groups who claimed that their "particular" death also belonged within the boundaries of the museum? How could the perpetrators be portrayed without glorification? More sensitively, how would America's role in the Holocaust be interpreted? For instance, many felt that President Franklin D. Roosevelt was guilty of inaction with regard to rescuing Europe's Jews, but that a federally funded memorial might be ahistorically apologetic for his actions or lack thereof.

Finally, there were profound spiritual dilemmas—relatively unheard of in the construction of other memorials—regarding the redemptive meaning of the Holocaust. For some, it was important that the museum be America's official "conscience-salving" symbol that offered the promise of hope and reconciliation and the vanquishing of evil. Insofar as Americans were complicit bystanders during the Holocaust, that guilt could be redeemed by a penitential act—federal support for the Holocaust museum. For others, visitors to the museum should leave challenged by the *lack* of redemptive meaning in the Holocaust. Even a "healthy" dose of chastisement and shame might arouse enough strong emotion to bring about a moral transformation. Some survivors even felt "defiled" by the mere request to cede their sacred stories to the brick and mortar of an impersonal museum. There was a fear that a physical installation might actually destroy human memory by reifying past events in an object.

The controversies did not end with the opening of the museum's doors. In the immediate weeks preceding our trip, for example, the museum went through two well-publicized storms. The first centered on a fourteen-minute introductory film, "Antisemitism," included in the museum's permanent exhibition. It introduces the Jewish origins of Christianity and the fact that some Gospel accounts seem to be "blaming the Jews and their leaders for the crucifixion." It recounts Christianity's rise to prominence following the Roman destruction of the Temple in Jerusalem. The film includes the invective of the early church fathers against the Jews "as agents of the devil and murderers of God" as well as snippets from Martin Luther's antisemitic diatribes of the sixteenth century. The film identifies Hitler as a baptized Catholic and quotes him as saying, "In defending myself against the Jews, I am acting for the Lord. The difference between the church and me is that I am finishing the job." After a brief review of the Holocaust, the film winds up with a two-sentence conclusion: "In the aftermath of the Holocaust, Christian churches are re-examining their teaching on the Jews and Judaism. In 1994, the Evangelical Lutheran Church in America rejected Martin Luther's writings on the Jews."

On December 5, 1997, six Jewish conservatives, among them Elliot Abrams, Michael Horowitz, and Michael Medved, sent a letter of protest to then director Walter Reich. The letter charged that "the film advances a profoundly inaccurate thesis: that Christianity and Christian leaders were the initial cause of anti-Semitism and have at all times been its major proponents. . . . The film takes the clear position that anti-Semitism originated with Christianity." "For all the sins of anti-Semitism committed in its name," the letter continued, "Christianity's historical effect has been democratizing and civilizing." They asked to meet with Reich "in order to set a process in motion" to evaluate the film and in hopes of seeing it thoroughly revised. The letter did not persuade Reich to set up such a meeting, although it did lead to a flurry of name-calling and finger-wagging.

A scathing column by literary editor Leon Wieseltier in the *New Republic*, for instance, called the letter "an ignorant and indecent document." "It is all kampf and no kultur, a model of the traduction of history by politics." Not to be outdone by Wieseltier's venom and vocabulary, Horowitz responded that the "signers of the letter critiquing the film have long dealt with smarter, less bloviated [sic] interlocutors than Wieseltier." Abrams took the baton for the next leg of the verbal riposte: "Leon Wieseltier's 'Diarist' screed—full of insults, name-calling, and sheer nastiness—appears to be motivated by personal animus of unknown origin. That his argument was *ad hominem* may be explained by the apparent fact that he did not bother to see the film in question before setting poison to paper."

Even conservative Christians looked up from whatever they were doing and added their two bits in support of the protest letter. In a commentary in the *National Review*, David Neff (executive editor of *Christianity Today* magazine) alleged that the film was another "historiographical enterprise bent on reducing Christianity to a history of oppression" and that this "historiography of oppression cannot afford to recognize the positive, democratizing, and liberating influences of the Church throughout the centuries." Another editorial in *Christianity Today* raised the question of "the inclusion of this anti-Christian message in a tax-funded national museum." "As a museum of conscience," the editorial continued, "the U.S. Holocaust Museum has a responsibility to report how Jews have suffered, in large part because of morally repugnant stereotyping. How ironic and sad that its own film should foster inaccurate stereotypes of Christianity!"

Raised again here was a debate that has engaged many Holocaust scholars for decades: To what degree did Christian beliefs about Jewish unbelief simply *set the historical stage* for the Holocaust and to what degree did they actually *contribute* to the Holocaust? In other words, exactly how much guilt should Christianity bear for the destruction of European Jewry? Unfortunately, the debate flamed out almost before it began—the shelf life of controversies at the U.S. Holocaust Memorial Museum is brief. These controversies have to resolve themselves, or be resolved, quickly because there is always another one waiting in line. This protest letter and the resulting discussion it aroused were quickly pushed out of the public spotlight when the museum became embroiled in yet another controversy.

The week before we arrived, the State Department "suggested" that Palestinian leader Yasser Arafat be given a VIP tour of the museum's permanent exhibition. The tour would grant Arafat the opportunity to become the first major Arab leader to visit the museum and thereby acknowledge the Holocaust and its role in defining the identity and aspirations of Jews today. However, Reich and other museum officials protested that such a gesture would be divisive and offend those Jews who consider Arafat a sponsor of terrorism. The museum withdrew its planned invitation. That snub of Arafat provoked a firestorm of protest from the Clinton administration. There were subtle and not-so-subtle reminders that, although American Jews founded it, the museum was a federally funded institution. After a closed-door, four-hour meeting on January 22, the invitation was reissued. Reich fought the invitation and refused to be part of the welcoming committee. "This is a matter of conscience for me," Reich said, "and this is a museum of conscience." Arafat was scheduled to tour the exhibition on Friday, January 23, the day we left Atlanta. But it was now Arafat's turn to take his ball and go home. His staff said he did not have time to visit the museum on this trip, but left open the possibility of doing so in the future. Reich was fired on February 19, 1998.

The primary missions of the U.S. Holocaust Memorial Museum are to advance and disseminate knowledge about the Holocaust, preserve the memory of those who suffered, and encourage visitors to reflect on the moral and spiritual questions raised by the events of the Holocaust and their own responsibilities as citizens of a democracy. The museum welcomes nearly two million visitors a year to participate in that reflection. The mission of the museum is advanced through three areas: permanent and special exhibitions, memorial areas, and resource facilities.

As Edward Linenthal describes, the building housing the museum itself can be perceived as a "code," a collection of Holocaust symbols that need to be identified and read. However, architect James Ingo Freed has said that he was wary of symbols in the design process. He wanted visitors to be free to find metaphors in what amounts to a collage of possible metaphors, but also free to find no metaphors at all. Regardless, the building itself does teach. One first notices that the benign outside is part of "official Washington," particularly in the way its skin of limestone (the most common building material in this part of Washington) and brick relates to its neighbors. Upon entering into the museum, though, visitors are removed from the comfort and familiarity of American space and plunged into a world of skewed lines and hard surfaces. Visitors take the first of several initiatory turns left and right, which both help to control pedestrian traffic and disengage people from the outside space.

The main floor, the Hall of Witness, is a large, three-story, naturally lit gathering place. This floor includes the hands-on exhibit recommended for grade school students, but equally well appreciated by adults, "Remember the Children: Daniel's Story." Overhead, the warped and twisted skylight tells visitors that, in Freed's words, "something is amiss here." Exposed beams, arched brick entryways, boarded windows, metal railings, steel gates, fences, bridges, barriers, screens, and a stairway that ominously narrows as it rises—all "impound" the visitor and are disturbing signs of separation. There is a definite sense of unease in this odd space. The interior mood and the insistence on how visitors move through the space coerces us to "leave" Washington, D.C. We begin to recognize that we are in a profoundly different place.

Our second removal occurs when we are herded into the intentionally ugly, dark gray metal elevators that take us to the beginning of the permanent exhibit on the fourth floor. While on the elevator, our attention is seized by a video monitor in the upper corner. On it is documentary footage of U.S. tanks rolling across a charred landscape toward a concentration camp. As we step off the elevator, we are confronted with a shocking photomural of what these American troops saw when they arrived at the camp. A life-sized image depicts American soldiers standing at the edge of a pit filled with naked and partially clad bodies of Holocaust victims. The Americans arrived at these camps not knowing of the Holocaust. Now we, the visitors, come upon the Holocaust for the first time.

As we make our way through the permanent exhibit, it becomes clear that this is a "story-telling" museum and not a collection-based museum. It is only dependent on artifacts (approximately one thousand in the exhibit) to the extent that they make concrete the elements of the story. What is the story told by the museum? Most historians use the term "Holocaust" to refer to the period of state-sponsored, systematic persecution and annihilation of European Jewry by Nazi Germany and its collaborators between 1933, when Hitler became Chancellor of Germany, and 1945, when the war in Europe ended. Statistics indicate that the total number of Jewish victims was more than 5.9 million. Although the Nazis also murdered about 5 million non-Jewish civilians (for example, homosexuals, Jehovah's Witnesses, Soviet prisoners of war, political dissidents), the Jews were the only group specifically targeted for total extermination.

The fourth floor of the exhibit, "Nazi Assault, 1933–1939," details the Nazi's rise to power—the early years of the Third Reich and the beginning of World War II. Most of the display texts are written in the past tense and third-person impersonal. Such language keeps us in the frame of a witness located outside the time and space of the Jewish victims of the Holocaust. It is also here that we see the much-discussed film "Antisemitism." The consensus of our group is that the film gives a very even-handed presentation of the relationship between Christianity and antisemitism. We also agree that what is most disturbing about the controversy surrounding the film is that it keeps the discussion rooted in the past rather than in the reality of the present. Both the film and the controversy make it too easy to believe that antisemitism is a historical artifact when, in reality, it remains a clear and present danger.

By the end of the exhibits on fourth floor, the Jews are stateless— divested of their citizenship rights in Germany and denied access to other countries. The third floor of the exhibit, "Final Solution, 1940– 1945," describes the ghettos, deportations, slave labor, concentration camps, and the implementation of the "final solution," extermination of the Jews. This area includes an "authentic" Holocaust boxcar and other memorabilia of terror. We are no longer the detached witnesses that we were on the fourth floor. Rather, we are encouraged to temporarily become one with the victims, to inhabit their space, to feel their pain. Nazi footage of executions and medical experiments in the camps is shown on monitors behind walls that are too high for children to see over. As we pass by, it is clear that many adults wish the walls were even higher.

Before descending to the second floor, a face is given to the victims of the Holocaust in one of the most compelling sections of the permanent exhibit. Ascending from the third floor through the fifth floor is a fifty-four-foot-high frame. It is a chimneylike space capped by a skylight. On the frame are 1,032 black-and-white and sepia photographs. They are photographs of the pre–World War II Jews of Ejszyszki, a town in Lithuania. The photos were collected by Yaffa Eliach, who lived in the shtetl as a child. For nearly nine hundred years, Jews had lived in Ejszyszki, an agricultural center for nearby Polish villages and a home to many rabbis and scholars. On September 25 and 26, 1941, nearly all of the four thousand people in the Jewish community of the town were shot to death by German mobile killing squads and Lithuanian collaborators. Only twenty-nine Jews, Eliach among them, survived. Today, there is not a single Jew among Ejszyszki's 12,000 residents.

Eliach's photographs make an incredibly moving exhibit on several levels—structurally and emotionally. One sees the vibrancy and complexity of a small shtetl. The exhibit is a living memory of the town. One sees town events, buildings, and streets. Some of these photographs are formal, others informal; some individual, others collective; some sacred, others secular; some amateurish, others professional—but all show people with "normal" lives. These are not prisoners, inmates, or victims. They are simply "people," like you and me. The people of Ejszyszki had dreams, hopes, fears, and insecurities. Life is present in these photographs—the faces tell us that. On another level, though, these same faces are excruciating because we are privy to their fate—a fate that they cannot even begin to imagine. It makes it nearly unbearable to look them in the eye.

The permanent exhibit concludes on the second floor. This area, "Last Chapter," chronicles the rescue, resistance, liberation, and survivors' efforts to rebuild their lives. Another sequence shows survivors of the death camps testifying at the Nuremberg trials. This area closes by depicting the founding of Israel and Jewish immigration to the United States. Here, several of us sit in a theater clad in Jerusalem stone and watch snippets of "Testimony," a seventy-seven-minute film made up of short segments of interviews with survivors. The stories are recalled from within the safety of either America or Israel, subtly emphasizing the role of both countries in preserving the eternal flame of Judaism.

After we leave the permanent exhibit, many of us stop in the Hall of Remembrance, a seventy-foot chamber of limestone. This hexagonal area with the eternal flame is America's national memorial to the victims of the Holocaust. Narrow, slit windows allow visitors to catch glimpses of the Washington Monument and the Jefferson Memorial. Writing in the *Washington Post*, Charles Krauthammer found these views important: "The juxtaposition is not just redemptive. It is reassuring. The angels of democracy stand on watch on this temple of evil. It is as if only in the heart of the world's most tolerant and most powerful democracy can such terrible testimony be safely contained."

The Hall of Remembrance is a solemn, simple space designed for public ceremonies and individual reflection. It is here that visitors are led directly from history to silence. It is here that the reality of the Holocaust begins to clench our hearts. It is here that all we have experienced in the past several hours has a chance to catch up and wash over us.

Later that evening, we reconvene at the Hirshhorn Museum on the mall for a special lecture by author Nathan McCall. In 1994, McCall burst onto the literary scene with his best-selling autobiography *Makes Me Wanna Holler: A Young Black Man in America*. The book traces his life from his early years in Portsmouth, Virginia, to his participation in violent criminal acts to his twelve-year prison sentence for armed robbery. While in prison, McCall worked as an inmate librarian and was so moved by Richard Wright's books that he decided to become a writer. After his release, he began a career as a journalist that led him to the *Atlanta Journal-Constitution* and, finally, to the *Washington Post*. Despite McCall's success, his is no triumphant memoir. It is frustrated, angry, and worried. His accounts of the hidden prejudice in seemingly liberal, integrated bastions of the newsroom are eye-opening and candid.

Tonight's presentation is an interview with McCall about his just-published *What's Going On: Personal Essays*. In this second book, McCall challenges blacks to "forget white America" and bring a critical eye to how they can solve their own problems. "Let's face it," he writes, "at our best we're as black and beautiful as beautiful gets. But at our worst, well, we be some ignorant niggas sometimes. Black-on-black crime, violence, pettiness, disregard for our children and elders, political apathy, disunity, and general chaos in black communities—you name it, we got it going on." I have yet to read the book in its entirety, but expect that McCall will challenge us with the same provocative edge he brought to his first book.

Unfortunately, that does not happen. McCall is not very provocative and, in contrast to the tone in his first book, seems incredibly restrained. I'm not entirely sure why the interview fell flat. I wonder if the success of McCall's first book and his rapid career rise has dulled his edge somewhat. Maybe he is too far removed from the hardscrabble authenticity that was the backbone of his first book. Or maybe he is just tired of being the latest "new black voice" that will transform race relations in America. Either way, McCall is not pricking the conscience of the audience in the way I expected. As we leave the auditorium, I wonder if the major part of the problem may be simply that we are drained from the emotional experiences at the U.S. Holocaust Memorial Museum. Maybe I heightened the students' expectations to a point that, given our emotional weariness, only extreme provocation would have reached us. Regardless, I wish he had yelled at us more tonight.

As we make our way down the mall for an informal night tour of the monuments, I think about the epidemic of young black men, like McCall, for whom prison is a rite of passage. In 1993, for instance, the National Center on Institutions and Alternatives discovered that forty-two percent of blacks eighteen to thirty-five years of age in the District of Columbia were under criminal justice supervision—in prison or jail, probation or parole, out on bond, or being sought on a warrant. In a 1998 follow-up study, the center found that the percentage of young blacks in the district under justice supervision had actually increased to nearly fifty percent. All told, the number of blacks in custody in Washington, D.C., is thirty-six times greater than the number of whites, relative to their population. The raw numbers are more astonishing—in 1997, the district's Department of Corrections held 8,153 blacks, but only 135 whites.

On a national level, nearly one in three young black men is currently under justice control on any given day. In the Watts neighborhood of South Central Los Angeles, seventy percent of black men between the ages of sixteen and twenty-five are on "some kind of paper," meaning they are in jail, on parole, or on probation. Data from the U.S. Department of Justice reveals that nearly three of every ten black men will be sent to prison in their lifetime. If jails were added to the calculation (the difference has only academic importance to the inmate), the figure rises to eight in ten.

Such figures have tremendous implications for the future of black communities in America. For instance, more young black men are locked up than are enrolled in our nation's colleges and universities. Washington, D.C.'s only public university, a prime opportunity for minority residents to pursue higher education, has seen its enrollment drop from more than 15,000 students in 1979 to just 7,000 today. In that same time span, the population in the city's prisons swelled from 3,000 to 8,500. In addition, one in seven black men have permanently or currently lost their right to vote as a result of a felony conviction. Excluding such a large segment of our society from voting further polarizes our country along racial lines and undercuts everything for which our country stands.

Some argue that these figures simply indicate high levels of black involvement in crime. Others suggest that they relate largely to law enforcement practices and social policies and note that blacks commit crimes at roughly three times the rate of whites nationwide, but that blacks are locked up at roughly seven times the rate of whites. How could this be? Many point to disparities in economic opportunity and the quality of public education. In addition, the selective enforcement of lesser crimes (for example, disorderly conduct) and discriminatory legal statutes impact the disparity. In a specific example of the latter, powder cocaine is purer than crack cocaine and worth more money. Yet, according to author Paul Kivel, one must possess five hundred grams of powder cocaine (worth $40,000 in 1994) to receive the five-year sentence that one possessing five grams of crack cocaine (worth only $250) would receive. The fact that whites are the main users of powder cocaine, whereas blacks primarily use crack, leads to fewer arrests and lighter sentences for whites than for blacks. Regardless of the explanation, one must be struck by the fact that a free nation would not tolerate it if half of the young white men in its capital were under justice control.

Ever since L'Enfant urged that Washington be lavishly equipped with "statues, columns, or other ornaments" to honor the nation's great, a continuous effort has been made to assure that no open space in the city lacks its representative monument. Within the District of Columbia alone, more than three hundred memorials and statues of varying size, purpose, and aesthetic merit have been raised. The most famous concentrated area of memorials and the repository of American identity is at the west end of the National Mall. After the McCall lecture, we begin a walking night tour of this area. It is a bit chilly, but, in our crowded itinerary, this is one of the few chances we will have to see the monument and memorials as a group. Besides, I think the monuments take on a different beauty and are even more impressive at night. Over the next two hours, we visit the "closed-for-renovation" Washington Monument,

Vietnam Veterans Memorial, Lincoln Memorial, Korean War Veterans Memorial, and new Franklin D. Roosevelt Memorial and take the long walk along the tidal basin to the Jefferson Memorial.

The monument and memorials are indeed striking. Like elsewhere on the tour, though, we have learned to view even this experience through a different lens. As we make our way back to the Metro, one student asks, "I wonder how different minorities feel upon arriving at our nation's capital? Can they accept and marvel at memorials that cause me so much pride, when they have been marginalized at times from their own political system? Can minorities relate to these different memorials when they have been both directly and indirectly oppressed by the government that used their tax dollars to erect them?" These are difficult questions with no easy answers, especially this late at night. However, they remind us all that the perpetual promise of America has a fine print that still excludes far too many people.

The night tour of the monument and memorials takes the place of that evening's debriefing. This is too bad because today—with the U.S. Holocaust Memorial Museum and the McCall lecture—deserves a debriefing. Regardless, our two-hour walk gives us some time for informal reflections. A couple of students were struck by how little they were moved by the U.S. Holocaust Memorial Museum. They recognize a sense of numbness that has come over them during the tour. They have seen and heard about so much pain that anything else just does not have a chance to stick. One student, in a painfully honest moment of introspection, finds a deeper source of her emotional distance: "I have found an alarming trend of unemotional responses [in myself] to sensitive and emotion-laden subject matter. The only emotion I expressed with any power or force was anger, harbored under a demeanor of aloof calm. In reflection, I see that this course of nonemotional approach to potentially painful stimuli is a recurring theme [in my life]. Used as a defense mechanism as a child and young teen to disassociate from my family, it now stands as a standard operating procedure for upcoming trials. . . . This results in my ability to walk through a museum of horror, sawed-off limbs, decayed bodies half-covered in flesh, walls of shoes of the dead, and countless other horrors without the bat of an eyelash. . . . I could not grieve. Only stare, absorb and move to the next exhibit. A sponge drinking it all in, but not tasting. Perhaps when I am wrung out I will respond someday with tears."

In truth, each of us is suffering from dulled sensibilities. Despite that, most of us still had some part of our heart and mind that was assaulted by what we saw at the U.S. Holocaust Memorial Museum. "As I looked at all the horrifying pictures of mutilated bodies and gruesome scenes worse than any horror film I had ever seen," one student said, "I wanted to hate someone for it. . . . Yet, I am annoyed at the reality of what I have been taught—that we are all capable of this. Maybe so, but I have to believe I am not, and those I love and am loved by are not. I have to believe that even at the worst point in life I could never do these things to innocent people."

Another student's journal testifies to the way in which the museum personalizes the suffering to such an extent that it is almost impossible not to leave unscathed. "The story I remember the most was given by a woman who explained that some of the young girls were upset because they were no longer menstruating. I was menstruating myself, and all of a sudden I realized how I take this human life process for granted. Sometimes I even despise it as an inconvenience. Here I was in this museum realizing that these girls longed for a sign of life and a feeling of being human. The woman went on to explain that the lack of menstruation really was a blessing, because they had nothing, not even underwear. I walked away from that room feeling differently about my body and thanked God that I was menstruating."

As we ask ourselves what to make of all we saw at the museum, one student says she found her answer carved on the wall in the Hall of Remembrance: "Only guard yourself and guard your soul carefully, lest you forget the things your eyes saw, and lest these things depart your heart all the days of your life. And you shall make them known to your children and to your children's children" (Deuteronomy 4:9).

As we wind our way through the impressive Roosevelt Memorial, the discussion shifts (ironically enough, given Roosevelt's lack of response to the Holocaust) away from the U.S. Holocaust Memorial Museum and to McCall's presentation. To my surprise, the depth of my disappointment with the interview is countered by the heights of their appreciation for the event. Where I saw McCall as not provocative or challenging enough, they saw him as compelling and incredibly provocative and challenging. For one student, McCall was the highlight of her time in Washington, D.C. "What an amazing speaker of truths and thoughts that draws the listener in with humor and keeps them with convictions," she said. Another said "He gave us the best presentation on the current state of racism that we've had." Where I had found the "brother" and "sister" language exclusionary, several of the students found it admirable. "When he commended the black 'sisters' for holding together the communities and embracing each other in sisterhood," one said, "never before have I wanted to be black so much as at that moment. Not only to be embraced by my sisters, but be referred to as a sister by a man I have never met—to be included in a group of people that treat one another as family. That is one thing I detest in our white culture is our damn determination to be independent."

As we hop down the cold marble steps of the Jefferson Memorial, I wonder if I could be wrong about the evening with McCall. Thinking that I surely cannot be wrong (I am an academic, after all), I first attribute the different reactions to the fact that I'm the only one who had read his first book and, thus, brought a different expectation to the lecture. If the students had read the book, surely they would have been more in line with my reaction. Even as I think that, I realize how egocentric I am being.

So, I fall back to the idea that the students liked McCall precisely because he *was not* brutally honest, provocative, or challenging enough. McCall, after all, spared whites a great deal by stressing that the black community needed to take a more active role in solving their own problems. We had seen that dynamic before on the tour and maybe we are seeing it again—if you can talk about race relations without making *us* feel too bad, we will repay the favor by liking *you.*

As I step on the Metro, though, I am struck again by my own arrogance. Maybe the answer is simply that the students *are* right—McCall was an insightful speaker and I, for whatever reason, just missed it. Why?

Perhaps it is because I bristle at anything that blames the victims of racism for their own suffering or, similarly, any hint that the victims must take the initiative to address their own plight. I know that some victims *are* responsible for their own suffering and that empowerment of victims *is* a key step in their recovery. But I just don't like the way that whites so quickly grab on to those concepts and won't let go. "Yes," we exclaim, "now you've got it! If you just work harder and pull yourself up by your bootstraps, you can achieve anything you want!" It lets us off of the hook too easily. McCall's perspective is important for the black community to hear, and I sense that his recent book and tonight's interview are directed specifically to that community. I just hope that my students, and whites in general, understand that McCall's advice to blacks is an adaptation to the reality of white apathy. He is not saying that blacks should not keep blaming whites because whites deserve no blame. He is saying that blaming whites is a dead-end road. We will not listen or accept that blame. So, the more effectual road to follow is a road of self-critique and self-sufficiency. In other words, it is blacks' best option when the only other one is waiting for white America to recognize its own racist tendencies and begin to eradicate the effects of those tendencies—a wait that McCall is wise to avoid.

January 27

Today is the last full day of our tour. It has been an incredible few weeks. It feels like we have been gone forever, but, at the same time, it seems as if it was only yesterday that we met at the airport in Los Angeles. In a jam-packed month, it is only fitting that our last day be one of our biggest.

The day begins with a briefing at the National Congress of American Indians. The organization was founded in 1944 in response to termination and assimilation policies that the United States forced upon the tribal governments. These policies were in direct contradiction of the tribal governments' treaty rights and status as sovereigns. Since its founding, the National Congress of American Indians has been working to inform the public and Congress of the governmental rights of American Indians and Alaska natives. Through its membership of 250 tribes, the congress uses its collective strength to protect the rights of all American Indian people.

We enter the conference room for our briefing with Jack Jackson, governmental affairs director, and John Dossett, general counsel, of the National Congress of American Indians. We have the preconception that the fall preparation course has left us fairly well informed about American Indian issues. We know, for instance, that at the time that Columbus arrived in the West Indies, there were about 15 million indigenous people in North America. As we enter the twenty-first century, American Indians number about 2.3 million in the United States (less than one percent of our total population), with about a half thought to live on reservations (although, like other minorities, they were vastly undercounted on the 1990 census). Today's American Indians represent more than 550 tribes, each with unique cultural, genetic, and sociodemographic characteristics. The states with the largest American Indian populations are California, Oklahoma, Arizona, New Mexico, North Carolina, and Washington.

We also know that American Indians remain the poorest and most disadvantaged of all racial groups. Indian reservations have a thirty-one percent poverty rate—the highest in America. Indian unemployment is six times the national average. In tribal areas, forty percent of the housing is considered substandard, compared to a national figure of just six percent. Twenty-one percent of homes are overcrowded, whereas the national average is less than three percent. Indian health, education, and income statistics are the worst in the country.

Some of the greatest distress falls on the youngest shoulders. The proportion of American Indian people who die under twenty-five years of age is 3.2 times greater than the national average. The alcoholism death rate for Indian youth aged fifteen to twenty-four years is seventeen times greater than national rates. The Sudden Infant Death Syndrome rate for American Indian infants is 1.8 times greater. The suicide rate for fifteen- to twenty-four-year-old Indians is more than twice that of the same group in the general population.

Indian national identities are threatened as their lands are being mined, logged, hunted, used for toxic waste dumping, and developed without permission or fair compensation. Recent data from the Justice

Department indicates that American Indians experience a much greater exposure to violence than other racial groups. A review of five years of data indicates that they are victims of violent crime at a rate more than double that of the rest of the American population. In seven of ten violent episodes against American Indians, the offender was reported to be a non-Indian. It is little wonder that Rennard Strickland, dean of the University of Oregon Law School, can say: "The most remarkable thing in the twentieth century is that the Indians survived."

Over the next hour and a half, however, Jackson and Dossett let us know how little we actually understand the major *political* issues facing American Indians today. They remind us that the single most important thing to know about tribes is that they serve as the governments on Indian lands. Self-government on Indian lands is the fundamental bargain that tribes struck with the federal government. This tribal self-government empowers the tribes to protect their cultures and identities and provide for the needs of their people. Specifically, tribes are responsible for education, law enforcement, justice systems, environmental protection, and basic infrastructure such as roads, bridges, sewers, solid waste disposal, and public buildings.

However, it is this very system of tribal government that has come under attack in the last few years. Just three months before our visit, Senator Slade Gorton, (R-WA), chair of the Senate Interior Appropriations Subcommittee, attached two particularly threatening riders to the FY 1998 Interior Appropriations bill. One rider would force tribal governments into an *unlimited* waiver of their sovereign immunity from civil lawsuits. This would deprive the tribes of a basic protection—now enjoyed by federal, state, and local governments—against frivolous and crippling lawsuits. No government could long operate under such a waiver of sovereign immunity. Another rider proposed a means-testing provision that would base federal assistance on tribal income. It was aimed at redistributing income from tribes that have made money from gaming operations. No other sovereign entity, state or local, has to endure such tests to receive its share of federal funds.

Fortunately, in this case, the National Congress of American Indians quickly mobilized a media protest and political counter-punch. Under heavy pressure from his Senate colleagues, Gorton agreed to remove these particular riders. In exchange, though, he was promised a hearing on the issue of sovereign immunity and has pledged that he will raise these issues again. As W. Ron Allen, president of the National Congress of American Indians, later wrote, "In simple terms, Indian Country's historical and present war with America is over control and jurisdiction. There are many who want to take away what little we have preserved and are threatened by our tribal governments' growing economic base and power."

Dossett also tells us that the National Congress of American Indians presently is embroiled in a legal suit over the mascot name of the Washington Redskins. As he talks, I am reminded of a conversation that I had last year with an American Indian activist. She had been called to mediate a debate in a local high school regarding their Indian mascot. In a painfully obvious way, she told me how the Indian mascot issue touches deep wells of resentment among American Indians. She explained that Indians see themselves as about the last racial group others feel free to mock without fear of reprisal. Whether it is the use of generic Indian names (such as Indians or Braves), specific tribal names (such as Seminoles or Apaches), idealized or comical Indian mascots, Indian paraphernalia, or Indian behaviors, most American Indians see it as no less than a mockery of their cultures. They see important aspects of who they are being co-opted for use in another culture's *game.* That is not fair and neither is the fact that these caricatures perpetuate stereotypes and racism to both Indian and non-Indian children.

American Indian groups estimate that more than six hundred schools, including Stanford University and Miami University of Ohio, have gotten rid of Indian mascots and names. In 1997, the Los Angeles School District decided to remove all Indian-themed mascots. Public schools in Dallas also banned the American Indian mascots used at nine of its schools—at a cost of about $40,000 to cover the changes in uniforms and school emblems on gym floors and walls. But more than 2,500 other schools around the country still employ such images. Some are embroiled in fights to retain those images. The University of North Dakota, for example, is fighting a resolution in the state legislature that would urge the school to drop the name "The Fighting Sioux." Professional sports teams, which are not dependent on public funds, continue to turn a deaf ear to the issue—as, apparently, have the Washington Redskins.

I have come, embarrassingly late, to the realization that the names, mascots, paraphernalia, and behaviors stolen from Indian cultures to use in our games can no longer be tolerated. It does not matter if we intend no harm, if we think these images convey a sense of honor, if we convince ourselves that we are helping to preserve another culture, or if we simply hide behind the veil of political correctness and hope the protests go away. What matters is that another culture feels disrespected and mocked by the use of these images. What meaning these images convey is *their* call, not ours. And they have made that call clear—for far too long, American Indian cultures have felt belittled by our use of these images.

In the closing period of discussion, I ask Jackson and Dossett about their views on President Clinton's advisory board on race relations. American Indians are the only major racial group not to be represented on the board. (As a matter of fact, until Clinton's July 1999 visit to South Dakota's Pine Ridge Reservation, no American president since Franklin Roosevelt had even visited an Indian reservation.) They both see the slight as just another way in which American Indians are marginalized throughout society. When they found out that we would be visiting with members of the board later this afternoon, Dossett says: "Make sure to ask *them* why there aren't any American Indians on their board."

After we leave the National Congress of American Indians offices, we have only two hours before we are due at the New Executive Office Building for our appointment with the representatives from the President's Initiative on Race. President Clinton announced the year-long initiative during a commencement address at the University of California in San Diego on June 14, 1997. Love him or hate him, commissioning this initiative placed Clinton as the first president since Lyndon Johnson to make race relations a cornerstone of his administration. Although, as Nathan McCall mentioned last night, the politically astute Clinton may not have been elected to a second term if he had announced the race initiative in the first term.

The goal of the initiative is "to strengthen our shared foundation as Americans so that we can live in an atmosphere of trust and mutual respect." This was to be done through constructive dialogue, study, and action. If you think the initiative sounds nebulous and ill-defined, you are not alone. From the beginning, both supporters and critics have wondered exactly *what* the initiative is about and exactly *what* the commission has been charged with. Over time—whether by design or happenstance—some answers appeared. It became clear that the initiative was primarily about increasing honest dialogue to confront issues about racism and race relations. It also became clear that the seven-member advisory board was in place to advise Clinton on potential policy changes and, where possible, to draw as much criticism to the initiative as they possibly could.

The board's first meeting, for example, was simply to be an opportunity for members to get to know one another. As such, it was an open meeting and occurred in front of reporters. However, Board Chairman John Hope Franklin, who is black, took the meeting in a different direction when he began outlining his vision of what the board would discuss in the coming year. Franklin's vision focused largely on the historical divide between black and white Americans. Another board member, Angela Oh, firmly suggested that the panel should take a broader view of race that would not overlook the nation's many minority groups. "Intellectually," Oh later said, "the President gets the idea of inclusion. [But] at an experiential and gut level, he really knows the black-white thing. I don't think he has an Asian-American friend." This initial exchange created an impression of discord among board members and raised the possibility that Clinton had allowed the board too much latitude in defining its responsibilities. It also served as a cautionary event that limited frank discussion during board meetings. To comply with federal law, all official gatherings of the board were open to the public, which limited how freely the panel could speak or debate different opinions without fear of being misinterpreted.

This, of course, was not the end of the criticism. The American Civil

Rights Institute, chaired by Ward Connerly, criticized the initiative for not including conservative viewpoints on issues like affirmative action. Others charged that the much-ballyhooed "honest dialogue" to be encouraged by the initiative was neither honest nor dialogue. Especially in the case of the three nationally televised town hall meetings, it was serial monologue; an airing of grievances and personal perspectives; a cliched jumble of policy prescriptions, platitudes, and anecdotes. Other town hall meetings produced a bland near-unanimity of opinion as selected panelists took turns preaching to the choir. As Orlando Patterson, a Harvard University professor of sociology, said: "Americans are very committed to the idea of dialogue, but are actually very awkward when it comes to engaging in it."

Many people were not surprised by the limits of honest dialogue. "We may place too much faith in dialogue," said Michael Eric Dyson, a Columbia University professor of African-American studies. "Conversation is not enough to leverage moral authority against racism. At the end of the day, you believe one thing and I believe something else. It's racial conversation as a one-night stand, a cheap thrill. When you converse in the context of a relationship then you can sustain something." Andrew Hacker, a professor of political science at Queens College, questioned how much people talk *honestly* about race. Instead, Hacker believes that the issue of race is so charged that we end up describing as our view the ideas and feelings we would *like* to have or believe we are *supposed* to have. For example, blacks might refrain from charging whites with racism because they know that sort of bluntness would end the conversation. Few whites want to talk openly about their suspicions that blacks may be genetically inferior—a suspicion that Hacker believes is widespread among the white community.

After passing through security and receiving some really nifty identification badges, we head for the briefing with representatives from the President's Initiative on Race. Leading the briefing is Michael J. Sorrell, special assistant to the executive director. With him is Maria Eugenia Soto, a communications assistant with the initiative, and several other staff members. Sorrell and Soto begin the briefing with a welcome and an introduction to the "One America" program. To be honest, this is pretty much all I expect the debriefing to be—an opportunity for them to tell us about their activities and solicit our support of the initiative.

To my surprise, though, Sorrell then asks for the group to tell him about our experiences on the tour, some of the things we have learned, and what directions we would recommend for the initiative to take. Even more to my surprise, he says that he wants to hear from *every single person* in the group. I start with a brief review of the course's history, purpose, and mechanics. Then, for the next two hours, the students take their turns sharing their impressions and recommendations with the representatives. I didn't expect this and, frankly, I'm nervous. I know some of the students will handle themselves well and be very articulate. But I am less sure of others. Just moments before one student had said to me: "I can't believe how nervous I am about this. I'm so tired and I don't want to think any more. This trip has completely exhausted me in every way. All I want to do is go home." In a flash of insecurity, I find myself worried about the image of Whitworth College, this tour and, honestly, me.

As usual, my insecurities are unfounded. The students express themselves clearly and convincingly. For the first time, I have a chance to step back and hear their perception, not mine, of what they have learned on the tour. I am impressed at some of the connections they have drawn and implications they have picked up. (I become a little self-conscious when every other one seems to mention my book. I hope the initiative staffers don't think that I'm giving extra credit for such comments—although I definitely will.) On the whole, I am proud of how they have processed their experiences to this point.

When the last student finishes, Sorrell and Soto are effusive in their praise. They say that they are inspired and energized by our work. They are impressed by the risks we took in reaching out of our comfort zones and say that it is these types of efforts that give our country hope for racial reconciliation. As I look around at the students, it seems that their reaction to these comments mirrors my own. In a long, draining, weary month, there is nothing better at the end of it than to be told "you done good." In one student's words: "I just thought it was so neat how interested they were in what we had to say. They really made you feel like your ideas had worth and they sincerely wanted to know what we thought and what solutions we could think of. . . . It's good to see that there are a lot of people out there, just like us, who want to make a difference." Another wrote, "I had been feeling a little overwhelmed and discouraged as to what we had accomplished as a group, but they were so quick to tell us they were impressed by what we had already done. . . . I realized we were so much farther along than when we started."

Both Sorrell and Soto, as well as the other members who have dropped in and out of the discussion, seem to be passionate and committed people. As we leave the New Executive Office Building, I don't know who to be more impressed by—my students or the idealistic group of young staffers committed to bringing racial reconciliation to America. Either way, you can't go wrong.

After fifteen months, three presidential town hall gatherings, eleven board meetings, and more than three hundred public hearings involving millions of Americans, the President's Initiative on Race reported its findings in September 1998. It is a document that contains no solutions, no policy prescriptions, and no sweeping program alternatives to mend the nation's racial divide. Instead, it simply urges the White House to maintain a race panel and keep the conversation going. Just keep talking. That trite phrase summarizes the essence of the lengthy report. Just keep talking. Although the initiative stimulated some new interracial initiatives and cast a dim spotlight on efforts already under way in some communities, it failed to move beyond conversation. Just keep talking.

The lack of substance from the board's work should not catch anyone by surprise. The board was handicapped by a lack of organization, an uncertain mandate, internal disagreements, and a president whose attention wandered—during a critical period of the board's work—from the task of fighting racism in America to the task of defending his political career. In addition, one White House aide even hints that the White House seal of approval was barely legible. "First of all, you have to understand that there were powerful and influential factions in the White House that never wanted [Clinton] to undertake race as the defining issues of legacy. . . . That faction was afraid that any discussion of race would put Clinton in the position of having to do something about race. They thought it just would be better to kill the idea at the outset." In the final analysis, the initiative was a well-meaning but ill-conceived plan that never really got on track.

Lest its final legacy be one of halting dialogue and marginal action, the vision of the President's Initiative on Race has now been picked up by the Joint Center for Political and Economic Studies. This organization, in collaboration with Fisk University's Race Relations Institute, is in the midst of launching an effort to link racial bridge-building activities in communities across the nation. The working title for this effort is the National Diversity Network.

After the meeting with the President's Initiative on Race earlier today, our final debriefing tonight is a bit anticlimactic. We have already heard each other's impressions of how the tour has impacted us. It has been a long day at the end of a long month, and most of us just want to watch the State of the Union address and then go to bed. We have a 3:15 A.M. wake-up call to make the first of our three legs of flights to Spokane. Besides, there is no "right way" to bring closure to such an experience as this. After a few logistical details, I close with an old Irish prayer of farewell: "And now, whether your road be uphill or down, know that the Lord will see to your going out and your coming in. Whether the wind be in your face or at your back, know that the Lord is in the wind. Whether your days be filled with darkness or light, know that the darkness and the light are the same to the Lord your God and even now He holds you in the palm of His hand."

AFTERWORD

*The purpose of education, finally, is to create in a person the ability
to look at the world for himself, to make his own decisions, to say
to himself this is black or this is white, to decide for himself
whether there is a God in heaven or not.*

James Baldwin, American novelist

The tour was a time so busy that we could not step back to see it until
several weeks or months later. We arrived back in Spokane on January
28 and the spring semester started on February 3. We barely had time to
unpack our clothes, let alone our experiences. For me, there was a mountain of correspondence that needed replies, syllabi to construct for the
upcoming semester, and a family with which to reacquaint myself. For
the students, there was the impending spring semester (for many of
them, the last of their undergraduate career) and the almost impossible-
to-answer question "How was the tour?" There also was the adjustment
of returning to a place as different people than when we left. In one student's words, "Everything seems meaningless here. After what we've
been dealing with and the intensity of living together with twenty-two
people, it feels like life has stopped." Over the course of the semester,
though, each of us began to sort out what we had learned and how we
could apply that learning to making our world a better place. I think it's
safe to say that we're all still processing those questions even now.

Our contact with the President's Initiative on Race continued. On
April 6, as part of a national "Campus Week of Dialogue" sponsored by
the initiative, we gave a one-hour presentation of the tour to more than
1,200 of our campus peers. The presentation was followed by a week of
small-group dialogues and larger town hall meetings in which we—as a
campus and as tour members—struggled with discussions of race and
exclusion in our community. When we returned from the tour, we had
been plagued with questions of "*What* do we do now?" Following this
week of dialogue, however, the questions became "*How* do we do what
we now know we need to do?"

In June 1998, we received word that our study tour had been selected
as a "Promising Practice to Promote Racial Reconciliation" by the initia-

tive and would be featured on their website. Promising practices are community-based and national efforts around the country that are designed to improve race relations and build one America. Our selection was an affirmation of the tour as well as an important way for us to share our ideas and strategies with others.

Just a few months after our return, I watched over half of our group file through a graduation ceremony and on to the next chapter of their lives. The following spring, the rest of the group would join them. Today, the students from the 1998 tour are scattered from coast to coast. Joy Crawford worked her way into an incredible research apprenticeship with an Israeli woman and is now enrolled in a graduate program at the University of Washington. Other students are working as liaisons in human rights offices; congressional aides in Washington, D.C.; youth ministers and teachers throughout the Pacific Northwest; AmeriCorps volunteers; and social service workers. Many are enrolled in graduate programs and one is even writing her first book. I have received wedding invitations from a few and regularly keep in touch with most.

As I put the finishing touches on this book, I realize that the tour was not a perfect experience. We should have spent more time interacting with community leaders and activists and less time reading museum placards. The debriefings should have been more frequent and more structured. The fall preparation course should have been more focused. Upon returning to campus, we should have had a better way of finding some closure to the intensity of our experiences during January. Despite all of this, I'm still struck by the meaning that the students took from the tour. Through it all, they learned and were challenged to see with the other's eyes. In their final journal entries, I asked the students to share what the tour meant to them and what it will mean to their futures. Their responses reflect the diversity of who they are, who they want to be, and who they are becoming. These responses are also merely a reflection of beginning of their journeys. In many ways, the most important lessons we take from our experiences on the tour may be ones that we won't even recognize until years down the road. In a book devoted to those experiences, it's only fitting that the students should have the last words.

"I don't know specifics right now. But I know that I will always see people differently. That no matter where I work, I will treat all members of my office with respect because they have a voice and they need to use it. They need to feel they 'can' in any situation. I will try to eat my elephant one bite at a time, but with the confidence that I will finish it before it goes bad. I think what I learned were things I'd been told before, but now I've stood in someone else's footsteps, I've sung the blues, I've eaten Chinese food with Uncle Guy, I've been on CNN and tested the power of the media, and now I know. I know that I have more questions and fewer answers; I know that I have more faith and less evidence; and I know that it takes believers to have a dream, and I'm a believer."

"The lessons I am taking from these experiences are lessons I will take with me for a lifetime, in who I am and who I become. In concrete ways, this means I will not tolerate racial slanders, prejudice, or discrimination toward any person. I will teach people I encounter about the hate I have seen and the sadness that it has brought. But most important, I will constantly seek to learn. I will ask people about their personal experiences and the changes they would like to see. I will ask questions; read books; and visit museums, organizations, and people who are contributing to change."

"I want to say something profound, like I will educate others about racism and eventually teach my children what it means to love and respect others. Although those goals are real to me, what is even more pressing on my heart is that I need to be a reminder. I need to live my life as though I am the only one who has been on this trip. I need to be in challenging situations and to never allow myself to choose the 'easy' way of not thinking or choosing not to be in situations where I always feel comfortable."

"I have realized that the problem [racism] is bigger than life. It exists in every corner of every alley. There is no escaping its reality. It consumes every person and will rear its ugly head if allowed. It exists. The question is, now that I have seen it and been face to face with the outcome of racism, what will I do? Reality says that I am going to go back to 'white' Whitworth and fall back into the role of a student where life is comfortable. I don't ever want to forget, though, the faces that have been worn or the hearts that have been broken due to prejudice and discrimination. I don't want to forget the feeling that I experienced in Los Angeles and Memphis of being different. I don't know what to do or how to respond. I can, and will, always remember what I saw and know in my heart that I am forever different and changed."

"What I saw this month was both a hurting and hating country filled with glimmers of hope for a better future. The road ahead is not an easy one by any means. As long as hatred is being taught and its expression tolerated, prejudice will continue to grow. But if we begin by teaching our children that everyone should be treated with respect, the disease of hatred will begin to be destroyed. This month of study was an awakening of an awareness that racism is still present in our thinking. Now, it is my responsibility to take that awareness and apply it to my everyday life. As I embark on an unknown future, I will have opportunities to teach tolerance to my children, to students, to coworkers, and to family members. I pray that I seize every opportunity afforded me."

"I will treat others with more respect. I will no longer be comfortable around people making jokes, poking fun, or putting down any person for the color of their skin or their facial or body features or their accent. I will, and already have, call attention to the fact that this kind of joking is wrong. I will no longer seek what is comfortable all the time, but will branch out, meet new and different people, and share in their experience and life. This trip taught me to listen, and I will continue to do so. But I will also voice my opinion. I will raise my children differently than I was raised. They will attend multicultural schools with children of all backgrounds and teachers of all backgrounds. And I will be active in getting educational tools into the classroom that promote diversity and understanding of other cultures including multicultural history books and classes. I will read them books written in other voices than the white voice here in America."

"In less than a month's time, I have seen more than my eyes have ever seen before. I saw the dark struggle of humanity. People who awaken each day to the nightmare of reality. There is no peace for the children growing up in the South Side of Chicago, as they continue to dodge bullets to get an education. There seems to be no hope for reconciliation between blacks and whites in the cities of Memphis and Birmingham, as both groups continue to depart in separate directions. One group migrates to the south and the other to the north. In Los Angeles, passing glances from passengers on the public transit systems tell you that you are not welcome there. There can never be a fair and just society. No matter how many laws are passed. No matter how many safeguards are developed by those appointed to protect us. We can never be protected from ourselves. We cut each other down day by day. With words and actions, we show that the human race has not evolved very far. And, on this study tour, I saw it with my own eyes."

"I was taken out of my comfort zone and put in situations where I was the minority, where people possibly couldn't like me simply because of my color. I was forced to examine my own mind and heart and face any prejudices I might hold. Emotionally, I forced myself to be exposed to some of the ugliest sides of our nation and humankind, not trying to hide from the realities of our world but, rather, face them head-on. Although this has been happening, to some degree, since I came to Whitworth, this trip, more than any book could do, challenged me to look at the ugly side of my race, my culture, and my ancestry and then to find that point of separation between the past and present where I am now and where I can make a difference."

"This whole trip, I've kind of felt weird because I seem to be the only one in the group that isn't going into some type of work like counseling, law, politics, teaching, where your life can really make an impact in changing people's views on these issues. I want to work in the health care field . . . but then I figured out that it's okay, not everyone has to go into a 'social science' type of work to make a difference. My attitude and actions will always be watched, and I feel I can teach many more people than I can ever sit down and talk to, by setting a good example. More than anything else, I think that how I now will raise my children will be the biggest impact this trip can make and, maybe, the most important. I think that children need to be in situations where not everyone is like them, so they can learn that difference in skin color or religion doesn't mean that you can't be friends with that person."

"What I lacked was the education that can only be gained from direct contact and conversations with people who are different from you. I don't remember ever having a class with a black person, until college. So you can imagine how many I had talked with—zero. No amount of book learning, in my opinion, can totally shatter the misconceptions you have about a group of people that you've never had contact with. That is why I feel so fortunate to have the experience of this trip."

"This trip has reaffirmed the legitimate role I believe the state has in bringing justice for all. I have really seen on this trip how all of our destinies are intertwined together in a web of complexities and trials. There is such a need today to seek justice, which I believe is even more crucial due to the growing racial tensions, the rise of conservatism, the moderate's complacency, and the mainstream disillusionment with the continuing need for all to sacrifice for equality. We are so much stronger together than apart; we do have universal concerns; we have the potential to find commonality in a postmodern world full of fragmented experiences. We all want equal opportunities to find happiness, we all desire justice, we all hate crime and violence, and we all want to see our families flourish in society. I hope with all my heart that I can take one bite at a time, working endlessly to consume the elephant of racism and injustice."

"Why did I do it? Why did I endure this month, which has been THE HARDEST one of my life? I didn't realize how full it would be. So busy. Not a minute to slow down. I didn't realize how difficult the material would be to grasp. I didn't know what living with twenty-one other people was going to be like. I didn't know my body would hate me so much for what I put it through. Why did I go through it all? What am I taking with me? And how, how in the world, do I communicate to others who I now am today? I want to be part of reconciliation in America. To be honest, though, I don't really know what that means for me. Does it mean volunteering in an urban shelter or organization? Does it involve my future career? What I do know is this—in every little way that I can, I will be striving to better race relations. Like the guy on the president's panel [Sorrell] said, it may simply be through a smile, a conversation, or a gift to someone who's been wronged in the past."

"Our trip has come to an end. Here I sit, on this plane filled with people I hardly knew twenty-three days ago. These people [and I] have since experienced some of our most influential, life-changing moments together. Nobody will be able to relate or understand as completely as they will. We have been faced with some extremely harsh realities, been forced to process and try to understand, and are now being sent out on a mission. This mission—to educate others, to spread the hope of a racially unified and culturally appreciative society. I am afraid. I am afraid I will lose the passion that burns so strongly in my heart right now. I don't want to devalue what we did, but I am not ready. I am not ready to talk to people who did not have our same experiences. I don't want to list off what we did because that is not what the trip was all about. How do you replay this for someone? How do you explain the way your heart was touched and began to ache for peace? I don't know. The trip is over."

Appendix A
Itinerary of the 1998 Tour

January 5

1:00 P.M. Rendezvous at LAX

January 6

10:00 A.M. Little Tokyo Guided Tour
244 South San Pedro Street, Suite 501
Los Angeles, CA 90012
(213) 620-0570
1:00 P.M. Japanese-American National Museum
First and Central Streets in Little Tokyo
369 East First Street
Los Angeles, CA 90012
(213) 625-0414
http://www.lausd.k12.ca.us/janm/main.htm

January 7

10:00 A.M. Wiesenthal Center Museum of Tolerance
9786 West Pico Boulevard
Los Angeles, CA 90035
(310) 553-9036 or (800) 900-9036
http://www.wiesenthal.com

January 8

10:00 A.M. House of Blues/Blues School House Program
8430 Sunset Strip
West Hollywood, CA 90069
(213) 848-2527
6:00 P.M. Leave LAX for SFO
7:19 P.M. Arrive SFO

January 9

9:30 A.M. Alcatraz Island
Pier 41/Red and White Fleet
San Francisco CA 94133
(415) 546-2803
http://www.nps.gov/alcatraz

January 10

10:30 A.M. Chinese Cultural Center
750 Kearny Street
San Francisco, CA 94108
(415) 986-1822
http://www.c-c-c.org
1:30 P.M. Chinese Historical Society of America
644 Broadway Street, Suite 402
San Francisco, CA 94133
(415) 391-1188
http://www.chsa.org/home.html

January 11

12:25 P.M. Leave SFO for Chicago
6:25 P.M. Arrive Chicago Midway

January 12

8:30 A.M. Red group meets with Arvis Averette
Black group meets with Donald Crumbley
2:00 P.M. Meeting with Wanda White,
Director of Development Initiatives
Chicago Housing Authority
616 West Jackson
Chicago, IL 60661
http://www.thecha.org

January 13

10:00 A.M. DuSable Museum of African-American History
740 East Fifty-sixth Place

Chicago, IL 60637-1495
(312) 947-0600
http://www.dusablemuseum.org
12:00 P.M. Lunch at Nuevo Leon Mexican Restaurant
1515 West Eighteenth Street
Chicago, IL 60608
(312) 421-1517
1:00 P.M. Tour murals in Pilson with José Guerro
Mexican Fine Arts Center Museum
1852 West Nineteenth Street
Chicago, IL 60608
(312) 738-1503
http://www.chicago-sidewalk.com/detail/18329

January 14

9:00 A.M. Meeting with Reverend Donald L. Sharp
Faith Tabernacle Baptist Church
Urban Life Center Offices
5240 South Harper Avenue
Suite A
Chicago, IL 60615
(773) 363-1312
http://www.urbanlifecenter.org
9:00 P.M. Leave Chicago for Memphis on Amtrak #59, *City of New Orleans*

January 15

7:38 A.M. Arrive Memphis

January 16

11:30 A.M. National Civil Rights Museum
450 Mulberry Street
Memphis, TN 38103-4214
(901) 521-9699
http://www.midsouth.rr.com/civilrights/

January 17

7:54 A.M. Leave Memphis for New Orleans on Amtrak #59, *City of New Orleans*
4:45 P.M. Arrive New Orleans

January 18

12:00 P.M. House of Blues Gospel Brunch
225 Decatur Street
New Orleans, LA 70130
(504) 529-2583

January 19

7:00 A.M. Leave New Orleans for Birmingham on Amtrak #20, *Crescent*
2:10 P.M. Arrive Birmingham

January 20

10:00 A.M. Birmingham Civil Rights Institute
520 Sixteenth Street
North Birmingham, AL 35203
(205) 328-9696
http://bcri.bham.al.us
2:09 P.M. Leave Birmingham for Atlanta on Amtrak #20, *Crescent*
7:07 P.M. Arrive Atlanta

January 21

10:00 A.M. Atlanta History Center
130 West Paces Ferry Road NW
Atlanta, GA 30305-1366
(404) 814-4089
http://www.atlantahistory.net

January 22

10:00 A.M. Martin Luther King Jr. National Historic Site
National Park Headquarters

502 Auburn Avenue
Atlanta, GA 30312-1525
(404) 331-5190 or 331-6922
http://www.nps.gov/malu

11:00 A.M. Martin Luther King Jr. Center for Nonviolent Social
    Change
449 Auburn Avenue
Atlanta, GA 30312
(404) 524-1956
http://www.thekingcenter.com

12:30 P.M. Underground Atlanta
Bounded by Wall Street, Washington Street, Martin Luther King Jr.
    Drive, and South Peachtree Street
http://www.underatl.com

2:30 P.M. Center for Democratic Renewal
Contact: Dexter Wimbish
P.O. Box 50469
Atlanta, GA 30302
(404) 221-0025
http://www.publiceye.org/pra/cdr/cdr.html

January 23

7:46 P.M. Leave Atlanta for Washington, D.C., on Amtrak #20, *Crescent*

January 24

9:33 A.M. Arrive Washington, D.C.

1:00 P.M. African-American Heritage Tour
Capitol Entertainment Services, Inc.
3629 Eighteenth Street NE
Washington, D.C. 20018
(202) 636-9203

January 25

11:00 A.M. Metropolitan Baptist Church
1225 R Street NW

Washington, D.C. 20009
(202) 483-1540
http://www.metropolitanbaptist.org

January 26

10:30 A.M. U.S. Holocaust Memorial Museum
100 Raoul Wallenberg Place SW
Washington, D.C. 20024-2150
(202) 488-0400
http://www.ushmm.org
6:00 P.M. Special lecture with Nathan McCall
Smithsonian African-American Studies Center
Independence Avenue and Seventh Street NW
Washington, D.C. 20560
(202) 357-3030

January 27

10:30 A.M. National Congress of American Indians
2010 Massachusetts Avenue NW
Second Floor
Washington, D.C. 20036
(202) 466-7767
http://www.ncai.org
2:00 P.M. Briefing with the President's Initiative on Race
The New Executive Office Building
725 Seventeenth Street NW
Washington, D.C. 20503
(202) 395-1010

Appendix B: Bibliographic Essay

These resources, which are extensive but not exhaustive, represent the significant books and articles I consulted while writing this book and are recommended for additional reading. In selecting these resources, I wanted balance in accessibility and perspective. Some of the resources are easily accessible to the lay reader, others are meant primarily for the professional scholar. I also tried to include as broad a range of perspective in the resources as possible.

General

The majority of the demographic data in the book—for example, population statistics, poverty rates, educational attainment—came from the well-maintained website of the U.S. Census Bureau (http://www.census .gov). Specific information for each city was culled from the archives of the major metropolitan newspapers: *Los Angeles Times, San Francisco Examiner, San Francisco Chronicle, Chicago Sun-Times, Chicago Tribune, Memphis Commercial-Appeal, New Orleans Times-Picayune, Birmingham News, Birmingham Post Herald, Atlanta Journal-Constitution,* and *Washington Post.* Much of this material was supplemented by websites maintained by the city governments or local chambers of commerce. In addition, some information came from the archives of the *New York Times* and *USA Today.* Finally, I occasionally drew from brief articles or tables in mainstream periodicals, such as *U.S. News and World Report, Time, The Economist,* and *Newsweek.*

Introduction

Much of the material on the rapidly changing face of Americans came from James H. Johnson Jr., Walter C. Farrell Jr., and Chandra Guinn's (1997) "Immigration Reform and the Browning of America: Tensions, Conflicts and Community Instability in Metropolitan Los Angeles," *International Migration Review* 31(4):1055–1096. The original inspiration for the "Prejudice across America" study tours came from Douglas

Brinkley's *The Majic Bus: An American Odyssey* (New York, N.Y.: Harcourt Brace and Company, 1993). For anyone interested in the history of Whitworth College, I recommend Dale E. Soden's *A Venture of Mind and Spirit: An Illustrated History of Whitworth College* (Spokane, Wash.: Ross Printing Company, 1990).

Chapter 1: The Preparations

The complete citations for the assigned texts for the fall preparation course are Martin Luther King Jr.'s *Why We Can't Wait* (New York, N.Y.: Penguin Books, 1963); Harvard Sitkoff's *The Struggle for Black Equality, 1954—1992* (rev. ed.; New York, N.Y.: The Noonday Press, 1993); Ronald Takaki's *A Different Mirror: A History of Multicultural America* (Boston, Mass.: Little, Brown and Company, 1993); James Waller's *Face to Face: The Changing State of Racism across America* (New York, N.Y.: Plenum Press, 1998); and Elie Wiesel's *Night* (New York, N.Y.: Bantam Books, 1982). The four objectives of the fall preparation course are distilled from the final chapter of *Face to Face: The Changing State of Racism across America* (1998). The quote from Paul Kivel is taken from his very helpful book *Uprooting Racism: How White People Can Work for Racial Justice* (Gabriola Island, B.C.: New Society, 1996).

Chapter 2: Los Angeles

I found the most helpful scholarly analysis of the racial demographic history of Los Angeles to be Camille L. Zubrinsky and Lawrence Bobo's (1996) "Prismatic Metropolis: Race and Residential Segregation in the City of the Angel," *Social Science Research* 25:335–374. From the wealth of material available about the 1992 Los Angeles riots, I recommend the following: Albert Bergesen and Max Herman's (1998) "Immigration, Race and Riot: The 1992 Los Angeles Uprising," *American Sociological Review* 63:39–54; Jeannette Diaz-Veizades's "A Social-Psychological Analysis of African American and Korean American Relations in Los Angeles," in Craig Summers and Eric Markusen's (eds.) *Collective Violence: Harmful Behavior in Groups and Governments* (Lanham, Md.: Rowman and Littlefield, 1999); Koft Buenor Hadjor's (1997) "Race, Riots and Clouds of Ideological Smoke," *Race and Class* 38(4):15–32; James H. Johnson Jr., Walter C. Farrell, and Dean S. Toji's (1997) "Assessing the

Employment Impacts of the Los Angeles Civil Unrest of 1992: Furthering Racial Divisions," *Economic Development Quarterly* 11(3):225–236; and Paul M. Ong and S. Hee's *Losses in the Los Angeles Civil Unrest* (Los Angeles, Calif.: UCLA Center for Pacific Rim Studies, 1993).

My comments on the Los Angeles political scene include data from two sources: Katherine Underwood's (1997) "Ethnicity Is Not Enough: Latino-Led Multi-racial Coalitions in Los Angeles," *Urban Affairs Review* 33(1):3–27 and the brief editorial "The Fading of Black Power: Los Angeles Politics," *The Economist* (May 16, 1998):26–27.

Regarding the internment of Japanese-Americans during World War II, there is probably no more accessible introduction than David Guterson's novel *Snow Falling on Cedars* (San Diego, Calif.: Harcourt Brace, 1995). For those looking for a more scholarly analysis, I recommend Jacobus tenBroek, Edward Barnhart, and Floyd Matson's classic *Prejudice, War and the Constitution: Causes and Consequences of the Evacuation of the Japanese Americans in World War II* (Berkeley, Calif.: University of California Press, 1970) and Ronald Takaki's *Strangers from a Different Shore: A History of Asian Americans* (Boston, Mass.: Little, Brown and Company, 1998). William H. Rehnquist's thoughtful and provocative analysis of the internment process can be found in his 1998 article, "When the Laws Were Silent," *American Heritage* October:77–89.

My summary of Jon Weiner's comments about the Museum of Tolerance come from his 1995 article, "The Other Holocaust Museum," *Tikkun* 10(3):22–23, 82–84. A summary of my work on perpetrators of the Holocaust can be found in my 1996 article "Perpetrators of the Holocaust: Divided and Unitary Self Conceptions of Evildoing," *Holocaust and Genocide Studies* 10(1):11–33. Finally, I drew the information about Roosevelt High School from Maria Fleming's (1998) "A Garden of Honor: Latino Students in East L.A. Plant a Tribute to Japanese Americans," *Teaching Tolerance* Spring:40–45.

Chapter 3: San Francisco

Much of the information related to San Francisco's racial and ethnic diversity came from James P. Allen and Eugene Turner's (1989) "The Most Ethnically Diverse Urban Places in the United States," *Urban Geography* 10(6):523–539 and Ramon McCleod's "Changing Face of the Bay Area" in the September 20, 1998 edition of the *San Francisco Chronicle*.

The most accessible account of the American Indian occupation of Alcatraz Island is Troy Johnson's *We Hold the Rock: The Indian Occupation
of Alcatraz, 1969 to 1971* (San Francisco, Calif.: Golden Gate National
Parks Association, 1997). Additional information on the Muwekma Ohlone can be found at http://www.muwekma.org.

   Some of the best recent work on the history of San Francisco's Chinatown can be found in George Anthony Peffer and Roger Daniels's *If They
Don't Bring Women Here: Chinese Female Immigration before Exclusion* (Champaign, Ill.: University of Illinois Press, 1999) and Victor and
Brett De Nee's *Longtime Californ': A Documentary Study of an Ameri-
can Chinatown* (Stanford, Calif.: Stanford University Press, 1994). Also
of help was Lani Ah Tye Farkas's *Bury My Bones in America: The Saga
of a Chinese Family in California (1852–1996)* (Nevada City, Calif.: Carl
Mautz, 1998). Regarding the birth of the "model minority" stereotype,
David Bell's 1985 essay can be found in "America's Greatest Success
Story: The Triumph of Asian-Americans," *The New Republic* 193:24–30.
Also of interest is Victor Low's *The Unimpressible Race: A Century of
Educational Struggle by the Chinese in San Francisco* (Providence, Utah:
East/West Publishing, 1982).

Chapter 4: Chicago

A readable introduction to Chicago's neighborhoods can be found in
Richard Conniff's (1991) "Welcome to the Neighborhood," *National
Geographic* May:50–77. For background material on the Great Migra-
tion, I am indebted to Alferdteen Harrison's (ed.) *Black Exodus: The
Great Migration from the American South* (Jackson, Miss.: University
Press of Mississippi, 1991) and Nicholas Lemann's *The Promised Land:
The Great Black Migration and How It Changed America* (New York,
N.Y.: Alfred A. Knopf, 1991).

   The classic psychological study in which a videotaped shove that
looked "playful" to most white people when done by a white man, but
much more often looked "violent" when done by a black man, can be
found in Birt L. Duncan's (1976) "Differential Social Perception and At-
tribution of Intergroup Violence: Testing the Lower Limits of Stereotyping of Blacks," *Journal of Personality and Social Psychology* 34:590–598.

   For an experiential view of life in Chicago's South Side, I recommend
Alex Kotlowitz's *There Are No Children Here: The Story of Two Boys*

Growing Up in the Other America (New York, N.Y.: Anchor Books, 1991).

A description of Tiffany Hogan and Julie Netzer's research on "approximating experiences" can be found in Joe R. Feagin and Hernan Vera's *White Racism: The Basics* (New York, N.Y.: Routledge, 1995:175–179). Peggy McIntosh's well-known work is published in *White Privilege and Male Privilege: A Personal Account of Coming to See Correspondences through Work in Women's Studies* (Working Paper no. 189, Wellesley, Mass.: Wellesley College, Center for Research on Women, 1998). A fuller account of Jody David Armour's concept of "intelligent Bayesians" can be found in his *Negrophobia and Reasonable Racism: The Hidden Costs of Being Black in America* (New York, N.Y.: New York University Press, 1997).

Chapter 5: Memphis

A concise introduction to the history and charms of Memphis can be found in Thomas Childers's (1998) "Memphis," *American Heritage* October:97–116. A more detailed analysis of old-fashioned and modern racism can be found in chapters 6–8 of my *Face to Face: The Changing State of Racism across America* (1998). Ralph David Abernathy's recollection comes from Howell Raines's oral-history collection *My Soul Is Rested: The Story of the Civil Rights Movement in the Deep South* (New York, N.Y.: Penguin Books, 1977).

For a history of blues music, I pulled from a wide variety of fascinating sources. Prominent among these were Charles E. Cobb Jr.'s "Traveling the Blues Highway," *National Geographic* April 1999:42–69; Gerald Early's (1999) provocative essay "Devil in a Blue Dress," *Books and Culture* September/October:11–13; Gerard Herzhaft's *Encyclopedia of the Blues* (Fayetteville, Ark.: University of Arkansas Press, 1998); Mark Jacobson's "Those Front Porch, Backyard, Juke Joint, Fife and Drum Blues," *World Music* October 1996:66–71; and Leon F. Litwack's outstanding chapter "Crossroads" in his *Trouble in Mind: Black Southerners in the Age of Jim Crow* (New York, N.Y.: Vintage Books, 1998).

Chapter 6: New Orleans

Much of the background material for the discussion of children dancers in the French Quarter came from Rick Bragg's "French Quarter's Black

Tapping Feet," *New York Times* (February 14, 1998):A6. Additional information about New Orleans' unique experiment with public housing can be found in Gary Boulard's (1998) "Public Housing Smarts: Two Universities Discover a Trove of Opportunity in New Orleans' Public Housing System," *Black Issues in Higher Education* 15(5):18–20 and S. C. Gywnne's (1998) "Miracle in New Orleans: What Do a Bunch of College Professors Know about Fixing Public-Housing Projects? A Lot, It Turns Out," *Time* 151(9):74. For a scholarly analysis of how a local black government influences black trust and confidence, specifically set in New Orleans, I recommend Susan E. Howell and Brent K. Marshall's (1998) "Crime and Trust in Local Government: Revisiting a Black Empowerment Area," *Urban Affairs Review* 33(3):361–381.

Chapter 7: Birmingham

For the material in this chapter, I am most indebted to the work of Glenn T. Eskew. The following were all indispensable: his book *But for Birmingham: The Local and National Movements in the Civil Rights Struggle* (Chapel Hill, N.C.: University of North Carolina Press, 1997), his 1997 article "'Bombingham': Black Protest in Postwar Birmingham, Alabama," *The Historian* 59(2):371–391, and his 1996 piece "The Freedom Ride Riot and Political Reform in Birmingham, 1961–1963," *The Alabama Review* XLIX(3). For a general history of the Civil Rights movement, I highly recommend the groundbreaking work of Taylor Branch—both *Parting the Waters: America in the King Years, 1954—63* (New York, N.Y.: Simon and Schuster, 1988) and his more recent *Pillar of Fire: America in the King Years, 1963—65* (New York, N.Y.: Simon and Schuster, 1998). An even more accessible overview can be found in Juan Williams's *Eyes on the Prize: America's Civil Rights Years, 1954—65* (New York, N.Y.: Penguin Books, 1987).

Information about the Sixteenth Street Baptist Church bombing can be found in any general history of the Civil Rights movement. For a specific review, I suggest Frank Sikora's *Until Justice Rolls Down: The Birmingham Church Bombing Case* (Tuscaloosa, Ala.: The University of Alabama Press, 1991). Quotes from Spike Lee are taken from Denene Millner's (1998) "Remembering Four Little Girls," *American Visions* 13:36. The reopening of the case was covered in most major newspapers and periodicals. I first read about it in Adam Cohen's (1997) "Back to 'Bombingham,'" *Time* 150(3):37.

Finally, I drew the information on the Austins' work in Metropolitan Gardens from Denise George's (1997) "Gerald and Gwen Austin, Good Neighbors," *Christianity Today* 41(13):33.

Chapter 8: Atlanta

With the arrival of the centennial Olympic Games, there was an explosion of interest in the history of Atlanta as well as in its contemporary racial climate. Among the many sources I consulted, the most helpful were Frederick Allen's *Atlanta Rising: The Invention of an International City, 1946–1996* (Atlanta, Ga.: Cox Enterprises, 1996); Ronald H. Bayor's *Race and the Shaping of Twentieth-Century Atlanta* (Chapel Hill, N.C.: University of North Carolina Press, 1996); Matthew Cooper's (1996) "Welcome to the Olympic Village: Atlanta Says It's 'Too Busy to Hate.' Is It?" *The New Republic* 215:14–18; Rebecca J. Dameron and Arthur D. Murphy's (1997) "An International City Too Busy to Hate? Social and Cultural Change in Atlanta, 1970–1995," *Urban Anthropology* 26(1):43–69; Arthur D. Murphy's (1997) "Atlanta: Capital of the 21st Century?" *Urban Anthropology* 26(1):1–8; Gary M. Pomerantz's fascinating *Where Peachtree Meets Sweet Auburn: A Saga of Race and Family* (New York, N.Y.: Viking Penguin, 1997); Charles Rutheiser's *Imagineering Atlanta: Making Place in the Non-Place Urban Realm* (New York, N.Y.: Verso Books, 1996); and Henry Wiencek and Jonathan Lerner's (1996) "The Road to Modern Atlanta," *American Heritage* April:82–92.

For my discussion of the 1906 race riot, I am indebted to Dominic J. Capeci Jr. and Jack C. Knight's (1996) "Reckoning with Violence: W. E. B. DuBois and the 1906 Atlanta Race Riot," *The Journal of Southern History* LXII(4):726–766. I found the most balanced analysis of the controversy surrounding the Martin Luther King Jr. National Historic Site to be in Ebba Hierta's (1996) "Overcoming the Odds," *National Parks* 70(7/8):40–46. The complete results of the *Ebony* survey can be found in the 1997 article "Which City Is the Best for Blacks," *Ebony* 52(11):67–72.

Two recent publications were very helpful in writing the section on the affirmative action debate. The first was a 1996 issue of the *Journal of Social Issues* entitled "The Affirmative Action Debate: What's Fair in Policy and Programs?" Edited by Paula R. Skedsvold and Tammy L. Mann, this issue brought together the current social scientific research and opinion in an accessible and helpful resource. The second was William G. Bowen, Derek C. Bok, Thomas I. Nygren, James L. Shulman, Stacey Berg Dale, and Lauren E. Meserve's *The Shape of the River: Long-Term Consequences of Considering Race in College and University Admissions* (Princeton, N.J.: Princeton University Press, 1998).

Finally, the 1997 report "Cause for Concern: Hate Crimes in America," which was commissioned by the Leadership Conference Education Fund and Leadership Conference on Civil Rights, can be found at http://www.civilrights.org/lcef/hate/.

Chapter 9: Washington, D.C.

There are a plethora of resources devoted to the history of Washington, D.C., and the construction of its racial identity. Among the ones I consulted are Kenneth R. Bowling's *The Creation of Washington, D.C.: The Idea and Location of the American Capital* (Fairfax, Va.: George Mason University Press, 1991); D. E. Gale's *Washington, D.C.: Inner-City Revitalization and Minority Suburbanization* (Philadelphia, Pa.: Temple University Press, 1987); Constance M. Green's *The Secret City: A History of Race Relations in the Nation's Capital* (Princeton, N.J.: Princeton University Press, 1967); and Robert D. Manning's (1998) "Multicultural Washington, D.C.: The Changing Social and Economic Landscape of a Post-Industrial Metropolis," *Ethnic and Racial Studies* 21(2):328–355.

Colbert I. King's comments can be found in his editorial of December 27, 1997, "The Sounds of Wounded Racial Pride," in the *Washington Post*. A complete description of James Jones's TRIOS model can be found in his "Racism: A Cultural Analysis of the Problem," in John F. Dovidio and Samuel L. Gaertner's (eds.) *Prejudice, Discrimination, and Racism* (San Diego, Calif.: Academic Press, 1986) as well as Jones's landmark *Prejudice and Racism* (2d ed.; New York, N.Y.: McGraw-Hill, 1997).

I found the best description of the machinations behind the development of the United States Holocaust Memorial Museum to be in Edward T. Linenthal's *Preserving Memory: The Struggle to Create America's Holocaust Museum* (New York, N.Y.: Penguin Books, 1995). Also helpful in the general realm of public memorialization was Linenthal's (1995) "American Public Memory on the Washington Mall," in *Tikkun* 10(3):20–21. The vitriolic controversy surrounding the film "Antisemitism" reached near-comic proportions. For the two sides of the issue, see

David Neff's (1998) "Faulty Memory: The Holocaust Museum Does a Disservice to Its Visitors and Its Cause," *National Review* 50(8):34–37 and the editorial "Did Christianity Cause the Holocaust?" in the April 27, 1998 issue of *Christianity Today* 42(5):12–13 versus Leon Wieseltier's scathing 1998 reply, "Epistle to the Hebrews," *The New Republic* 218(32):42. For reviews of the museum's architecture and mission, I consulted Michael Berenbaum's *The World Must Know: The History of the Holocaust as Told in the United States Holocaust Memorial Museum* (Boston, Mass.: Little, Brown and Company, 1993); Greig Crysler and Abidin Kusno's (1997) "Angels in the Temple: The Aesthetic Construction of Citizenship at the United States Holocaust Museum," *Art Journal* 56(1):52–65; Leon Wieseltier's (1993) "After Memory: Reflections on the Holocaust Memorial Museum," *The New Republic* 208(18):16–26; and Brendan Gill's (1993) "The Holocaust Museum: An Unquiet Sanctuary," *The New Yorker* April 19:107–109.

The complete references for Nathan McCall's two books are *What's Going On: Personal Essays* (New York, N.Y.: Vintage Books, 1998) and *Makes Me Wanna Holler: A Young Black Man in America* (New York, N.Y.: Demco Media, 1999). Much of the data on black men under justice supervision came from Eric Lotke's (1998) "Hobbling a Generation: Young African American Men in Washington, D.C.'s Criminal Justice System—Five Years Later," *Crime and Delinquency* 44(3):355–367. Also helpful was Andrew Hacker's *Two Nations: Black and White, Separate, Hostile, Unequal* (New York, N.Y.: Ballantine Books, 1992). The material on sentencing discrepancies between the possession of powder and crack cocaine was taken from Paul Kivel's *Uprooting Racism: How White People Can Work for Racial Justice* (Gabriola Island, B.C.: New Society, 1996:195).

Finally, for more information on the controversy surrounding Indian team mascots, I recommend Barbara Munson's (1999) "Not for Sport: A Native American Activist Calls for an End to 'Indian' Team Mascots," *Teaching Tolerance* Spring:41–43 and Sue Anne Pressley's February 18, 1999 article, "Indian Mascot Debate Becomes a Federal Case," in the *Washington Post*.

Index

Abernathy, Ralph David, 146, 150
Abrams, Elliot, 256–57
Affirmative action, 220–25
African American Civil War Memorial, 242
Alabama Christian Movement for Human Rights, 178–79
Alarcon, Richard, 54
Albany, Ga., 181–83
Alcatraz Island, 80, 83–88, 290
Ali, Muhammad, 115, 241
Allen, Ivan, Jr., 218
Allen, W. Ron, 272
American Civil Liberties Union, 59
American Civil Rights Institute, 274–75
American Indian Foundation, 83
Amistad, 126–29
Amtrak, 139–40, 159
Anacostia Museum, 241
Anti-Defamation League, 229
Antisemitism, definition of, 22
Antisemitism (film), 256–58, 260–61
Arafat, Yassar, 258
Armour, Jody David, 124–25
Arrington, Richard, 185, 195
Association of Community Organizations for Reform Now, 105
Atlanta Committee for the Olympic Games, 220
Atlanta Compromise, the, 206–07
Atlanta Cotton States and International Exposition, 206
Atlanta History Center, 203–04, 211, 212, 292
Atlanta History Museum, 204
Atlanta Project, the, 212
Atlanta riots (1906), 207–08, 213
Auburn Avenue, 213–14
Austin, Gerald and Gwen, 197
Averette, Arvis, 107, 110–12, 114–16, 117, 120–21, 122–23, 133, 290

Baldwin, James, 125–26
Ball, Thomas, 242
Barger, Don, 216
Barnett, Camille Cates, 250–51
Barry, Marion, 249–50
Baxley, William, 191
Bayor, Ronald, 210
Bennett, William, 106
Bergesen, Albert, 48–49
Bethune, Mary McLeod, 242
Bevel, James, 184
Bey, Lee, 114
Birmingham Civil Rights District, 185
Birmingham Civil Rights Institute, 185, 188–90, 196, 197, 292
Birmingham Housing Authority, 196
Blanton, Tommy, 192
Blues, the, 152, 153–56; whitening of, 155–56
Bond, Julian, 199, 218
Boutwell, Albert, 180, 187
Bracero Program, 79
Bradley, Tom, 45, 53, 55
Branch, Taylor, 182, 194
Brinkley, Douglas, 8–9
Brown vs. Board of Education (1954), 113, 148
Bureau of Indian Affairs, 88
Burroughs, Margaret T., 126
But for Birmingham (Eskew), 180

Cabrini Green, 113–14, 119
Campbell, Bill, 210, 211, 218–19, 220
Campus Affiliates Program, 171
Capitol Entertainment Services, 239, 293
Carlos III, King of Spain, 43
Carter, Jimmy, 255
Cash, Herman, 192
Cause for Concern: Hate Crimes in America (LCEF/LCCR), 229

Center for Democratic Renewal (CDR), 225–28, 230, 232–33, 293
Center for Urban Missions, 197
Chambliss, Robert Edward, 191, 193
Chavis, Benjamin F., Jr., 199
Cherry, Bobby Frank, 192
Chicago Defender, 109, 114
Chicago riots (1919), 108
Chicago Sun-Times, 114
Chicago Housing Authority (CHA), 111–12, 117–20, 290
Childers, Thomas, 141–42, 151
Children's crusade, 184–85
Children's Rights Council, 247
Chinatown, 88–91, 94–96
Chinatown Community Development Center, 96
Chinese Cultural Center, 91, 290
Chinese Exclusion Act (1882), 55, 89, 95
Chinese Historical Society of America, 290
Choy, Philip, 90
City of Chicago Percent for Art Program, 131
Civil Liberties Act (1988), 60
Civil Rights Act (1964), 44, 174, 194, 195
Civil Rights Bill, 218
Civil Rights Project, 211
Civil War, 71, 204–06, 212, 242–43
Cisneros, Henry, 118
Clark, Lenard, 115
Clinton, William "Bill," 196, 213, 258, 273–74, 277–78
Cobb, Charles E., Jr., 154
Collins, Addie Mae, 192
Community Affairs Committee, 196–97
Connerly, Ward, 275
Conniff, Richard, 106
Connor, Theophilus Eugene "Bull," 174, 179–80, 184–85, 187
Cox, Bryan, 98–99
Cronkite, Walter, 191
Crumbley, Donald, 107, 112, 116–18, 122–23, 133, 290

Dakota: A Spiritual Geography (Norris), 33

Daley, Richard, 113, 150
Dameron, Rebecca J., 235
D.C. Democracy 2000 Act, 246
de Neve, Felip, 43
de Soto, Hernando, 141
Dearborn Homes, 110–11
Dearborn Homes Resident Management Corporation, 111
Devine, Joel, 167–68
Different Mirror: A History of Multicultural America, A (Takaki), 20–21
Discrimination, definition of, 22
District of Columbia Financial Responsibility and Management Assistance Authority. *See* Financial Control Board
Dobson, James, 227–28, 232
Dossett, John, 270–72
Douglass, Frederick, 240–41
Drake, James, 185
Duarte, Hector, 131–32
DuBois, W. E. B., 207–08
Duke, David, 232
Durr, Floyd, 113
DuSable, Jean Baptiste Pointe, 103
DuSable Museum of African-American History, 126–29, 290–91
Dyson, Michael Eric, 275

Early, Gerald, 153
Eastman, Zebina, 103
Ebenezer Baptist Church, 216–17
Ejszyszki, 260–62
Eli, Look Tin, 90
Eliach, Yaffa, 261–62
Emancipation Proclamation, 182, 242, 244
Encyclopedia of Chicago History (Grossman), 116
Equal Employment Opportunity Commission (EEOC), 194
Eskew, Glenn, 180, 195
Ethnic diversity index, 234
Eto, Mamoru, 60
Evers, Medgar, 192, 199
Evers-Williams, Myrlie, 199

Face to Face: The Changing State of Racism Across America (Waller), 21

Faith Tabernacle Baptist Church, 132–34, 291
Farrakhan, Louis, 53, 115, 132
Farver, Jo Ann, 50–51
Feagin, Joe, 5
Federal Immigration Act (1965), 79
Financial Control Board, 245–46, 250–51
Fire Next Time, The (Baldwin), 125–26
Fisk University's Race Relations Institute, 278
Forrest, Nathan Bedford, 159
Four Little Girls (Lee), 192
Franklin, John Hope, 274
Frederick Douglass National Historic Site, 240–41, 248
Freed, James Ingo, 259
Freedom Riders, 178
Fugitive Slave Law, 242

Gaston Gardens, 185
Gaston Motel, 187
Gautreaux v. Chicago Housing Authority (1968), 117, 119
Geller, Elaine, 66–68
General Accounting Office, U.S., 170
Giants in the Earth (Rolvaag), 34
Girl "X," 113–14
Goodwin, George, 218
Gore, Al, 217
Gorton, Slade, 271
Grady, Henry, 206
Great Migration, 71, 107–08, 157, 208, 239, 244
Grossman, James, 116
Grunwald, Michael, 156
Guerrero, José, 130–32, 291

Hacker, Andrew, 125, 275
Hadjor, Kofi Buenor, 46
Hall, Tony, 133
Hampton, Carol, 37
Handy, W. C., 154
Harris, Ryan, 113
Hart-Cellar Act (1965), 6, 55
Hartsfield Atlanta International Airport, 219–20
Harvard, Beverly J., 219

Hate Crimes Statistics Act (1990/1996), 229
Herenton, Willie, 157
Herman, Max, 48–49
Hernandez, Mike, 54
Hicks, H. Beecher, Jr., 252
Hirshhorn Museum, 262–63
Hitler, Adolf, 256, 260–61
Hogan, Tiffany, 120
Holocaust, 27, 31, 63, 65–67
Holocaust Memorial Museum, U.S., 67, 254–62, 263, 266–67, 294
Homosexuality, 27, 28
hooks, bell, 169
Hoover, J. Edgar, 192
Horowitz, Michael, 256–57
House of Blues: Los Angeles, 70–72, 289; New Orleans, 168–69, 292
House Resolution 108 (1953), 81
Housing and Urban Development, U.S. Department of, 170, 196
Housing Authority of New Orleans (HANO), 170–71
Hutchinson, Earl Ofari, 47

Ida B. Wells Homes, 120
Indian Claims Commission Act (1946), 83
Internment Camps, 59–60, 73
Invaders, the, 146
Issei, 59

Jackson, Andrew, 141
Jackson, Jack, 270–72
Jackson, Jesse, 115
Jackson, Mahalia, 150
Jackson, Maynard, 218, 219–20
James Irvine Garden, 56
Japanese-American Cultural and Community Center, 55–56
Japanese-American National Museum, 59–62, 73, 289
Jefferson County Committee for Economic Opportunity, 196
Jefferson, Thomas, 149
Jimmy Carter Center and Presidential Library, 211, 212–13, 215
Jodoshu North American Buddhist Mission, 56–59

Johnson, Robert, 71
Johnson, Troy, 80
Joint Center for Political and Economic
    Studies, 278
Jones, James, 251

Kaskey, Raymond, 185–86
Keimi, Hal, 59–62, 67
Kelly Ingram Park, 177, 184–86, 189,
    195
Kennedy, John F., 178, 194, 218
Kim, J., 54
Kincaid, Bernard, 195
King, A. D., 216
King, Colbert I., 251
King, Coretta Scott, 214, 215
King, Dexter Scott, 214
King, Martin Luther, Jr., 21, 24, 68,
    121, 135, 145–46, 149–51, 159, 174,
    177, 178, 179, 181–84, 185, 189, 193,
    213–14, 218, 244
King, Martin Luther, Sr., 216–17
King, Rodney, 45, 47, 49
Knight, Jack, 207–08
Krauthammer, Charles, 262
Ku Klux Klan, 144, 158–59, 187, 191,
    193, 229

Lang, Laura, 243
Lawler, Jerry, 157
Lawson, James, 145
Leadership Conference Education Fund
    (LCEF), 228–29
Leadership Conference on Civil Rights
    (LCCR), 228–29
Lee, Spike, 192
L'Enfant, Pierre-Charles, 243, 265
Lentz, Richard, 182
Lerner, Michael, 67
Letcher, Donald, 147–48
Letter from a Birmingham Jail (King,
    Jr.), 21, 183, 189
Levson, Leon, 128
Lewis, John, 218
Lincoln, Abraham, 240, 241–42
Linenthal, Edward, 254–55, 259
Little Tokyo Business Association, 55
Lomax, Lewis E., 181
Lorraine Motel, 146

Los Angeles riots (1992), 45–50
Luther, Martin, 256

Makes Me Wanna Holler: A Young
    Black Man in America (McCall), 263
Malcolm X, 32, 149, 182
Malcolm X Center for Self-Determina-
    tion, 193
Mankiller, Wilma, 85
Martin Luther King Jr. Center for Non-
    violent Social Change, 214–16, 231,
    293
Martin Luther King Jr. National His-
    toric Site, 214, 230, 292–93
Mason, Ronald, 170–71
Masumoto, Mas, 59–62, 67
McCall, Nathan, 262–64, 265–66, 268–
    69, 273, 294
McGill, Ralph, 218
McIntosh, Peggy, 121
McKenzie, Richard, 82–83
McNair, Carol Denise, 192
McNair, Chris, 195
Medved, Michael, 256
Meeks, Catherine, 24
Meredith, James, 149
Metropolitan Atlanta Rapid Transit
    Authority (MARTA), 203
Metropolitan Baptist Church, 252–54,
    293–94
Mexican Fine Arts Center Museum,
    291
Mfume, Kweisi, 199, 200
Model-minority stereotype, 92–94
Modern racism, definition of, 143–44
Molina, Gloria, 54
Morgan, Chuck, 191
Morial, Marc H., 199
Mount Zion Harmonizers, 169
Mount Zion United Methodist
    Church, 5
Murphy, Arthur D., 235

National Anti-Klan Network. See Cen-
    ter for Democratic Renewal
National Association for the Advance-
    ment of Colored People (NAACP),
    198–200

National Civil Rights Museum, 144, 145, 146–51, 152, 188, 291
National Congress of American Indians (NCAI), 269–73, 294
National Council of Negro Women, 242
National Council on Indian Opportunity, 82
National Diversity Network, 278
National Museum of American History, 239
National Parks Association, 87–88
National Park Service, 87–88, 214, 215–16, 217, 230
National Voting Rights Act (1965), 149
Naturalization Act (1790), 80
Netzer, Julie, 120
New City Church, 197
New Otani Hotel, 56
Night (Wiesel), 21
Nisei, 59, 61
Nomura, Kenjiro, 61
Norris, Kathleen, 33
Norton, Eleanor Holmes, 245–46

Oakes, Richard, 83–85
Obgfemi, Ahmed, 193
Ohlone Tribes, 77–78, 87–88
Old fashioned racism, definition of, 143
One America program, 276

Palmer, Parker, 25
Parks, Rosa, 148, 192
Patterson, Orlando, 275
Peabody Hotel, 151–52
Peci, Dominic, 207–08
Percy, Walker, 166
Pettigrew, Thomas, 26
Pilsen, 129, 130–32
Pitts, Leonard, Jr., 133
Plessy vs. Ferguson (1896), 208
Porter, Rufus, 113
Portes, Alejandro, 235
Prejudice, definition of, 22
Preserving Memory: The Struggle to Create America's Holocaust Museum (Linenthal), 254–55

President's Initiative on Race, 233, 273–78, 281–82, 294
Problem fatigue, 164
Project C, 182–84
Promise Keepers, 228, 232
Proposition 187 (CA), 54–55
Proposition 209 (CA), 223–24

Racism, definition of, 22
Raines, Howell, 190
Rebuild L.A., 48
Rehnquist, William H., 59
Reich, Walter, 256–58
Riordan, Richard, 53
Robert Taylor Homes, 112
Robertson, Carol Rosamond, 192
Rodriguez, Richard, 49
Rolvaag, Ole, 34
Romanowski, Bill, 98–99
Roosevelt, Franklin D., 255, 267, 273
Roosevelt High School, 73
Rowan, Carl, 5
Rudy Lozano Branch Library, 130–31

Sandhu, Daya, 94
Scott, Emmett J., 107
Scott, Krashaun, 48
Serra, Junipero, 43
Shapiro, Walter, 145
Sharp, Donald L., 132–34, 145, 212, 291
Shaw, Robert Gould, 242
Sherman, William Tecumseh, 205–06
Shores, Arthur, 195
Shuldiner, Joseph, 118
Shuttlesworth, Fred, 178–79, 182, 194
Sitkoff, Harvard, 21, 151
Sixteenth Street Baptist Church, 21, 185–86, 190–93, 195, 200
Smith, Jacqueline, 146–47, 152
Smithsonian National Museum, 241
Smyer, Sidney, 179
Sorrell, Michael J., 275–77
Soto, Maria Eugenia, 275–77
Southern Baptists International Mission Board, 132–33
Southern Christian Leadership Conference (SCLC), 182, 184, 187, 198
Southern Poverty Law Center (SPLC), 229

Spaulding, Chandler, 233
Spielberg, Steven, 126–27
Stand Up for Democracy Coalition, 250
Starr, Kevin, 72–73
Stepick, Alex, 235
Stereotypes, definition of, 22
Stewart, Kordell, 98
Stokes, J. J., 98
Stowe, Harriet Beecher, 241, 248
Strickland, Rennard, 271
Struggle for Black Equality, 1954–1992, The (Sitkoff), 21

Takaki, Ronald, 20, 89, 108, 207
Tauber, Laszlo, 255
Taylor, Ella, 127–28
Thomas, Rufus, 142
Thompson, Barbara Guillory, 168
Thompson, Mark, 250
Thorpe, Grace, 85–86
Till, Emmett, 192
Trail of Tears, 204–05
Tulane University, 170–71
Tuttle, Elbert, 218

Uncle Tom's Cabin (Stowe), 241
Urban Life Center, 291

Vera, Hernan, 5
Voting Rights Act (1965), 195

Walker, Wyatt, 182
Walker-Moffat, Wendy, 93

Wallace, George, 196
Washington, Booker T., 206–08
Washington, George, 243
Waters, Maxine, 53
Watts riots (1965), 44–45
Wesley, Cynthia, 192
What's Going On: Personal Essays (McCall), 263
White privilege, 121–22
White, Wanda, 117–20, 290
Whitworth College, 9–11
Why We Can't Wait (King, Jr.), 21
Wiencek, Henry, 215
Wiener, Jon, 66–67
Wiesel, Elie, 21
Wieseltier, Leon, 257
Wiesenthal Museum of Tolerance, 21, 63–67, 149, 188, 289
Williams, Anthony A., 251
Willie, Edward, 86
Wilson, Amy, 149
Wilson, Pete, 224
Wimbish, Dexter, 226–28, 293
Wright, Richard, 108, 263

Xavier University, 171

Young, Andrew, 218
Young, Guy, 90–92, 94–96, 97–98
Young Men's Business Club of Birmingham, 191